MICHIGAN STATE UNIVERSITY
LIBRARY

AUG 14 2025

WITHDRAWN

OVERDUE FINES:
25¢ per day per item

RETURNING LIBRARY MATERIALS:
Place in book return to remove
charge from circulation records

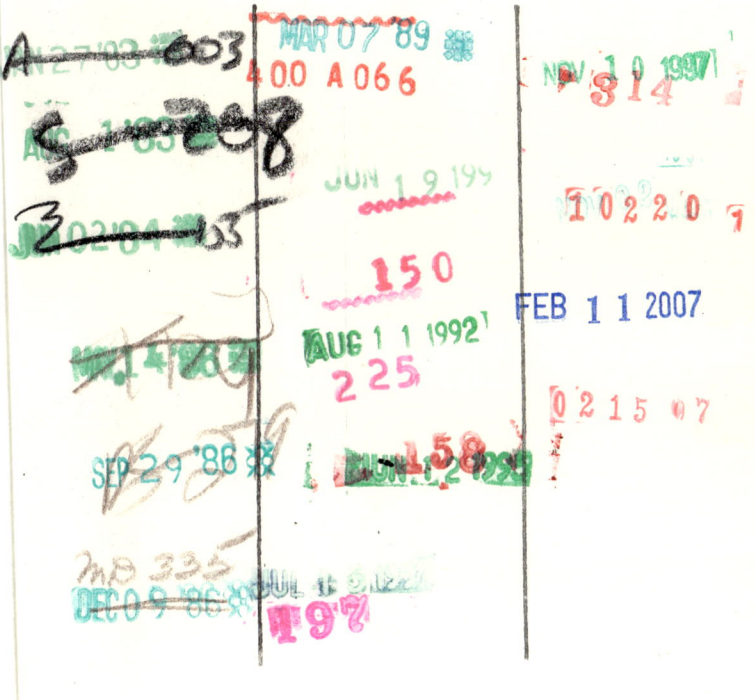

The MONTESSORI WAY

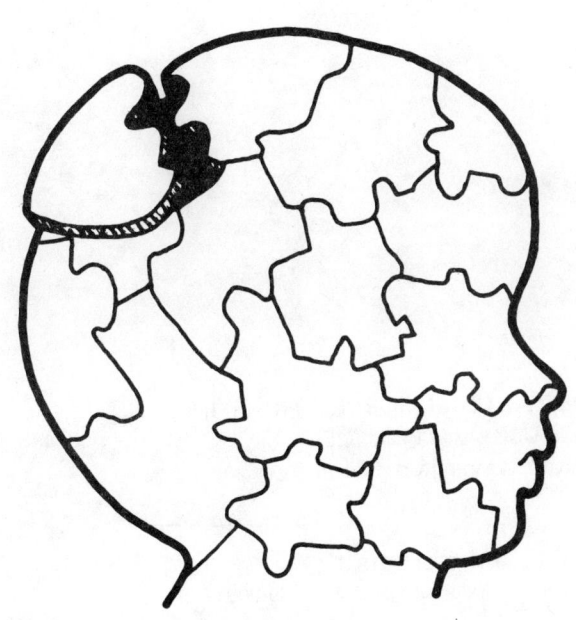

LENA L. GITTER

SPECIAL CHILD PUBLICATIONS, INC.

LB
775
·M8
G49
c.2

© 1970   SPECIAL CHILD PUBLICATIONS, INC.
        4535 Union Bay Place N.E.
        Seattle, Washington 98105

Standard Book Number: 87562-018-3
Library of Congress Catalog Card Number: 69-20317

All rights reserved. This book, or parts thereof, must not be used or reproduced in any manner without written permission. For information address the publisher.

Printed in the United States of America

TABLE OF CONTENTS

Biographical Note on Maria Montessori   7

Introduction   9

An Experience in Humanity   11

The Underachieving Child   30

The Role of the Teacher   40

The Unbroken Circuit   59

Exercises of Practical Life   75

Formation of Concepts   128

The Development of Language Skills   164

The Number Environment   208

Advancing the Curriculum   233

Bibliographies   251

MARIA MONTESSORI

BIOGRAPHICAL NOTE ON MARIA MONTESSORI

Maria Montessori was born to middle-class parents in Chiavalle, Italy, in 1870. While still a young girl she became interested in a medical career. Since this was unthinkable for a woman at that time, she met great opposition but her determination was unshakeable, and she was admitted to the Medical School of the University of Rome, although with conditions to assure the maintenance of her feminine modesty which seem rather quaint today. When she graduated at the age of 26, she received a double honors degree.

As a young doctor she visited asylums which developed her interest in mentally retarded children and led her to the work of Itard and Seguin, using an approach that was sensory and concrete, and her success was remarkable.

At the same time Montessori was revealed to be an observer of genius. In one of the essays in his book BASIC VERITIES, Charles Peguy wrote: "One must always tell what one sees. Above all, which is more difficult, one must always see what one sees." Montessori saw clearly, drew conclusions correctly and told accurately, and the rare combination of these three abilities turned her into a seminal figure in the history of education.

Government officials listened sympathetically to Montessori's request to educate these retarded children, feeling that little could be lost in such a hopeless experiment. Working through her first understanding of the power of the hand in education and carefully studying the brilliant work of the French doctors Itard and Seguin, whom she named as her predecessors, Montessori devised the first of her special pieces of equipment and, by trial and error, discovered that her children could indeed learn—could learn well enough, in fact, to pass the state examinations given to normal children in their first year of school.

Montessori was not only a theoretician but a disciplined observer who learned through doing and submitted herself to the child. Gradually she devised materials and equipment to realize her goals and formulated an underlying philosophy based on the dignity and spiritual worth of the child. Between 1912 and 1917 she put her ideas into five key books: THE MONTESSORI METHOD, PEDAGOGY AND ANTHROPOLOGY, DR. MONTESSORI'S OWN HANDBOOK, THE ADVANCED MONTESSORI METHOD, Vols. I and II.

Between 1917 and the end of her life she wrote twenty additional books and pamphlets on various aspects of her educational theory and practice.

In addition, Dr. Montessori traveled extensively to give training courses and to supervise additional schools as her method spread throughout the world. She lived for some time in Spain and found an especially warm welcome in Holland and, during World War II, in India where she was interned as an Italian but where the authorities gave her freedom to teach and to open schools, so that much of her most fruitful work was done in India.

Dr. Montessori died in Holland in 1952 at the age of 82 and was buried in Holland, her adopted country, whose love of freedom and concern for education she particularly valued.

Since her death her works have achieved greater popularity than ever before and the growth of Montessori schools in the United States is reaching phenomenal proportions. More and more, psychological research is confirming Montessori's observations about the unfolding of learning in the child.

INTRODUCTION

For forty years I have been a Montessori teacher. I began my work in Europe and continued it in America. I have taught in Viennese schools and in those of suburban Maryland. I have worked with poor children and middle-class children, with retarded and emotionally disturbed children, with gifted children. I have taught in Headstart programs, conducted workshops for parents and teachers as well as workshops for disadvantaged adults in Mississippi. I have worked in and studied classes in parochial and private schools as well as in public schools from one end of this country to the other. I have organized and participated in Montessori training programs and seminars in many colleges and universities.

Through all these years and experiences, I have seen a steadily increasing demand for more knowledge of the methods of Maria Montessori. Parents, educators, and social scientists, on hearing her name, read her books and are excited by them, but they remain puzzled about how to apply her words to contemporary situations and problems.

Nowhere is this interest greater than in the field of special education. Montessori started her work with retarded children, and her apparatus, as well as her underlying philosophy, was born of this fruitful work. She was able to observe, in slow-motion, as it were, the sensitive periods which govern the development of the normal child, and she applied this knowledge to her later work.

But there does not exist one comprehensive book to help those interested in special education in the Montessori way, a book which gives the practical guide for using Montessori's ideas along with the philosophy which permeated every step of her work.

This book attempts to fill that gap. It does not pretend to be a complete guide to Montessori — how can it be when Montessori herself wrote more than 20 books, and her disciples many, many more? But it is a thorough basic guide for anyone concerned with the special child — teachers, psychologists, therapists, parents. It gives the essentials of Montessori's philosophy of the child and his development, views that the findings of modern psychology have confirmed.

This book gives a large selection of Montessori exercises and materials. These exercises are not limited to the ones devised by Montessori but combine her work with my own. The Montessori system is not a rigid doctrinaire way of approaching education but, at its best, an open-ended system that allows each teacher to build creatively on the solid foundation already laid down by Montessori and her first followers.

I *have* limited the exercises, however, to the ones which my own experience has verified. They *do* work. I have tried all of them out in different learning situations over many years of teaching and I know from my own observations that they make a difference in the child's development.

Many of the exercises *do* require the background of a Montessori training course and I have eliminated those, since this book is intended for the many people who wish to use the Montessori method without formal training. A great deal of the method can, however, be assimilated without the need for this training once the attitude of Montessori is understood.

I have tried to convey this attitude so that it will become available to all who are interested in Montessori. In keeping with my aim, therefore, I have chosen exercises which do not require more background in Montessori than this book provides.

My last consideration was: can the materials required be made or constructed by the teacher or by interested parents? Of course, the equipment can be obtained from special supply houses. Sometimes, however, money is not available. Even more important is the sense of achievement that comes from making the equipment oneself. When I was in Mississippi working with desperately poor rural children and adults in the Headstart program, and when I returned later to work with Negro women in Natchez, I discovered anew the thrill that comes from making things with one's own hands.

Since the work of the hand is crucial in Montessori's philosophy and since she recognized how basic to learning the work of the hand is, it is only appropriate in a book dedicated to Montessori's work that emphasis should go on the actual making of the materials needed. It is then that the wonderful simplicity of the apparatus stands fully revealed, to be appreciated not only by the head but also by the hand.

In my native language, German, the verb *greifen* is used in two senses — for the physical and for the mental grasping of something. The closest equivalent in English is the word *grip;* the hand *grips* a tool, the mind *grips* or *is gripped by* an idea. It is easy to forget the literal meaning of *to grip* as we use the metaphorical one, but in Montessori both meanings operate simultaneously and literally, as the child *grips* or *grasps* learning through his hands.

I myself have *grasped* Montessori through a lifetime of experience in the field. Through all the changes in my own life as well as in the life of our society, I have seen this kind of education prove itself again and again.

We are only now at the beginning of yet greater changes in education, especially in special education. More sophisticated diagnostic techniques, advances in medical care, advances in psychological understanding, all combine to bring excitement and challenge to special education. But Montessori remains valid.

It is my hope that this book will demonstrate that validity to many others.

AN EXPERIENCE IN HUMANITY

Historical Background

Discovery of the handicapped child had to await the discovery of the child. Not until childhood was seen as a separate stage in human development could anyone focus on the specific problems of the handicapped. I would therefore like to follow this historic development by speaking of the discovery of the child in general, relating Montessori's work to this history, then going on to consider the underachieving child in further detail. It was no coincidence that the awareness of childhood came at the same time that retardation was differentiated from insanity and insanity itself was seen as a medical rather than as a religious problem.[1] Man's picture of the world changed radically in the 18th century. What had not been seen previously now seemed new and exciting.

Jean-Jacques Rousseau was the pioneer in the discovery of the child. Until Rousseau children were seen as small adults.[2] With schooling limited to upper-class boys, children worked side by side with adults on farm and in household tasks from an early age. If any differences were admitted, they were linked to the belief that children were naturally more evil (as shown by their behavior) and had to have this evil beaten out of them by rigorous punishment.

Rousseau, on the contrary, proclaimed that mankind was naturally good and was made evil by society. Deficient education was responsible for the thwarting of childhood's naturally beneficent impulses, and in *EMILE* he drew up a plan for the education of the young.

Rousseau's ideas are not followed today but he is still seen as the single most influential writer in changing mankind's impressions about the value of childhood. Pestalozzi, an early worker with quite small children, was a fellow Swiss, and Froebel, founder of the kindergarten, was familiar with the work of Rousseau and Pestalozzi.

Economic considerations favored the extension of education in the 19th century. Children of workers continued to work alongside adults, often in appalling conditions, in the

---

[1] Foucault, Michel, MADNESS AND CIVILIZATION. N. Y.: Pantheon, 1965.
[2] Aries, Philippe, CENTURIES OF CHILDHOOD. N.Y.: Knopf, 1962.

mines and mills of an industrializing Continent and in England, but children of the growing middle-class were sent to school for longer years and had to master the subjects which were the mark of their status. The growth of professions and the need for business men of many kinds in the complex urban societies of the West, created a demand for teachers, and this climate encouraged some experimentation.

While this work was going forward, two French doctors, Gaspard Itard and Edouard Seguin, were pioneering in the treatment of the retarded so brilliantly that all subsequent work in the field rests firmly on their work. Itard's classic WILD BOY OF AVEYRON described a long-range attempt to educate a mute savage found in the wild forests of Aveyron where he had apparently been abandoned before speech had appeared. The child had survived by living with animals but had not learned to speak when he was found in his late pre-adolescence.

Itard took the child to live with him and devised ingenious methods for teaching Victor, as he called him. Although he never could teach Victor to speak and became convinced that the child was retarded, not merely suffering from lack of exposure to society, he achieved remarkable results in many other areas, and his book is an extraordinary record of a great intellectual achievement.

Itard's contributions to the "New Education" were enormous:

> The genetic concept of education; education by progressive stages of individual development.

> Adjustment by the teacher of his methods to the peculiar needs of the student.

> The notion that a relaxed environment with suitable stimuli can become a potent factor in education.

> The use of the educational material with a view to its having a direct bearing upon the development of the child, rather than, as propounded by John Locke, to facilitate the teaching process and to endow it with a playlike quality.

Seguin, a pupil of Itard, developed his methods further in the treatment of the retarded and wrote about his work in IDIOCY: AND ITS TREATMENT BY THE PHYSIOLOGICAL METHOD (published 1866), another landmark in the field of special education. It was Seguin who systematically developed materials and techniques for teaching the retarded through a system of physiological education. He believed his system embodied the true principles and the best methods of normal education.

In 1837 he began the education of an idiot boy and after 18 months, he had taught the boy to make use of his senses, to take care of himself, to speak, and to write. In 1839 he opened his school for idiots in Paris, the first of its kind. His successful work attracted French and foreign educators and philanthropists. Schools of this kind were established in England and several continental countries.

In 1850 he and his family emigrated to the United States. A small beginning had been made in the establishment of institutions as a result of the influence of his work. He acted as director of the Pennsylvania School for Idiots, inspected many schools for defectives and often wrote unfavorable criticisms. He was the founder and first president of the American Association for Mental Deficiency and the true father of this field in America.

His physiological method of education is not limited to defective children but is a system formulated with a view to helping all the developmental needs of the normal child. He felt that his work contained new ideas, not only for the education of idiots but also for education in general, and time has proven him right.

Seguin's physiological method recognized the relationship between sensory perception and muscular activity. He applied his physiological method very successfully with mentally deficient children. His techniques have orderly sequences: from passive to active; gross to refined; sensation to perception; observation to comparison; known to unknown; teaching in context and teaching by relationship rather than rote; mobility with immobility; activity with rest.

Seguin recognized the love of the retarded for routine. He based discipline on order, using materials and experiences of daily living for moral and intellectual education. He opened and closed the day with songs and happiness.

Dr. Seguin is often called the father of the educational toy. He developed a number of simple toys. These were designed to educate the retarded children, to help them stimulate the senses, and to classify their impressions. He believed that each toy or game should have only one difficulty or challenge, not several.

He believed the education of the child must begin with the training and development of his muscular and sensorial powers. At first sight all children look much alike; at the second their countless differences appear like insurmountable obstacles; but better viewed, these differences resolve themselves into groups easily understood and not unmanageable.

The hand is an aggressive power in its power to work. The girl who begins to wipe the dishes, the boy who picks up stones in the field are above all helping to save themselves from the horrors of idiocy.

> *One of the earliest and most fatal antagonisms taught to a child is the forbidding of using his hands to ascertain qualities of surrounding objects of which is sight gives him but an imperfect notion, if it be not aided by touch; and of breaking many things as well to acquire the proper idea of solidarity. The youngest child, when he begins to totter on his arched legs, goes about touching, handling, and breaking everything. It is our duty to foster and direct the beautiful curiosity, to make it the regular channel for the organization of correct perceptions and tactile accuracy. As for breaking, it must be turned into desire of preservation and the power of holding with the will; nothing is so simple.* IDIOCY (p.204)

> *Perceptions are acquired by the mind through sense, not by the senses. This is proved anew every time a new sense is created or an old one improved by some discovery such as spectacles, telescopes, microscopes, algebra, compressors, elec-*

> tric motors, etc. *It is not that artificial sense which perceives, it is the mind through it.*
> IDIOCY (p. 199)

Some of Seguin's Conclusions

> That the senses and each one in particular can be submitted to physiological training by which their primordial capability may be indefinitely intellectualized.
>
> That one sense may be substituted for another as a means of comprehension and of intellectual culture.
>
> That the physiological exercise of a sense corroborates the action as well as verifies the acquisition of another.
>
> That our most abstract ideas are comparisons and generalizations by the mind of what we have perceived through the senses.
>
> The education of the modes of perception is to prepare pablum for the mind proper.
>
> The sensations are intellectual functions performed through external apparatus as much as reasoning, imagination, etc. through mere internal organs.
> IDIOCY (p. 20)

In addition to building upon the work of Itard, Seguin also discovered the practically unknown Jacob Rodriguez Pereira (1715-1780), who had devoted many years to the study and education of congenital deaf mutes.[3] Pereira's work was in many respects beyond Itard's and Seguin was amazed by the practical results Pereira achieved with his education through the senses. Pereira, like Itard and Seguin, conducted his work in a careful, scientific manner, so that further work could be built upon it.

The validity of Seguin's principles — as well as the influence these had on Montessori's mind — can be seen even in brief extracts from a speech he gave in 1869 summarizing some general results of his work:[4]

> *The first problem is to disengage and develop the mind of an idiot, which has hitherto been as if hidden beneath the useless muscles and the insensate nerves, components of his weak and inefficient body. The second problem, though by no means the last, is to apply this partially liberated intellect to the acquisition of useful knowledge and good habits.*

Seguin also made clear his belief that the way to educate the retarded was by "educating the mind through perceptions instead of by pre-arranged reasonings. . . .The organs of sensation being within our reach, and those of thought out of it, the former are the first that we can set in action. . . .The physiological education of the senses must precede the psychical education of the mind."

---

[3] See Fynne, Robert, MONTESSORI AND HER INSPIRERS. London: Longmans, Green, 1924.

[4] All quotations on this page from: Seguin, Edward, "New Facts and Remarks Concerning Idiocy," a lecture delivered before the New York Medical Journal Association, October 15, 1869. N.Y.: Wm. Wood & Co., 1870.

From his own experience, then, he made the classic formulation: "The physiological education of the senses is the royal road to the education of the intellect: experience, not memory, is the mother of ideas."

Finally, in this same speech, as in his other works, Seguin pointed out what Montessori also realized, that the same principles which make education of the retarded effective will assist in the education of the normal child. It is surely remarkable to consider that Seguin published the results of his work a century ago and they remain as fresh as ever in their formulation of the problem, observation and methods of training!

Maria Montessori

The final impetus to work with children was provided by Sigmund Freud with his studies of the importance of early dreams, memories and experiences in the formation of the adult personality. He probed back to the earliest period in human development, before the age of three, to reveal that basic personality structures were formed long before the "age of reason," which was the earliest period to capture the close attention of most educators.

The work of Freud and his followers also focused attention on the child *as child* in his deepest personality modalities. In his classic paper "On Memory and Childhood Amnesia," Ernest Schachtel analyzes the absolute differences that exist between childhood and adult perception of experience.[5]

Maria Montessori was a contemporary of Freud's and took part in the intellectual revolution of European thought from 1880-1914, a revolution which has shaped modern man.

The determination Montessori manifested while at the Medical School of the University of Rome, coupled with years of hard work to prove that she could do as well as her male colleagues, stood her well in the intellectual adventures of her later life.

The World of the Retarded

Her introduction to the world of the retarded came quite by accident. When she was a resident at the University Hospital, she had to take her turn in providing patients for clinical study and was sent to an asylum for the insane in search of suitable "subjects." While she was there she noticed a group of children kept in an entirely empty room and was told that they were mental defectives. At that time, such children were kept with the insane.

Observing these children, Montessori noticed that they had made tiny pellets of bread crumbs left from their meals and had turned them into toys to occupy their minds. Much impressed by the resourcefulness of these defectives in manufacturing play materials from a barren environment, Montessori began to study literature on the subject of mental retardation at the same time that she was slowly formulating her own ideas on the importance of sensory stimulation.

---

[5]Schachtel, Ernest, METAMORPHOSIS, N.Y.: Basic Books, 1963, pp.279-322.

Indeed, her own work followed her principles, for when she came upon Seguin's book on idiocy, she copied it by hand, feeling that she would better remember the pages if they literally flowed into her mind through her hand and through the active muscle response of copying.

Calling into play once more her powers of determination, Montessori requested and received permission from the Ministry of Education to form a school for the retarded to test her theories. Education officials felt that they had nothing to lose, since nothing was expected from such children, and so the Orthophrenic School began its work.

Montessori herself summarized these first experiments in the Lectures on Pedagogy delivered at the Scuola Magistrale Ortofrenica in 1900 (see Appendix). From these lectures we can see how closely Montessori observed the children and how early she hit upon the basic sensorial motivations which, following Seguin, she saw as the means by which the mental abilities of the children could be developed.

For example, in the section on General Rules, she writes:

> *To attract the attention of defective children, strong sensory stimulants are necessary. The lessons, therefore, should be eminently practical. Every lesson should begin with the presentation of the object to be illustrated by the teacher in a few words distinctly pronounced with continual modulations of the voice and accompanied by imitative expression. The lessons should be made as attractive as possible and, as far as practicable, presented under the form of games, so as to arouse the curiosity of the child... But however amusing the game may be, the lesson should always be stopped while the child is still willing to continue... To fix ideas, lessons should be repeated many times.*[6]

Montessori modified many of her theories as she worked with a wide range of children over the years, but her basic principles remain sound almost 70 years later because they were based on precise observations of how children actually function.

What happened next? Montessori's "defectives" improved so radically that they were able to pass the state test given to admit normal children into the primary school! Far from being overly proud of her accomplishments, Montessori was driven to reflect on the inadequate preparation given to normal children if her defectives could reach the required standard with no further instruction than that provided by her methods. So she went one step further and requested to teach normal children. The story of her first Children's House is celebrated in the history of education, but what is important for those in the field of special education to realize is that Montessori's work started with retarded children, who provided the first test of her method's success.

Montessori's method in general — as it applies to mentally retarded, socially disadvantaged and normal children—has been receiving more and more recognition over the years, not only from educators but also from those who have no particular interest in promoting one method but who see the viability of the insights which characterized her work. Paul

---

[6]Montessori, Maria, THE ADVANCED MONTESSORI METHOD. N.Y.: Frederick A. Stokes, 1917.

Weiss, Sterling Professor of Philosophy at Yale University, speaks of Montessori in his "galaxy of geniuses" who persuaded the world that a child is a child. Later in his book, THE MAKING OF MEN, Weiss formulates in his own language the central preoccupation of Montessori's lifetime of work.

> *To see the child as a child does not mean that it is to be left childish, an unformed ed creature which lives through experiences, but neither investigates nor matures. It must be given work that is appropriate to its powers and its possible satisfactions. Sometimes it must be made to think and to act, to attend and to work in direct opposition to its express desires. But that does not preclude giving it interesting material; it should not preclude its being taught by someone interested in it.[7]*

In her terminology, Montessori spoke of the true freedom of children which does not consist in untrammeled disobedience but rather in disciplined obedience coming from within to serve the good of the child's development. The interesting material Montessori provided was, of course, her sensory apparatus with their bright colors and careful construction, appealing to eye and to motor development as well as training specific skills.

Montessori developed what she called the "prepared environment" which already possesses a certain order and disposes the child to develop at his own speed, according to his own capacities, and in a noncompetitive atmosphere in his first school years. "Never let a child risk failure, until he has a reasonable chance of success," said Montessori, understanding the necessity for the acquisition of a basic skill before its use in a competitive learning situation. For the retarded child competition means terror and failure, where the opportunity to work alone at his own speed under the watchful eye of a teacher who assists him only when he needs it can be life-enhancing.

Basic Principles

Fundamental to the Montessori method are the absorbent mind, sensitive periods, liberty within limits, freedom in the prepared environment, order in the prepared environment, autoeducation.

Montessori Materials And Activities

Montessori materials and activities are divided into four general classes: 1) exercise of practical life, grace, and courtesy; 2) sensorial materials; 3) language arts and the development of the mathematical mind; and 4) development of character and spiritual life.

Exercises of practical life include learning to pour (starting with dry materials such as beans, rice, and progressing to pouring liquids); polishing glass, brass, silver, shoes; washing hands, tables, clothes; sweeping and mopping the floor; dusting; arranging flowers; putting the room in order; and working with dressing frames.

Sensorial materials are not intended to "train the senses" but to give children experience

---

[7] Weiss, Paul, THE MAKING OF MEN. Carbondale, Ill.: Southern Illinois Univ. Press, 1967, p.20.

in using their senses to make fine discriminations. Eyesight may not be made sharper through exercise, but a child can becomes interested in making fine visual discriminations through working with materials that demand visual acuity. An attitude of discrimination and appreciation of fine differences can be learned, and the sensory exercises aim to spark a child's interests in so using his senses.

Academic teaching materials for the three R's are graded in difficulty, designed to require a minimum of teaching and to allow maximum "autoeducation."

Through the psychological prepared environment, character and spiritual life are developed.

The most important features of Montessori educational materials are 1) isolation of difficulties; 2) a clear indication from the structure of the material of its intended use; 3) "control of error" built into the system, so the child can see from the results of his work whether or not he has succeeded.

Montessori was able to systematize the work of her predecessors and add to it many unique observations, because she was able to actually see children as they were, not as adults spoke about them. Nor did she foist her own preconceptions on them. Her essay on "Child Character"[8] is only one example of the brilliance of her clarity as she observed children.

The same recognition of Montessori's grasp of the essentials in childhood education is made by men in other professions who have come to these same essentials by different disciplines. Riley W. Gardner, a psychologist with The Menninger Foundation discussed Montessori's achievements from the viewpoint of one interested in the psychological health of children.

> *Understanding of the sensory-motor nature of the young child's intelligence seemed to stem. . .from uniquely astute observations of young children. It was the genius of Montessori to sense that this was true, to employ it in the training methods she used with young children, and to understand that only by using methods appropriate to the age level (or the level of retardation) could maximum acceleration of cognitive development be achieved.*[8]

Gardner went on to make a point especially relevant to work with retarded children:

> *. . . I will note there that what the Montessori method seems to do is to put the child into effective coordination with certain features of external reality in such a way that he becomes the instigator of his learning. It seems to me worthy of note that a common general axiom concerning learning seems to guide this approach and the approach often involved in effective psychotherapy.* [9]

---

[8]Gardner, Riley W., Ph.D., "A Psychologist Looks at Montessori." THE AMERICAN MONTESSORI SOCIETY BULLETIN. Vol. 4, Nos. 1 & 2, 1966.

[9]Ibid.

Since so many retarded children are suffering from emotional impediments to learning, the approach which Gardner links to psychotherapy can serve effectively to handle children with such difficulties.

Montessori in America

After years of growth elsewhere in the world, Montessori has only lately come into its own in the United States, although the first Montessori school was founded here more than a half-century ago.

> *Great as lay interest was in the Montessori methods, there was no lack of professional endorsement. In addition to the approval given by Henry W. Holmes of Harvard, the United States Commissioner of Education, Dr. P. P. Claxton, stood with Montessori. Nor was this professional approval simple faddist enthusiasm. . . .By 1898 Dr. Montessori was the leading European student of special education for mentally retarded children. Her study of medicine, psychology, and anthropology — the latter two fields in their first empirical undergirded research on the mentally handicapped and identified Dr. Montessori as among the very first European proponents of a scientific study of education — scientific in a quite modern sense of the term. It was no penchant for faddism, then, that won such educators as Anne E. George to Montessori. Miss George, recognized in the United States as the foremost authority on the kindergarten, learned Italian and translated into English. . .THE MONTESSORI METHOD. Further, Miss George offered to operate a school in the United States and in accordance with Montessori theory and using the Montessori "didactic materials."*
>
> *. . .The pupils were not retarded; Montessori had moved from thought on training the intellectually handicapped to the schooling of the normal child.*[10]

That first school was founded in 1913 by Miss George. Her own report of this work is of great historical interest — it shows how, beneath the inevitable trappings of her own time, the timelessness of Montessori's work comes through. How little of this is marked by the passage of time — and nothing solid is touched at all! When we consider how quickly the new becomes the outworn, this achievement is even more remarkable, pointing up the essence of Montessori's method, which is bound neither to one class nor to one country — indeed, her influence spread outside the boundaries of Western civilization when she made her great impact in India.

Despite the success of the George School and others and the great appeal of Dorothy Canfield Fisher's A MONTESSORI MOTHER, this initial flurry did not lead to large numbers of schools or any sustained influence. Why did this happen?

In his study of the history of Montessori in America, Gilbert Donahue quotes Robert Beck, who asserts: "For the first time in modern history of the American public, genuine

---

[10]Donahue, Gilbert E., "Montessori and American Education Literature: An Unfinished Chapter in the History of Ideas". Distributed by the American Montessori Society, 1962.

lay enthusiasm had been engendered but died in the face of professional opposition."[11] And we must not underestimate the influence of Montessori's chief critic, William Heard Kilpatrick of Teachers College, Columbia University, at that time the fountainhead of American educational wisdom.

It is difficult to isolate particular reasons, but a general over-view of the social situation in the United States will explain some factors mitigating against the spread of Montessori schools. Shortly after the founding of the first Montessori schools, America became involved in World War I. The war and its aftermath changed the United States into an international power and helped to erase much of the provincialism that had marked an earlier America. The changes that occurred in American society in the 1920's were great enough to involve much of the psychological energy of the people and leave very little for educational innovation and reform.

Montessori was not the only educator to fall victim to this eclipse. John Dewey and his followers in "progressive" education suffered not from neglect but from misunderstanding and misapplication of their ideas which led, finally, to the rejection of their methods based not on experience but on inadequate trials of not-quite-grasped principles. There seemed to be no time for the careful observation that was necessary to make even a small start at renewing our educational system. And, in fact, there were not many people who could see the necessity for such renewal — what was good enough for their parents was good enough for their children.

The work of Freud first reached the United States via the expatriates of the 20's but here, too, misinterpretation was the order of the day and people reacted in horror from what they imagined to be Freud's idea — complete permissiveness and sexual license. In the midst of all this confusion, it was difficult to see children as they actually were, rather than in the light of certain preconceived notions of how they had to be.

Popularization of the work of John Watson and his school of behaviorists and the influence of Gesell on ideas of upbringing fostered the belief that children developed in a fixed way as they reached "readiness" ages and nothing much that anyone could do would change this rate of development. The belief also prevailed that intelligence was fixed at birth and gradually revealed itself as the child grew and nothing much could be done about that, either.

Some nursery schools were established according to Dewey's principles of education, but the Great Depression of the 30's effectively brought a stop to the spread of pre-school education as the struggle for a bare living consumed the time and energy of most of the population. Nor was money available.

Then came preoccupation with the rise of Hitler and the great effort of fighting World War II. Small wonder that little time or money was available for research in child development!

[11]Beck, Robert H., "Kilpatrick's Critique of Montessori's Method and Theory," STUDIES IN PHILOSOPHY AND EDUCATION, Vol I, No. 4, 1961, pp. 153-162.

However, just at this time several things were happening in America that prepared the ground for the postwar excitement over pre-school education. First, the Nazi persecutions drove to America large numbers of Freud's disciples and students; they presented to the United States a full picture of the work done by psychoanalysis and through their teaching and translating activities, replaced earlier half-truths and misunderstandings with a more complex view of Freudian theories of early childhood development. The controversies that swirled around differing interpretations of Freud's words served to bring this field more and more to the attention of educated people.

The war itself necessitated the employment of large numbers of women outside the home; the day care center grew up to fill a need that had not previously existed in more than a few cases. Mothers could *see* that their young children were thriving where the day care was good and they began to press for a continuation of pre-school education after the war.

Then, in the immediate postwar period, several radical changes in American society brought a sudden demand for nursery schools and a genuine interest in the education of the young child. The baby boom, coupled with the millions of returning veterans who took advantage of the GI Bill to pursue college education, meant that all over the country couples with small children depended on the working mother to make ends meet. College began opening nursery schools to provide for the care of these children.

The fact that many of these millions of young people—who most likely would not have considered a college education before the war—were broadening their horizons in so many ways created an awareness of the importance of the early years of life and a demand that nursery schools help make the most of these early years by providing trained teachers and play equipment parents could not afford.

After graduating from college, these men and their young families went where the jobs were, often far from home and grandparents. They moved into the burgeoning suburbs, far from urban amenities, and young mothers found themselves without any possibility of getting away from their young children for necessary rest and recreation. All around were similar couples. The solution, in community after community was the cooperative nursery school, which would care for young children for a small fee and some outlay of time on the parents' parts. This way the children would be receiving developmental experiences of great importance while mothers would be relieved of the constant burden of child care.

It is important to remember, however, that by the early 1950's this growth of nursery education was middle-class and upper middle-class. There was as yet no realization of the needs of the poor.

In a way this is not surprising. It had taken many centuries before people had been able to see that children were not simply small versions of adults, and the writings of the great "liberators of the child" still had not penetrated into many segments of society. This was a genuinely new idea and the ramifications were barely understood. The concept of fixed intelligence remained and the growth of IQ testing seemed to confirm this belief, since IQ test scores remained relatively constant over the years as children were re-tested. Understanding and absorption of new discoveries took time.

But the demand for nursery schools and for trained pre-school teachers had set the stage for the remarkable developments of the late 1950's and the 1960's. There was increasing research into learning (some specific examples will be given in the following section), and they pushed the learning process back earlier and earlier in life. Sputnik created a panic in America, a panic which lead to a re-examination of our educational systems and purposes. Not all of the results were fortunate, but the time was suddenly ripe for renewed interest in the work of Montessori as part of the demand for better ways of educating our children.

How can we account for this sudden burst of interest specifically in Montessori? The immediate cause was surely the work of Nancy Rambusch, who studied the Montessori method in Europe and came back to America ready to found Whitby School in Connecticut and to organize the American Montessori Society. Her articles and speeches all over the country, plus the evidence of success achieved at Whitby, brought Montessori to the attention of many people in a dramatic way. An entire generation of young parents who had never heard of Montessori before began looking into her work with fresh eyes.

This time, too, Montessori suffered through misunderstanding. Parental demand in many cases was for early reading and Montessori was often advocated as a way to have your child reading and writing at age three or four. Fortunately, the structure of Montessori and the requirement that the child develop through use of the sensorial material enabled teacher and children to resist a great deal of this pressure.

Although Montessori had started her work with retarded and disadvantaged children, this new Montessori foundation was middle-class. It was not until society as a whole woke up to the extent of poverty in this country and to the educational poverty whose long-range effects are so destructive both to individuals and to the society as a whole, that it was possible to see again the value of Montessori as a way of educating those children who were out of the mainstream of American life.

Slowly, people in education turned back to Montessori's own writings and began to apply them in programs for children with learning problems, in programs for disadvantaged children. There is still much misunderstanding (as well as honest disagreement, of course), based in part on mis-reading, based also on the rigidity of some Montessorians who have an "all or nothing" approach.

My own belief is that such an approach is unfortunate, and I think the pages which follow will demonstrate how flexible Montessori actually is if applied with imagination and sympathy. What is essential is that the Montessorian follow the great Italian educator in actually *observing* children, for the basis of Montessori's work springs from the scientific exactitude of her observation, an observation which has no room for sentimental preconceptions of how children should behave or how children ought to learn. As the French essayist Charles Peguy wrote: "To write about what one sees is difficult; even more difficult is to see what one sees." And indeed this is the case;

like the people in Poe's "The Purloined Letter," we do not see what is just under our noses.

Contemporary research is helping us to see. Belief in a fixed intelligence has been replaced by an understanding of the role of the infant's earliest experiences in creating psychological attitudes toward learning and life, attitudes which can either help or hinder the development of intelligence. A great deal of work is being done on the role of sensory deprivation as a hindrance to intelligence. We are becoming increasingly aware of the class bias in IQ tests and the factors which determine performance on such a verbally-oriented test. Cognizance is being taken of the variety of childhood emotional disorders which can temporarily or permanently affect the expression of intelligence. Minimal brain dysfunction and dyslexia, unrecognized even a decade ago, are being analyzed by growing numbers of skilled persons in the fields of psychology and medicine. Educators can turn to published assistance from many fields of learning.

Benjamin Bloom has presented evidence of the small but significant growth in IQ that occurs in early years when a more favorable environment replaces an unfavorable one (STABILITY AND CHANGE IN HUMAN CHARACTERISTICS). And in a paper entitled "The Psychology of Mental Retardation," Dr. Ronald R. Koegler, of the UCLA Neuropsychiatric Institute, summed up the result of many years of work by different experimenters, when he wrote:

> *In recent years there has been a tremendous change in our concept of the development of intelligence. It is no longer regarded as a fixed, stable quantity which is given us at birth and remains unchanged for our lifetime. This, therefore, means that mental deficiency also is not always a permanent diagnosis, and is always merely a description of the current result of an interplay between heredity, environment, and the IQ test.* [12]

A considerable amount of work has been done in this area by the psychologist J. McV. Hunt, who wrote the introduction to the contemporary reprint of THE MONTESSORI METHOD, showing how Montessori's discoveries were being repeatedly confirmed by investigators with more sophisticated tools of analysis than she had when she made her inspired observations.

Koegler goes on to speak of the implications of such work in the realm of education for the retarded.

> *In order to fully develop a program for the retarded, it is extremely important that the mutability of intelligence be recognized, and the infinite possibilities for further development of intelligence understood.... The contemporary emphasis on the rehabilitation of the mentally retarded has come at a time when we have the scientific evidence to show that significant alterations can be made in individual intellectual ability,*

---

[12] Koegler, Ronald R., M.D., "The Psychology of Mental Retardation." Paper delivered to the American Montessori Society Seminar, Washington, D. C., 1964.

especially among children....This does not mean that we are going to cure Mongolism with education. It certainly does mean that we can improve upon our present methods of treating the young, apparently retarded child. An enriched sensory-motor experience will result in intellectual advances that may change the final outcome from "trainable" to "educable," or from "educable" to "non-retarded and functioning usefully in society![13]

This change in the concept of a fixed intelligence and replacement of pessimism by guarded optimism in the diagnosis and treatment of mental retardation is the result of increased experimentation with mentally retarded and normal children. At the same time the value of IQ tests has been shown to be questionable when socio-economic background has not been taken into consideration, and there is growing awareness of the socially causative factors in seeming retardation. The aim of Head-start programs was to reverse the process whereby children from socially disadvantaged backgrounds fell further and further behind as they went through the grades.

There is growing interest in education for all children from the age of three on; psychologists working on a wide variety of experiments involving learning in children and infants are arriving at results which indicate that the optimum learning period begins almost at birth and extends to the years when school conventionally begins. The work of men like Omar Moore and Professor Skinner with programmed learning has pointed to ways in which the child's natural abilities can be fully developed through disciplined cooperation with his maturing powers and through the use of learning programs specifically designed to challenge the child while providing consistent experience of success as he learns.

Still more work is going on which tends to prove the concept of the "self-fulfilling prophecy"; that is, the child will perform as he senses he is expected to perform. If a teacher treats him as dull, he will respond dully; conversely, treated as a person with unusual abilities, he will respond accordingly.

All of this is only a brief outline; even a slightly fuller report would be a book in itself. I would like to turn now to a more detailed examination of a few research findings which confirm Montessori's observations of 60 years before. It is important that we realize to what extent Montessori's work is being confirmed by a variety of independent research workers so that we see her system (as she herself maintained) solidly based on scientific understanding. Montessori thought of her work as contributing toward a "science of man," and the research discussed below provides exciting confirmation of her accuracy.

SOME SUGGESTIVE RESEARCH

Some extremely interesting material dealing specifically with problems of mental retardation—although not limited in its implications to this specific area—can be found in results reported in MENTAL RETARDATION ABSTRACTS, published by the National Institute of Mental Health in Bethesda, Maryland.

[13] Ibid.

The following are a necessarily limited selection of results reported in the 1964 volume which show clearly the relation between Montessori's ideas and quite independent work being done today.

For example, E. C. Neuhas, writing in REHABILITATION RECORD (1964, 5, 32-35), on audiovisual job training, lists the following principles as the ones which guided supervisors training retarded people to hold jobs; 1) the skill had to be broken down into as many independent job steps as possible; 2) repetition of job steps was important; 3) verbal instructions need to be brief and easily understood; 4) reinforcement of feedback must be supplied.... Here we see virtually the entire **rationale** behind the basic Montessori approach to learning!

Similarly, G. Tarjan, writing on rehabilitation of the mentally retarded for the JOURNAL OF THE AMERICAN MEDICAL ASSOCIATION (1964, 187, 867-870), recommends that academic education of the retarded, rather than being directed to scholastic knowledge, be geared to provide concrete achievements of well-learned simple technical tasks, which the retarded person can often learn well through repetition and rote memory.

In another area of development, findings reported by J. L. McCarthy in MENTAL RETARDATION (1953, 2, 90-96) reinforce another basic Montessori learning device. McCarthy writes that labeling is the first developmental step of language. Reasoning is the implicit trail and error in which man shoves symbols around in his head rather than physical objects in the environment. Here McCarthy has provided some of the rationale for the matching and labeling work done by Montessori students and for the extensive use of sensorial materials, where the child begins by "shoving symbols around in the physical environment" **before** he begins shoving them around in his head. For the retarded child, who may never leave the stage of needing the physical object, such experience is especially valuable, but the normal child also needs this sensorial prelude to true reasoning.

A most suggestive dissertation by H. Van De Riet, "The effects of praise and reproof on paired-associate learning in educationally retarded children" (DISSERTATION ABSTRACTS, 1963, 23, 1250-1251), reports the results of experiments conducted with underachieving subjects to test the hypothesis that "children with generalized learning disabilities are so threatened by success that praise of their performance is detrimental to further learning. Success constitutes a threat because these children have a need to fail." The conclusion pointed to the fact that "while formal praise may hinder immediate performance, reproof may have long range consequences detrimental to learning. Therefore, the avoidance of both praise and reproof for learning achievement may be the wisest alternative."

Without having experimental proof Montessori was aware of this hindrance to learning when she devised her self-correcting materials. The child using Montessori equipment depends on the teacher only to learn proper use of the equipment; otherwise, he can judge his own performance through the self-correcting nature of the device itself, thus avoiding the necessity for either externally awarded blame or praise.

Finally, one of the most interesting reports was made by C. C. Nelson in MENTAL RETARDATION (1963, 1, 28-31), because it reads almost like the very words a Montessorian would use!

> *If adjustment* [of the mentally retarded] *is to be effective, the self-concept should be positive and reality-oriented. The Nation's 5 million mentally retarded children and millions of children handicapped in other ways* [i.e. socially disadvantaged] *are limited in developing a positive self concept in at least two ways: society tacitly expects the same behavior of the handicapped as it expects of all persons, and educational programs are traditionally built upon the presupposition that all participants are normal and capable of profiting from similar educational experiences. The mentally retarded child in the normal classroom tends to absorb and develop the aspiration level of his normal peers and since his handicap will not permit him to reach this level, he experiences failure and tends to devaluate himself so that he develops strong feelings of unworthiness and holds his abilities in low esteem.*

Having taught in special education classes for many years, I can confirm the precise observations of Nelson in this regard. And when we remember that, in addition to diagnosed retardates, millions of children suffer from social handicaps, emotional disabilities, minimal brain damage, dyslexia and similar problems which result in impaired learning, we can see the importance of developing educational programs which are programmed to allow for individual accomplishment so that all children can develop a positive self-concept in place of the rigid, academically-oriented classroom where only one criteria for successful performance is allowed.

Two Important Research Projects

The major research projects, conducted over a long period of time, provide valuable information on the worth of a Montessori pre-school education for the normal child, information which will undoubtedly affect the estimation of Montessori pre-school education in the future.

The first Study, MONTESSORI PRE-SCHOOL EDUCATION, was conducted under an Office of Education Grant by Dr. Urban H. Fleege, Professor of Education at DePaul University in Chicago, Dr. Michael S. Black, Chief of the Division of Psychometrics & Biostatistics of the Institute of Juvenile Research and John A. Rackauskas, a research associate at DePaul, who assisted Dr. Fleege. The full report is available from DePaul University.

When the study began in 1963, there were no objective reports on the comparative effectiveness of Montessori pre-school programs, only personal and subjective observations. Dr. Fleege and his associates set out to study, as carefully as possible, two sets of children, those attending a good, other-than-Montessori pre-school and their paired associates from the same community and the same socio-economic, cultural and educational level home attending an average, perhaps slightly-below-average Montessori school.

Are there any differences between these two groups of children? Are they noticeable by their parents? By the teachers in the public and parochial schools at the first and second grade level to which they transfer?

After exhaustive analysis of the relevant material, including numerous questionnaires plus the results of a number of tests plus observation, and after making appropriate statistical analyses, the conclusions of Dr. Fleege and his associates, drawn from their report, are as follows:

> Analysis of variance...confirms statistically the superiority of gains in verbal ability made by Montessori trained children over gains made by a matched group of other than Montessori trained children....

> Ninety-four percent of Montessori trained children five to five-and-one-half years old were ready to enter first grade as compared with only 50 percent of this age group in the Control group. The comparable percentages for reading readiness were 67 and 30 percent respectively, thus indicating a higher maturity and greater readiness level produced in the Montessori trained children.

> Children in the public and parochial primary grades who had attended Montessori pre-school were found to be superior, at a statistically significant level, to their peers who had attended pre-schools other than Montessori, in inter-personal relations, in learning ability and interest in learning. No significant differences were found, however, between the groups in creativity, both groups having made equal progress.

> Parochial and public school primary teachers reported no particular adjustment problems "peculiar to Montessori pre-school trained children." The majority rated children who had attended a Montessori pre-school as more independent, less in need of the teacher and as evidencing more leadership than their non-Montessori trained peers.

> Nearly twice as many Montessori parents as other-than-Montessori pre-school parents noted a definite carry-over and implementation on the part of the child in the home of many of the pre-school intended outcomes.

Results in this project are confirmed generally by quite a different kind of project conducted by Dr. Thomas J. Banta at the University of Cincinnati. Dr. Banta is not concerned with comparing non-Montessori and Montessori pre-school education as such, but in studying how children behave in learning situations when they are not told what to do but must actively discover what is wanted.

In his Progress Report of January-November 1966, as reported in the March-April 1967 issue of CHILDREN'S HOUSE, Dr. Banta discusses some of the tentative findings of his project. He and his associates have tested over 300 children "from different kinds of pre-kindergarten classrooms and from different income groups..." to arrive at three main groupings. "1) children from low income families who did *not* attend pre-kindergarten; 2) children from low income families who *did* attend pre-kindergarten, and 3) children from above average and high income families who *did* attend pre-kindergarten."

His findings have been extensive even at a stage only part-way through, but the results which are of primary interest point to the following conclusions:

> Privileged children, as might be expected, are far superior in innovative behavior; pre-kindergarten can modify this condition but privileged children have a considerable headstart. Dr. Banta also discovered that the best results among disadvantaged children were obtained in a Montessori classroom.
>
> Analytic thinking can be trained in pre-kindergarten classrooms, but again the privileged child has the advantage. Once again, a Montessori class showed the greatest improvement, and it was a large one.
>
> Learning processes are greatly improved through pre-kindergarten experience, and under certain conditions disadvantaged children do slightly better than privileged children. Dr. Banta does not yet make further statements on this point, but research undertaken by others, which backs him up, points to the necessity of providing those pre-kindergarten learning conditions which will enable the disadvantaged child to achieve his potential, both for his own good and for the good of society as a whole.

It is not surprising that such detailed experimental work supports Montessori's discoveries and recommendations, for she spoke of her work in similar language: "It is by scientific and rational means also that we must facilitate that inner work of psychical adaptation to be accomplished within the child, a work which is by no means the same thing as 'any external work or production whatsoever.'"(From DR. MONTESSORI'S OWN HANDBOOK.)

Her way of proceeding fits in well with the scientific temper of the age, for she based her judgments and her methods on careful observation of how children actually learned and grew—the same procedures followed by later investigators like Drs. Fleege and Banta. Her division of education of the young child into three basic parts is still valid today for all children: motor education, sensory education, language.

As Jerome Rothstein writes: "Most educators now recognize that teaching retarded children demands a developmental rather than a remedial approach."(MENTAL RETARDATION, p. 165. New York, Holt, Rinehart & Winston, 1961.)

Montessori offered more than a technique or a catalog of equipment, however. In the pages of her books, as in the operation of her Children's Houses, is made manifest a philosophy born of profound respect for the spiritual dignity of the child and for his right to obtain the best possible education so that he may realize himself to the limit of his capacities.

The pages which follow give in fuller detail the necessary philosophical and practical information to make a Montessori education a reality in the classroom for large numbers of children, especially those with learning difficulties. However, all children everywhere can benefit from contact with Montessori.

THE UNDER-ACHIEVING CHILD

There has been a growing concern among educators and the public alike of regarding the academic retardation evidenced by children from culturally and economically underprivileged homes. They have frequently shown an inability to adjust to the demands which have been expected of them in kindergarten and first grade. Testing by researchers has shown that there has been a constant process of retardation from a few months below grade level at the end of the first year to several years below grade level at the end of six years. In many cases children have not been ready to move into the first grade after a year of kindergarten experience.

Research has shown that these children have been particularly deficient in skills which are involved in the learning process. Notably lacking are language skills—both in expression in communicating with others and in comprehension of communication from others. Marked deficiencies have also been noted in concentration or attention focusing and auditory and visual discrimination.

Handicapped by these deficiencies the culturally deprived child has little opportunity for rewarding successes in school. He faces a succession of failures which increasingly dwarf his motivation until he becomes apparently listless and dull while merely serving his time until he can drop out of school. To such a child it is not surprising that school becomes an unpleasant and distasteful experience.[1]

The roots of under-achievement and the much later "drop out" problem have their beginnings early in life. Leonard Miller of the U. S. Office of Education has this to say:

There is evidence that academic under-achievement is present in the earliest school years and that it is a fairly consistent characteristic of the pupil throughout his school career. Any attempt to reduce

---

[1] McDermott, John J., Professor, Department of Philosophy, Queens College of the City University of New York; former Member of the Board of Directors of the American Montessori Society. From a lecture at the Fairleigh Dickinson University Montessori Training Program, September 1963.

the problem of under-achievement must be based upon an acceptance of the broad implications of individual differences. For example, school personnel must recognize that there are readiness levels for all types of learning....The elementary school teacher who works with the under-achiever and recognizes the child's personal needs will attempt to provide a classroom atmosphere which will give the child a feeling of acceptance and a sense of security.[2]

I believe, however, that under-achievement may be found even earlier, particularly if a child is prevented from learning at a point of sensitivity. I believe, further, that Montessori methods, through recognition of sensitive periods, can substantially reduce under-achievement.

Although there are many causes of under-achievement among students of average or better ability, one cause is often cultural deprivation. The child may have had poor experience before being introduced to school, and does not in fact understand the demands of school or its values. The parents may have been unable to provide for the child; they may have had little or no education, or it is not possible for them to change a marginal way of living. The parents also may be unable to recognize the special needs of their under-achieving child, or to recognize his emotional needs. The child has had little intellectual stimulation, and often has experienced rejection by brothers, sisters, and playmates. This is a great cultural distance from the well-loved, well-cared-for children in our own homes, but it was, in fact, such children as these that Maria Montessori had in mind when she evolved her philosophy and principles of education. Although the description of parents just given is often true of the parents of the culturally deprived child, the parents of the educable mentally retarded child present much the same picture.

The child of retarded mentality does not fit into the conventional classroom. His abilities are often not geared to the abstractions of the academic program, and his needs are not met by such a program. In a sense, his under-achievement is in areas other than academic, since it is probable that he will not achieve as much academic learning as an average student. His capacity is limited, and he will probably leave school at the legal age of 16.

Under-achieving children are often disturbed and almost compulsive in movement. The Prepared Environment, therefore, has an important value in "legalizing" movement. The child is free to move his material and furniture and has a free choice of location. Although Montessori training is structured to some extent it does give the child a freedom from guilt when he uses movement or exercises. In a Montessori classroom he is free from required static place while in a conventional classroom he is expected to remain in his seat.

A small child needs a repetition in learning. Often an older child may have a compulsive need to repeat an activity but is inhibited from doing so. The Montessori method

---

[2]Miller, Leonard M.(ed.), GUIDANCE FOR THE UNDERACHIEVER WITH SUPERIOR ABILITY, U. S. Department of Health, Education, and Welfare, OE-25021 No. 25, 1961, p. 72.

permits such necessary repetition. The child is able to work out his compulsive needs without feeling guilt or bringing a reprimand upon himself. The Montessori method gives him a framework within which he can work out his needs.

Dr. Montessori's feelings toward a disturbed child permit him to express himself freely. There is a learning of the acceptance of the needs of the child. The Prepared Environment with different work centers gives to the under-achieving child an opportunity to develop his skills in areas in which he can achieve. His poorer performance in other areas also can be taken care of within the suggested three year age span. The imbalance in make-up can be taken care of with these different materials, but a conventional classroom often gives a child no opportunity to have his lags taken care of and his skills strengthened at the same time. There is no shame attached to working at a level below his age group in a Montessori classroom because of the nature of the materials available.

Self-help activities, not only for the deprived child but also for the mentally retarded or poorly coordinated child, give the child an opportunity to master those activities which will help his esteem. The frames provide practice without exposing his lack of skill. It doesn't create an atmosphere of exposure but instead gives him an opportunity to learn the skill in a more neutral emotional climate.

It is the responsibility of the teacher and school to provide educational materials within the grasp of the student. Often a class may be treated as groups within the class, but this has the distinct disadvantage of the children soon learning that the "robins" and the "bluebirds" are using different materials or information of different difficulty levels. Grouping the children provides more suitable competition, and the content of the lessons may be more satisfactorily geared to the group, but the Montessori method of individualized instruction is far better. With Montessori techniques, it is less obvious and less important to the children who is the "best" or "slowest," and the approval or disapproval of a child's performance is a matter for the child to deal with, not the class.

There are questions asked by research scientists today that lead to the conclusion that mental retardation is not entirely hereditary, but is influenced by environment as well. Jerome S. Bruner in his book, ON KNOWING, has said:

> *The child is father to the man in a manner that may be irreversibly one-directional, for to make up for a bland impoverishment of experience early in life may be too great an obstacle for most organisms. Indeed, recent work indicates that for at least one species, the utilitarian rat, too much gray homogeneity in infancy may produce chemical changes in the brain that seem to be associated with dullness. One wonders, then, about the issue of the appropriate exercise of mind early in life as a condition for fullness later.*[3]

---

[3]Bruner, Jerome S., ON KNOWING. Cambridge, Mass.: Belknap Press of the Harvard University Press, 1962, p. 7.

Mentally retarded children are often fearful and failure to benefit from a school program has an adverse effect upon their confidence. I have found that slow learners also may have problems with self-help activities. Ten-year-olds who cannot manipulate buttons or shoelaces, and who lack the coordination for self care, are in no position to establish good relationships with their playmates, or with their families either, for that matter.

These children have a particular need to work at their own level. In many special education programs, particularly in schools dealing with disturbed children, teachers trained in early childhood development are especially suitable. These teachers have a good understanding of the child and can better "take the learner from where he is," and stoop down to help the child. The conventional teacher may be bothered by a lack of progress in academic work while the nursery teacher can take fumbling and inattention more in stride. As CHILDREN LIMITED had said in commenting on progress made at the Seaside Regional Center in Connecticut," Because a child hasn't made progress doesn't mean he can't." They say further:

> *To accept as absolute an estimate of the child's future abilities without proof that the child has been given ample opportunity to develop these abilities is tantamount to dooming him to a life of inactivity, idleness, frustration, and lethargy.*[4]

The Montessori classroom provides an atmosphere of acceptance of the individual as he is. Verbal demands are kept to a minimum, and learning is achieved without comparison to others in the group. Within the array of materials available, there are sure to be some that will suit the child's special needs. There is little stress on verbal approval or disapproval of a child's efforts, but satisfaction is achieved through knowledge of a job well done, and the self-correcting features of the apparatus. The under-achiever, who is also mentally retarded, is as apt to be an under-achiever in social skills as well as he is in academic skills, and the former are more important. Time should be spent helping these children to gain mastery of the environment in which they live. It is necessary, therefore, that these children receive from an early age an educational program geared to their needs, and which will give them tools to provide for themselves, both socially and economically. Time spent learning merely to read and write and gain control of abstractions cannot give full profit until the other more concrete areas of the environment can be taken in stride. Exercises in self-care skills, using frames for buttoning, working zippers, and tying bows, are more effective when conducted in the less emotionalized atmosphere of the classroom, and without the child having to fumble with his own clothing.

The Montessori Method provides an opportunity for these children to establish with the teacher a one-to-one relationship. The emphasis on show, not tell, is ideally suited to their abilities. Repetition, as much as is needed, is also permissible in the class. But more than this, choices must be made, and the fundamental steps toward self-help and decision-making are laid. Respect for one's self through self-care, and respect for equipment, and appreciation of a job well done through care of the

---

[4]CHILDREN LIMITED. "Seaside's Program Geared to Individual Child's Potential." April-May, 1963, p. 18.

classroom and apparatus, develop a strong sense of responsibility. There are places in this world for these children when they reach adulthood, but only when personal qualities also are considered.

A case I know shows the problems that may arise when abstract learning is stressed to the expense of the practical considerations of living. A local church hired a mentally retarded man as custodian of the church. He had been carefully taught to read and write—skills that the minister didn't really require for the position—but no one had taught him how to sweep or to take pride in his work. He was unable to do even the simplest job carefully or well, because he had not been taught to be careful in performance. He also had difficulty in choosing which of his duties to perform.

In a more reality-oriented frame of reference, from earliest training, Montessori techniques give a child an opportunity to make choices. The child learns to recognize his inner needs, and to balance them. Choices are not made for him by the teacher deciding when and how much of a subject is to be studied, or how long it is to be worked on. As the child grows in maturity, his needs come in balance and he has had experience that prepared him for management of his resources in life.

It is important for the child to learn on his own. As Jerome Bruner has said:

> *One encounters repeatedly an expression of faith in the powerful effects that come from permitting the students to put things together for himself, to be his discoverer...discovery is in its essence a matter of rearranging or transforming evidence in such a way that one is enabled to go beyond the evidence so reassembled to new insights...to the degree that one is able to approach learning as a task of discovering something rather than "learning about"iit, to that degree the child will be...rewarded by discovery itself.*[5]

It is through the Prepared Environment that Montessori made discovery possible for these children. Materials are displayed and kept in a way that makes it easy for the child to orient and organize himself. This gives him a feeling of security. The Prepared Environment is designed to give him freedom, and apparatus that he can use quietly without fear of mistakes being exposed, so that he may have a comfortable, rewarding experience. The children are not initially ready to work in groups and the Montessori materials permit each child to work alone, and yet learn to take turns on equipment. The fact that someone else may be working on a piece of equipment creates interest and incentive, but the child must wait until it has been returned to its proper place before he can take it out and use it.

Concentration and self-discipline are almost unknown for most of these children. Built into the Montessori system are techniques for encouraging both of these qualities. Maria Montessori emphasized silence as a most profound experience, which can be taught through the Silence Exercises. In learning control and mastery of themselves through them, they become more calm and better able to assimilate learning.

[5]Bruner, op. cit.

The exercises that call for self control, attention, and coordination of muscles teach the children the complete meaning of silence. The exercises give the teacher an opportunity to check the child's hearing and to help him formulate listening habits of value.

Montessori philosophy in the early grades will place culturally deprived children in an atmosphere of acceptance, and teach them in areas that will make them more socially at ease. Montessori training is not the answer to all problems, but surely it should not be overlooked as an important contribution to this difficult and knotty problem.

> *I feel I can say, both from my development as a teacher and from objective study of Montessori's system, that there is no need to claim that the Montessori Method offers only the choice of accepting it as a whole, or rejecting it altogether. It has to be fused with a system of psychology to give assistance to the teacher as individual development does not proceed according to the book. Parts of the Method can also find their places in an eclectic system of education, particularly if used with exceptionally gifted children or with children who have difficulties in learning, or a sensory deficit. The respect and understanding for spontaneity as well as for order, are essential prerequisites.*[6]

The under-achiever is exposed to his peers. Children are realistic, almost to the point of cruelty. Adults have a way of politely hiding the deficiencies of others, but children will actively exclude another from their group if he cannot do his work or play their games. The under-achiever, therefore, has his feelings of failure amplified, and feels further frustration through this discrimination. Such frustration can lead an under-achiever to give up trying. Again, it is easier to fail. The play group also tends to echo the criticism of the teacher.

Another common practice that adds frustration to the life of the under-achiever is the practice of grading papers with red pencil and thus clearly identifying for everyone the child who cannot do his work. Such a mass of red pencil marks can act as a fear stimulus to the child, who then is so identified as a failure by his companions that a vicious circle begins. Under-achievement contributes to a lack of acceptance by his peers, and frustration from lack of acceptance leads to an inability to concentrate on his work. In some cases, the under-achiever will blame the teacher or other factors for his failure. His companions may tantalize him for this, and hostility results. When the school thus provides an academic atmosphere that the child is unable to assimilate, further frustration and under-achievement result. Montessori, by providing concrete materials to teach abstractions, makes this method of teaching more acceptable to children from an alien culture of one kind or another.

Montessori training in early years has a confidence building effect that gives an intellectually limited or culturally deprived child the best opportunity of achieving up to his maximum ability.

[6]Plank, Emma N., REFLECTIONS ON THE REVIVAL OF THE MONTESSORI METHOD. Journal of Nursery Education (New York), May 1962, Vol. 17, No. 3, p. 134.

Montessori philosophy in a classroom, even in the absence of apparatus, can substantially contribute to the progress of the under-achiever.

In those cases complicated by poor early management, emotional problems, or previous failure, Montessori training serves as a therapeutic tool.

WHO IS THE UNDER-ACHIEVING CHILD?

The Pre-School Child

Under-achievement because of *intellectual limitation* is met in the true mental defective, children suffering birth defects, physical trauma, and developmental defects causing mental retardation.

The *emotionally disturbed* child may, as a result of true psychosis, neurosis or traumatic experiences know under-achievement.

The *culturally deprived* child may also under-achieve. Lack of experience, both sensory and verbal, may lead to under-achievement. Parental attitudes toward education may be negative and lead to under-achievement in an unencouraged child. Lack of a common understanding with the school and peers may lead to under-achievement, and lack of preparation by the parents compound this experience.

Motor deprivation experienced by certain children leads to an appearance of under-achievement. Lack of opportunity for exploration may lead to thwarting the child's ability to learn. Restriction of needed sneosry exploration can occur at all economic levels with the same restrictive result in achievement.

The *physically handicapped* child may also be an under-achiever. Lack of physical coordination may make learning more difficult, with adverse results in achievement.

The School Age Under-achieving Child

All five groups of pre-school under-achievers grow to school age and bring their pre-existing problems with them to the classroom. Failure is almost predestined for them since they do not share—because of physical, emotional, or cultural lacks—the same experiential background as "normal" children and they therefore do not respond to the normal teaching procedure.

The average classroom provides a too-restrictive environment for these children and does not take their differences into consideration. The static, "sit still" expectations of the average classroom are impossibly difficult demands for these children, and excess verbalization cannot reach them. In contrast, the Montessori classroom that provides freedom of movement, a range of materials within a three-year age span of difficulty, and activities to fill the needs of children previously denied life experiences, as well as the stimuli that can develop their higher skills to their utmost, presents a challenge within their level to grasp it. Montessori's emphasis on doing rather than verbalization develops confidence within these children, habits of success, and successfully permits them to keep their lacks and defects in an unimportant position.

THE SCHOOL'S IDENTIFICATION OF THE UNDER-ACHIEVING CHILD

Testing

I.Q., ability, achievement, and tests of intellectual capacity administered to children tend to be verbal in nature. Culturally deprived children, therefore, are apt to be underestimated by such testing programs. Testing may identify those children who will have difficulty with symbolic learning, however, and schools use these tests as a means of roughly grouping together those children who will be expected to learn at about the same pace.

Certain children do not learn as much material presented in the classroom as the I.Q. tests indicate might be expected of them. This group of children may include those with emotional disturbances, those from culturally deprived homes, or those who reject learning, among other reasons.

Classroom Performance

The teacher often identifies an under-achieving child through his lack of satisfactory performance in the classroom. Daily work may be left undone, assigments done poorly or not at all, tests of knowledge previously taught may be failed, and answers to classroom questions may indicate a lack of understanding and attention to the subject. Inattention, hostility, lack of pertinence of answers also may indicate under-achievement.

Behavior and Conduct

Rejection of the child by his peers, inability of the child to adjust to the group, to keep up with their games, or associate with them; hostility of the child to authority; withdrawal from reality; excessive fantasy; physical incoordination; aggressiveness; excessive compliance. Any or all of these symptoms may indicate to the teacher that trouble may be indicated for this child and under-achievement may be the result.

Parental Reports

The parent may be instrumental in identifying the under-achieving child by reporting to the teacher changes in his home behavior. Unhappiness, or any deviation from the child's usual home conduct, may indicate a response to school pressures that the child is unable to accept.

TREATMENT OF THE UNDER-ACHIEVING CHILD

By the School

The school identifies the under-achieving child through its teaching program, testing, teacher-parent contacts, observation of classroom and playground behavior, and from reports received from community agencies.

Adjustments for the less severely under-achieving may be made within the classroom. Groupings may be made within a "normal" class with brighter children given more work, or more advanced work, and the slower learners given material presumably within their grasp. For children unable to keep up in a regular classroom special classes are sometimes provided. In other cases referral to diagnostic clinics, or for a visiting teacher service may be recommended.

By the Parent

By reporting home behavior to the teacher the parent can cooperate in providing a cooperative environment for the child. Parents of under-achieving children may have all reactions, from hostility and guilt to sympathy and cooperation. The emotional attitude of the parent often contributes greatly to the ultimate ability of the child to achieve up to the level of his ability.

By his Peers

Discrimination and rejection by his peers can make the problems of the under-achieving child greater. The severely retarded child often fares quite well in a classroom with normal children, who can be taught to understand his true inability to compete with them; in some cases the severely retarded child may be "adopted" as a "class pet." Frustration in dealing with his peers may lead to the under-achieving child no longer trying.

By the Community

Groups can help the under-achiever. Scout troops and church groups are beginning to understand the problems of the under-achiever and to accept him in a helpful manner.

THERAPEUTIC USE OF MONTESSORI FOR THE UNDER-ACHIEVING CHILD

Montessori training in early years has a confidence-building effect that gives an intellectually limited child the best opportunity to achieve up to his highest level of ability. It prevents complications to the problem in later years. Montessori philosophy in a classroom, despite a lack of equipment and apparatus, can substantially contribute to the learning process. In those cases complicated by poor early management, emotional problems, or failure in other endeavors by the child, Montessori training can serve in a therapeutic role. Parents, by providing an attitude of understanding at home and cooperation with the teacher can substantially help the under-achiever. For children of culturally deprived or sensorially deprived home environments, the Montessori apparatus and Practical Life Exercises can help substantially.

Defense mechanisms often used by the neurotic child include compensation, projection, rationalization, regression, repression and denial, sublimation. The transformation of anxiety into bodily symptoms can result in conversion hysteria.

Fear with great intensity, or long duration, and which interferes with everyday living may be thought of as a phobia, and may be considered neurotic when it interferes appreciably with everyday life. A fear of snakes, for example, would hardly be considered a phobia or neurotic unless it interfered with the child's life, for example by having the child refuse to leave his bed because of his fear of perhaps meeting a snake.

Montessori defined the deviate child as

> *... an individual in whom the development of physical and mental capacities has gone awry, leading to conflict and unrealized potential; a generic term for a child whose behavior is symptomatic of disturbance.*
> (A MONTESSORI GLOSSARY.)

The opposite of the deviated child is the normalized child. Montessori called the first phase of the child's emergence into discipline "normalization" and considered discipline the most important single achievement of her method.

"Normalization" is the

> *... Self-preparation by the child, through response to education, constituting the first step in education. Stimuli in the prepared environment; the process by which the child becomes the active agent of his learning.*
> (A MONTESSORI GLOSSARY.)[7]

A "normalized" child is one who shows self-discipline, enjoys involvement in work, and begins to develop the social feelings of helpfulness and compassion for others. Yet this is not the point of arrival for Montessori. A normalized child is one who is ready and able to develop himself further. He is on his way to the next stage, discipline.

In order to help the child, Montessori prepared an environment in which the child could find himself immersed in experience. He could take in what he needed in order to unfold his potential. If the child was to achieve this, he had to have a teacher with a new approach.

[7] Rambusch, Nancy. "A Montessori Glossary." Unpublished paper. New York: American Montessori Society, 1963.

THE ROLE OF THE TEACHER

> The Montessori teacher could be characterized briefly in this way: He does not tell, he shows. "If the child is to increase, the adult must decrease," Montessori says. A Montessori teacher must have experienced a conversion, a transformation, if he is to be a condition rather than an obstruction for the child's learning. Children learn, with or without teachers. They absorb knowledge from whatever environment they are in. The type of environment conducive to children's learning depends largely on adults. Adults have always professed to love children. Less often have they professed a need to respect them. Many are the adults who believe that the role of the child is to respect the adult and not the reverse. Maria Montessori believed that any effective education of the child must necessarily involve a modification of the adult.[1]

It is always the case in any Montessori classroom that the teacher plays a role decidedly different from the one played by the teacher in the usual class, but the role of the teacher in special education is intensified because her responsibility is so much greater.

The Montessori teacher does not stand in front of the class and lecture, she does not take a piece of knowledge as one might an interesting rock, and display it for the class as a whole, then transmit facts about this rock. Quite the opposite! She will appear rather as a passive observer of the children, although this appearance is deceptive, for she is anything but passive. However, she remains in the background as quietly as possible, for her chief function is to observe and to assist unobtrusively whenever she perceives that a child needs help.

This observation, to be effective, must be profound, not superficial, for she must eventually know each child well enough to be able to distinguish from his behavior

[1] Rambusch, Nancy McCormick, LEARNING HOW TO LEARN, Baltimore: Helicon Press, 1962.

whether he is capable of moving on to more complex materials, whether he is suffering from emotional difficulties, whether he is having an unusually tense day because of a family situation, whether he is developing such mental powers as he has in the most fruitful manner, and so on. Such knowledge is not attained all at once, nor does it come from studying written records or tests, but it is rather the result of careful, patient observation of the individual child combined with the thought that will link behavioral phenomena into a meaningful pattern.

The following schematic guide to the teacher as observer should be helpful; I have found it useful in my own work. Disciplined observation is a great skill and a valuable quality in those working with children. The great child psychologist Jean Piaget made his brilliant contributions to the study of child development by observing his own children and grandchildren in their "natural habitats."

The teacher should be wary of forcing this pattern, however. In this area, as in many others in the Montessori classroom, patience and tranquillity are to be preferred to anxious pushing for results. Gradually, the pattern of a child's development will be unfolded to the teacher, and as she comprehends the meaning of a child's responses and interests, difficulties and triumphs, she will be in a position to truly assist this child to make his own discoveries. And this role of watchful waiting is by no means an easy one, not with normal children and certainly not with our special children, who often tax one's patience. However, once the teacher has experienced for herself the rewards which come from understanding the nature of the child rather than imposing herself and her ideas, she will be willing to discipline herself.

The Montessori teacher is more than an observer, however, much more. She is also a model and it is necessary to emphasize the importance of her role as a model when she is dealing with children in special education programs, for these children learn less from verbal communication than they do from non-verbal signs and behavior. Thus the teacher will instill lessons of grace and courtesy only by first mastering them herself, by treating the children with dignity and respect so that they will learn how to treat their classmates. This knowledge is not the subject of a lecture but should radiate freely from the teacher's own gestures and manners as she goes about her classroom activities. Here she follows the precept: show, not tell. Does she appear clean and neatly dressed? Is her voice soft and pleasant? Does she use language correctly? Does she move with a minimum of fuss and upset? Is her presence tranquil and comforting? It is thus that she creates a classroom atmosphere appropriate for learning.

And that leads us to the consideration of another role the teacher plays in the Montessori class. She is the protector of the child's right to know, not a representative of an enemy world. The creation of order and serenity is not an end in itself—far from it—but the necessary prelude to the process of learning. No child can learn in chaos; the retarded or disturbed child may not be able to function at all without an orderly environment. This environment is provided by the teacher. Each child must feel that his rights are guaranteed, that the teacher will not permit another child to interfere with him or to take the materials he is working with or to create a disturbance. In turn, the child comes to understand that he is required to return his materials

(Photo courtesy of the National Gallery of Art, Washington, D.C.)

"... the teacher will instill lessons of grace and courtesy only by first mastering them herself, by teaching the children with dignity and respect..."

"The Young Governess" by Chardin

to their proper place when he is finished with them so that another child can use them. And he must leave other children alone when they are working. He comes to recognize mutuality as necessary for the provision of order.

This order is not for the convenience of the teacher but is provided so that all the chidlren may be freed for intellectual work. If the teacher can maintain physical order in the classroom and assure that the children cooperate in the maintenance of this order—materials returned to their proper places, equipment kept clean, the room swept and dusted—then she has prepared the ground for emotional order. And without emotional order, the special child is seriously hindered in learning.

Thus, the Montessori teacher is in reality very busy, although she may seem quiet and she may seldom intervene in the class. It is her responsibility to make the children understand that all the materials belong to everyone in the class and that all are equally responsible for their proper use. Then there is no opportunity for those cries of, "this is my pencil," or "my letters," that can so easily disrupt a classroom. And each child is assured of his turn with the materials when he is ready and willing to use them and to return them to their proper places.

Generally, the children quickly assume responsibility for this physical order and the teacher discovers that her role is minimized. However, at times the children need assistance in creating this order, and the teacher must learn to judge the situation and give this assistance when it is required as pleasantly as possible in a quiet, self-assured way. Perhaps her observation has shown her that a particular child is over-tired or unusually stimulated or disturbed. Then she must have the understanding to lay aside the rules which determine that the child shall return his materials to their places by himself so that she can assist him. Only if she imagines that her authority is being tested by such a situation will she find difficulty in helping, and this difficulty will vanish if she remembers that her primary goal is the preservation of an atmosphere of order and serenity, not the imposition of her will.

These roles make great demands on the Montessori teacher. Her task is not an easy one, especially in classrooms with retarded or disturbed children. But she will be rewarded by success: the children will display confidence in themselves, they will respond positively to the environment and to her, and they will learn.

In order to fulfill her various functions, she must be an honest model. If she is bothered by something, she must admit it, verbalize it, cope with it. Since children can read non-verbal indicators, they will not be fooled—only the teacher will.

There is no doubt that all of this is difficult—but, as Dr. Jerome H. Rothstein says in his MENTAL RETARDATION (New York, 1964): "There is no greater challenge in the realm of human engineering than learning to deal effectively with the menally retarded." (p.99)

PREPARATION OF A MONTESSORI TEACHER

While I was working with the Child Development Group of Mississippi on Headstart projects, I came upon the expression of the Montessori point of view on teacher training from a completely different perspective. The CDGM people had no prior interest in adhering to *any* philosophy; their aim was "the best program for poor children in the United States," in the words of Polly Greenberg, who was in charge of the Teacher Development and Program for Children. But when Mrs. Greenberg wrote the following words, she was very close to the Montessorians in spirit:

> *We think* qualities *are vitally important, whereas* qualifications *are not. We look for* human qualities *such as warmth, affection, high spiritedness, conviction, sense of humor, and eagerness to learn new ways to work with* these *children* in the particularly difficult context in which they live. *These qualities may be found in teachers and in parents. We do not write up arbitrary requirements and regulations that prohibit us from taking in high quality people when we find them, wherever we find them.*[2]

Seguin's Ideas on Teacher Preparation

> *Seguin, in his glorious treatise on scientific pedagogy, dedicates a chapter to the training of the teacher of defective children. The teacher of abnormal pupils is not an educator, he is a* creator; *he must have been born with special gifts, as well as to have perfected himself for this high task. He ought, says Seguin, to be handsome in person, and strong as well, so that he may attract and yet command; his glance should be serene, like that of one who has gained victories through faith and has attained enduring peace; his manner should be imperturbable as that of one not easily persuaded to change his mind. In short, he ought to feel beneath him the solid rock, the foundation of granite on which his feet are planted and his steps assured. From this solid base, he should rise commandingly, like a magician. His voice should be gentle, melodious, and flexible, with bursts of silvery and resounding eloquence, but always without harshness. Seguin describes the methods by which the teacher should educate his own voice, speech and gesture; he should take a course in facial expression and declamation, like a great actor who is preparing to win favor of the select and critical public of the proudest capital.*
>
> *...But the perfect teacher must possess something more than physical beauty and acquired art; he must have the loftiness of a soul ardent for its mission; yet even this may be cultivated and perfected....Well, this is more or less what is demanded of the teacher of abnormal children. He ought to be conscious of his personal dignity and human virtue, and of a sincere love for the children whom it is his task to redeem; his own greatness must overcome their wretchedness. And if he continues to perfect himself and to mount toward the moral altitudes, cultivating at the same time a love for his own mission, he will, as if by magic, become an educator; he will feel that a magic power of suggestion goes forth from him and conquers; the work of redemp-*

[2]Taken from: "Basic Philosophy of CDGM in Teacher Development."

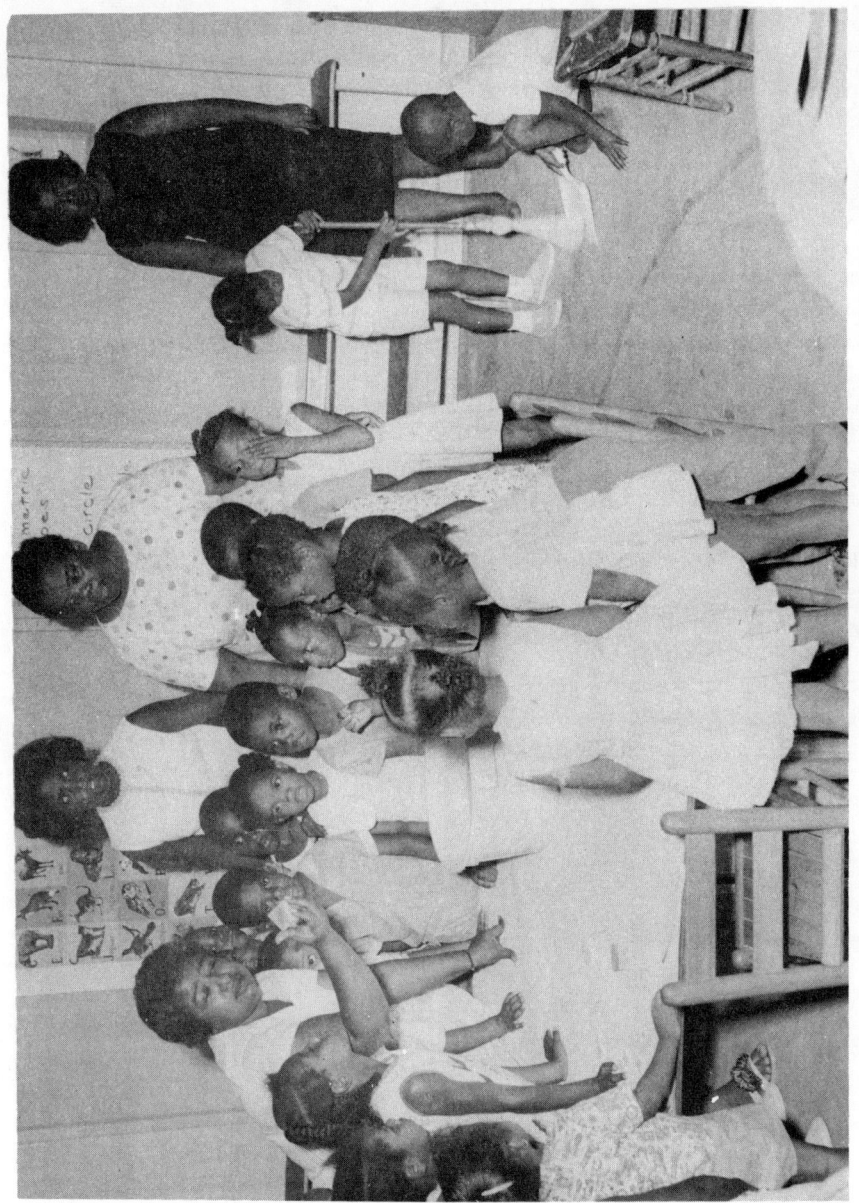

(Photo courtesy of Montessori Workshop, Mosspoint, Mississippi)

A Teacher "Filling the basic role of 'Demonstrator'"

> *tion will then seem to accomplish itself like a conflagration which has been kindled from some central point and spreads in rolling flames through the dried undergrowth.*[3]

Montessori devoted considerable time and thought to the subject of teacher preparation. Her essay summarizes her essential thought on the "new mistress." It only remains for us to translate her language into contemporary terms to see how her words remain relevant.

What sort of training is necessary for teaching the Montessori Method? Montessori training school, university, teacher training college, may help. Experience with children may also be a help. But to teach the Method successfully after we have been accustomed to conventional methods means a complete change of outlook, and it is not easy to alter attitudes and habits we have grown up with. Everyone grows up with these ideas, they are part of our civilization. A real change of heart is necessary, and this is why Dr. Montessori used to speak of the "spiritual preparation" of the teacher. Study by itself is not enough.

Montessori looked upon the teacher as filling five basic roles: 1) model of appropriate speech and behavior, 2) programmer of the entire environment, 3) demonstrator of the material to be learned, 4) observer of the child's activity, and 5) protector of the child's right to learn. This is an especially important task in a class with children with learning problems.

In order to fulfill these roles the teacher must also be an expert in self-analysis. This is necessary so that she can prepare and rehearse her lessons to achieve maximum effectiveness. The following are some general rules to serve as guidelines in preparing a lesson, any lesson, to be presented to a child:

> Do the action in your usual way and as fast as usual.
>
> Repeat more slowly, looking for defects.
>
> Look for the following defects in the action:
> Is it noisy?
> Does it damage the materials?
> Are you using the minimum force?
> Has action any unnecessary parts?
>
> Repeat corrected movement several times with attention to its sections, making sure that each is completed before starting the next.
>
> Repeat with pauses between these sections.
>
> Repeat, slowing down those parts difficult to see when done quickly.
>
> Remember that there is no need to imitate others or to stereotype an action, since most actions can be done in many different, but equally efficient, ways.

[3] Montessori, Maria, PEDAGOGICAL ANTHROPOLOGY, pp. 449-450.

> In giving the lesson, do not overteach but seek the minimum needed by each individual child. Never speak or move simultaneously.

Montessori spoke of the teacher as a role model. A contemporary writer, Leland B. Jacobs, Professor of Education at Teachers College of Columbia University, writing for an NEA Publication,[4] speaks of the teacher's "image," and he has this to say:

> *Whatever the popular image of the teacher at the moment, it can and will change, for an image is not stable. It has within itself the seeds of disintegration or modification.*
>
> *Those who teach in the elementary school are making the future image of the teacher moment by moment in their classrooms. Teachers' most perceptive image makers sit before them in blue jeans and pigtails. The teacher would do well to step back and take inventory of the image he now projects, strengthen the good in it, eliminate the bad, and then take hold of his destiny with vigor, dignity, and deepened insight into the teaching act.*

The perspective is not quite the same as Montessori's, but the goal certainly is.

When the teacher sees herself as the protector of the child's right to learn, she can appreciate the help Montessori provided in her conception of freedom. Freedom is not a point of departure but a point of arrival.

GROUND RULES AND EMOTIONAL SECURITY

The child must have external help to internalize his behavior. To aid in this process, Montessori established **ground rules** of classroom behavior and the teacher, in her role as protector, must enforce them:

> A child is only free as long as he is not disturbing anyone else. This is one of the times when teacher can intervene.
>
> Any object removed from its place must be returned to the same place in the same order.
>
> If one child is working with the material, another child can enter into this activity only if he is invited to. The teacher must also be invited by the child. She might ask the child if she can help if her observation shows that he cannot manage, but she must never jump in to help without asking. Even a child with a motor handicap must be allowed to ask for help!

Following these ground rules is very important for the child. They provide a grounding in obedience to the laws of the larger society and an awareness of how laws work in actual situations. This is necessary preparation for adult life.

[4]"The Image of the Teacher," N.E.A. Elementary Instructional Service Leaflet (Washington, D.C.), 1964.

In addition these rules give the child emotional security; he knows what he must do and feels secure within those limits.

At the same time she creates the emotional climate in which learning is possible. This might mean moving a child who is disturbing another one or having a child sit close to her. In each situation she asks herself: what is needed? what can I do to help?

Each child has an equal right to her protection. If she cannot handle a particular child, she may need the help of a psychologist. If at all possible, however, she can create an alternate solution to the problem of the child who is disturbing the class by giving him some way out—beating a drum rather than another child, pounding clay rather than hitting, etc. The teacher thus needs to have an understanding of the function of true discipline.

Disciplinary problems may arise from a child who cannot in fact control his behavior because of deep-seated psychological or neurological impairment. The Montessori teacher who feels that she is facing such problems should not hesitate to call in a psychologist for assistance or to follow the following:

Recommendations Made by School Psychologists[5]

Explore possibilities of neurological impairment.

Further evaluate personality factors related to educational problem.

Get a social casework report.

Consider validity of present educational placement.

Determine whether anxiety is the source of inattention and confusion.

Let the child express his hostility through working with clay and paints.

Stretch the child's horizons.

Help parents to develop a less critical attitude.

Provide remedial help.

Provide varied curriculum.

Provide short-term goals.

Find ways to build the child's prestige with peers.

Encourage mother to give her child more freedom.

[5] Taken from Mental Health Monograph 5, 1965.

Give other types of ability tests.

Orient teacher to child's problem.

See if probation officer can conduct a non-court investigation.

Refer the parents to an agency for psychotherapy for themselves and the child.

Have a home-school conference with psychologist-teacher-parent.

Provide a home-teacher for awhile.

Determine what the stressful situations are.

Ask parents to get a complete physical examination for the child.

Have the school nurse make a home call and offer help to assist with planning a more adequate diet.

A Case History

All those who work with children know the frustration of seeing the work undone each day by a parent who cannot or will not help his child. Sometimes intervention is helpful; parents and teacher (or psychologist or social worker) can communicate and discover new ways of helping a child. All too often, however, intervention is fruitless. There is a tendency to blame the parent—and it may be clear that the parent *is* positively harmful to his child. The parent may blame the professional worker or the school—and there may be good reason for such blame. In either case, though, the child is suffering.

So—rather than go through mutual recriminations, I have found that the best thing I could do as a teacher when such a situation came along, was to try to help the child as much as I could. My experience with Carolyn shows a little how a teacher can help, despite unfortunate influences at home.

Carolyn was a little redheaded girl who entered school with a cleft palate and consequent inability to communicate. There is no doubt that this experience marked her. It took a very long time before the principal, school nurse and speech therapist were able to persuade Carolyn's mother to seek medical help, and this difficulty pointed the way to further problems with the mother. Surgery was finally performed but by this time, Carolyn's image of herself was negative; not only was she unable to meet classroom standards but also she could not meet her mother's requirements, since her mother lacked any understanding of how to deal with Carolyn's problems and indeed seemed to feel there were no problems.

Carolyn entered school in the first grade just one month before her seventh birthday. Although it became evident that she needed special placement, there was no class in her area until she reached ten years of age. When she was extensively tested, her IQ was 68 with a possibility of higher level functioning.

It became evident that Carolyn's main emotional difficulties involved her mother. Her father was a laborer, the mother stayed at home and occupied herself mainly in making herself attractive. She dressed stylishly but did not show much concern for her children, who often had impetigo, who had burns on their hands because they were expected to fix their own meals, who showed evidence of meager care. The mother thought Carolyn should wash and set her own hair and do her own laundering and ironing; she showed no awareness at all that the child was incapable of doing these things. Quite often Carolyn came to school unkempt and dirty because the mother would not help. Carolyn was expected to go to the store and was beaten if she lost any money.

We at the school realized that we would have to supply some of the "tender, loving care" that Carolyn's mother would not give. The speech therapist took an interest in Carolyn's appearance, washing and combing her hair and doing the things a mother should do to assure good grooming.

We had a class grocery store, and Carolyn's often painful shopping experiences for her family enabled her to shine in making change and remembering amounts without any help from me. This initial success helped a great deal in overcoming her negative self-image. Her speech improved and communication became easier. She was also able to analyze her own feelings in words rather than reacting to frustration by kicking or screaming. She became able to concentrate, to finish work, to bring her oral reading to an acceptable level.

What was necessary in each of these victories was for me, the teacher, to provide the reinforcement denied her by her mother. I could not change the mother but I could change Carolyn, at least to some extent, and by concentrating on the child, rather than on anger toward an unsatisfactory parent, I was able to give, in some measure, what was lacking at home.

Discipline

Discipline has become an unfashionable word with parents and teachers as well as with artists and theologians. It is as if they have become so enamored with the broad sweep of the very word "freedom" that they have not been able to think closely about how to realize this freedom. What do we mean when we speak of a person being free? Is the person who is at the mercy of his emotions a free being? We can see clearly that an individual in economic bondage suffers serious impairment of his freedom, but what of the individual in bondage to ignorance or fear? We see that it is not simple, that freedom can evolve only under certain conditions and, while we cannot in fact create freedom, we may be able to provide the conditions under which freedom may flourish. And we begin to see that, paradoxically, freedom begins in discipline.

It is not surprising, therefore, that I have found in my visits to schools a recurring question from young teachers: "How do I create the serene atmosphere so essential to growth and learning?" And these teachers are equally preoccupied with questions of practical discipline which come up constantly in class when one child hits another or creates a disturbance which upsets the order essential to the work of all. It is apparent that many of these teachers experience feelings of guilt which inhibit them from expressing the assured firmness in restraining the undisciplined child that is necessary not only for class order but also for the unruly child himself. Yet she must be able to say: "We do not hit other people but we may hit this clay," and lead him to the materials on which he can displace his anger.

Bernard Bergonzi writes in the January 20, 1966 issue of THE NEW YORK REVIEW OF BOOKS: "At the risk of sounding square, one can...reaffirm the weary truism that it is not the business of art to use chaos to express chaos." Teaching is surely an art, and failure to impose discipline results in chaos. To think otherwise is to misunderstand the nature of discipline, to fall into the error of imagining discipline as punitive when it is properly the means by which we introduce order into chaos.

To answer the many questions of teachers who wished to exercise their art without enduring or expressing chaos themselves, Dr. Montessori wrote an article on the subject which has long been out of print. She expresses clearly and emphatically the successful methods of establishing rather than imposing a serene atmosphere through discipline.

Some Montessori Techniques

How are the Montessori children, one and all, induced to exert themselves to do their work? The standard of activity in a Montessori class is in most instances very high. Much is expected of the children. Yet there are *no rewards* for them to hope for, and *no punishments* for them to fear. How, then, are those who are by nature less energetic or less persevering than the rest to be challenged to rise to the level of the child's capabilities or potential?

To begin with, it is incorrect to say that there are no rewards or punishments in a Montessori class. Outward rewards and outward punishments are entirely unknown; but there are inward rewards to be had for the seeking, and inward punishments to be feared. What induces the child to work is his delight in his work.

Montessori developed what she called the "prepared environment" which already possesses a certain order and disposes the child to develop at his own speed, according to his own capacities, and in a noncompetitive atmosphere in his first school years. "Never let a child risk failure, until he has a reasonable chance of success," said Montessori, understanding the necessity for the acquisition of a basic skill before its use in a competitive learning situation.

For the retarded child, competition means terror and failure, whereas the opportunity to work alone at his own speed under the watchful eye of a teacher who assists him only when he needs it, can be life-enhancing.

SOME PRACTICAL IDEAS

The following goals are those to be kept in mind by the Montessori teacher working in special education. Following those are certain practical techniques which form the basis of the entire learning system in Montessori's method and which are of enormous benefit to all teachers as they analyze learning and teaching.

Goals the teacher should keep in mind for the retarded:

>An environment for their intellectual development.

>Sequential development.

>Continual success at small jobs.

>Positive human interaction.

>Concrete teaching objects.

>Structured learning materials.

>Organization to speed sequential learning.

>Development of intrinsic motivation from successful self-correcting materials.

>Development of inner rewards. No extrinsic rewards and incentives.

THE THREE-PERIOD LESSON

The formal method for handling learning difficulties as devised by Montessori is known as "the three-period lesson." The three-period lesson was initially developed by Seguin in his work with retarded children and was adopted by Montessori with certain refinements of Seguin's basic pattern. It is a valuable method for teaching all children but especially important for the retarded child, who cannot cope with a verbal barrage by blocking out the unnecessary words, as can the normal child. By substituting concrete material and practical example for the flow of language, the teacher can isolate the matter to be taught and can test the child's comprehension. In addition, the three-period lesson gives the teacher a diagnostic way of discovering speech defects and other learning difficulties which may be present.

This teaching technique is not limited to Montessori by any means. A chapter by Dr. Carl Bereiter and others printed in Fred Hechinger's PRE-SCHOOL EDUCATION TODAY (Doubleday, 1966), presents the essentials of Montessori's three-period lesson in discussing language development through repetition of patterns, giving as an example the following sequence:

    Teacher: "This block is big."
    Child: "This block is big."

Then, in the second step:
> Teacher: "Show me the block that is big."
> The child touches the big block.

Then the most difficult step, for the child must supply his own vocabulary:
> Teacher: "Tell me about the block."
> Child: "The block is big."

Here is an example of a lesson conducted according to the principles of Montessori's **three-period lesson.**

The First Period—Linking the sense-perception with the name. Teacher speaks clearly, showing the object: "This is a triangle. This is a square."

The Second Period—Recognition of the object corresponding to the name. Teacher says: "Point to the triangle. Point to the square."

The Third Period—Remembering the name corresponding to the object.
> Teacher: "What is this?" Child: "This is a triangle."
> Teacher: "What is that?" Child: "That is a square."

In this connection I have found excellent for use with normal children the three periods of which the lesson according to Seguin consists:

First Period. *The association of the sensory perception with the name.*

For example, we present to the child, two colours, red and blue. Presenting the red, we say simply, "This is red," and presenting the blue, "This is blue." Then, we lay the spools upon the table under the eyes of the child.

Second Period. Recognition of the object corresponding to the name. We say to the child, "Give me the red," and then, "Give me the blue."

Third Period. The remembering of the name corresponding to the object. We ask the child, showing him the object, "What is this?" and he should respond, "Red."

Seguin insists strongly upon these three periods, and urges that the colours be left for several instants under the eyes of the child. He also advises us never to present the colour singly, but always two at a time, since the contrast helps the chromatic memory. Indeed, I have proved that there cannot be a better method for teaching colour to the deficients, who, with this method were able to learn the colours much more perfectly than normal children in the ordinary schools who have had a haphazard sense education. For normal children however there exists a period preceding the Three Periods of Seguin—a period which contains the real sense education. This is the acquisition of a

> *fineness of differential perception, which can be obtained only through auto-education.*
>
> *This, then, is an example of the great superiority of the normal child, and of the greater effect of education which such pedagogical methods may exercise upon the mental evelopment of normal as compared with deficient children.*
>
> *The association of the name with the stimulus is a source of great pleasure to the normal child.*[6]

FUNDAMENTAL LESSON

The retarded or brain-damaged child as well as the emotionally disturbed child presents a problem which must be met before any learning can take place. This child is easily disturbed by the presence of extraneous objects, as he is by the sound of many words, because he lacks the power to discriminate between what is important and what is not important. Therefore, a way must be found to isolate the material we wish him to learn, to create an empty space around the child except for what is being taught at the time.

The fundamental lesson is thus the start for all Montessori learning and forms the necessary preparation for the three-period lesson. The table on which the child is to work should be clear of all materials, flowers, plants, etc., for what forms a pleasant background for the normal child becomes a disturbance for the special child.

Preparation for the Lesson

The teacher's movements as she prepares the table and the child's chair should be quiet and simple. The chair is placed gently by the table. Then the teacher walks to the place where the material to be used in the lesson is kept and shows the child the material and how to carry it to his workplace.

The teacher should make certain that the child's interest is engaged in this work. If not, she will wait for a better moment and proceed from the very beginning.

When the material is placed properly on the otherwise empty table, the lesson can start. The child may work with his material for as long as he wishes after the teacher has demonstrated the correct way of using it. This demonstration will be marked by very little talk. Rather, the teacher will show by appropriate gestures, moving as economically as possible, what is to be done, then will refrain from offering additional comments or assistance until the child requests help.

With the special child a great deal of demonstration may be necessary initially, but the teacher should be careful not to repeat unnecessarily and to wait patiently until the child clearly reveals a need for further instruction. The teacher must also

---

[6]Montessori, Maria, "Education of the Senses," Chapter XII, THE ADVANCED MONTESSORI METHOD - THE MONTESSORI ELEMENTARY MATERIAL. New York: Frederick A. Stokes Co., 1917, pp. 177-178.

be certain to demonstrate the primary purpose of the material, ignoring all of the interesting variations possible in favor of the main use. Another time will serve for additional points of interest. In this, too, she will be guided by the expressed interest of the child.

When the lesson is completed, the materials are returned to the proper place on the shelf by the child as soon as he has learned to do so.

Especially for the child with learning problems, the environmental clarity provided by the Fundamental Lesson is essential. There should be no distractions—visual, aural, tactile, or emotional. Within the child's range of awareness should be only the material needed for the immediate lesson.

In the Fundamental Lesson the teacher creates the one-to-one correspondence with the child which is so important to the impaired learner. Once the child is tranquil and prepared to learn the material, the teacher is in a position to present the material in the best possible way. The lesson to be mastered should be broken down into steps which follow each other in sequence, working from the easiest to the most difficult. Montessori called this method the "isolation of difficulty."

OBSERVATION

> *It is obvious that the possession of senses and of knowledge is not sufficient to enable a person to observe. It is a habit which must be developed by practice...Such preparation should generate in our consciousness a conception of life capable of transforming us, of calling forth a special activity and an attitude which will make us efficient for our task.*[7]

Schematic Guide to Observation

A certain acquaintance and familiarity with the Montessori Method, its principles and its recognition of the child, should naturally be present before the real exercises in observation can commence. During a certain period of time one should limit oneself to only one child.

> **One child only** (succession of activities: of concentration in work; of its movements (disorderly, orderly, attentive) and their succession; repetitions of the activity, etc.)

> **One material only** (an arbitrarily chosen part of the apparatus as it passes from child to child or remains out of use; repetitions around it)

> **Care of the environment** (out of an inner urge or after discovery of an outer need; the inanimate or animate environment, plants, animals)

---

[7]Montessori, Maria, THE ADVANCED MONTESSORI METHOD. Vol. 1 (The Preparation of the Teacher).

Social behavior (examples of co-operation, how it started, around which activity; helpfulness, when, by whom, to whom; how it started (spontaneously or by request) and how it finished; "leadership" and following among the children; interest for an admiration of the work of others, spontaneously or by request).

Choice of activities (how a child chooses; how it expresses its needs of a presentation, of a change of work, of an activity on a higher level).

Errors (attitude toward an error committed, in different fields; movement, sensorial, intellectual, moral, social; how errors are corrected; when interest for the control of error is awakened).

Fatigue (expressions of physical or mental fatigue; how they are expressed; how they are overcome).

Obedience (when obedience becomes manifest; the "three degrees of obedience" (accidental, directed, constant and with joy; how it is expressed; in connection with what; towards whom (adult, companions, strangers).

Abstraction (how abstraction is reached; when; when the child himself "discovers" to have reached it, i.e., to be working with using the apparatus; how this discovery is expressed; how and when a particular material is permanently discarded).

Expressions of will (positive; negative; perseverance).

Imagination (with regard to what; in which form; with what technical perfection; on the basis of what experience; as protest).

Emotions (joy; sorrow; depression; exuberance; affection; serene calm; anger, slow and persistent or flaring up; irritation; plaintiveness; patience; impatience, etc. in whom; when; in connection with what or with whom; how long; how often).

Particular attitudes (in work; in sensitivity; in social behavior; in moral behavior; in attachment, etc.).

Nice, interesting and surprising anecdotes should also be recorded carefully.

Guide for Psychological Observation[8]

Work

1. Note when a child begins to work, with constancy, at a particular task, what the task is and how long he continues working at it (the period of time from start to finish, repetition of the same activity).

[8]Op. Cit., Montessori, Vol. I, Chapter III.

2. Individual peculiarities in application to particular activities.

3. To what activities the child applies himself during the same day and and with how much perseverance.

4. If the child has periods of spontaneous industry and for how many days these periods continue.

5. How he manifests his need to progress.

6. What activities he chooses in their sequence, working at them steadily.

7. Persistence in spite of stimuli in the environment which would tend to distract attention.

8. If after forced interruption, the child resumes the activity which was interrupted.

Conduct

1. Note if the child responds to the invitation when he is called.

2. Note if and when the child begins to take part in the work of others with an intelligent effort.

3. Note how obedience to a summons becomes regular.

4. Note how obedience to commands becomes regular.

5. Note when the child obeys eagerly and joyously.

6. Note the relation of the various phenomena of obedience in their degrees (a) to the development of work; (b) to changes of conduct.

The GUIDE is grouped around three headings which deal with three of the most important characteristics of the child's life in the prepared environment; spontaneous constructive activity, normalization of his personality and behavior, inner discipline as its most splendid result.

Each point of observation indicated stresses moment of development and presupposes profound study and knowledge of Dr. Montessori's own observations, of the conclusions she drew from them and of the practical preparation of the environment based on them (organization, directions for behavior, the directness and the relations between her and the children's means of development).

Montessori said that the teacher must observe the child as one would a living pedagogical text, in his natural environment. This is most important when working with inefficient learners.

In developing an educational strategy based on this philosophy, the teacher, naturally, must involve the parent. She can learn from them about the child at home and in turn, explain to the parents her goals for the child in the classroom environment. She can also help the parents learn to observe and understand their child.

The teacher and parents can work together for realistic goals for their children and can work together to find a place in the community where their children can make a valuable contribution with their limited abilities.

THE UNBROKEN CIRCUIT

> *Let us first recognize that excellence is not limited to those of high capacity. Far too often we are prone to rationalize our lack of achievement by hiding behind real or imagined inadequacies. I am reminded of a young man whose intellectual gifts were indeed limited and who was issued a certificate of attendance at the end of the legally required number of years of formal schooling. John, however, was a sincere individual and a man of principle. Some two years after he finished school, a former teacher met him on the street and inquired as to his well-being. John proudly stated that he had a very important job in a local factory. He explained that scrap from the metal lathes fell to the floor of the shop and that his task was to keep the floor clean. "I must sweep carefully," he said, "for if I fail, some of the scraps can get into the machines and cause them to break down. This can cause men to be out of work. Yes," he said, "I have a very important job and I do it well." John was using his gifts, limited as they were, in an excellent manner.*[1]

Montessori would have been in complete accord with the sentiments in this quotation. We have seen its application to special children in earlier pages, but here we will turn to the parental role and the way in which parents and school must work together for maximum accomplishment. This quotation has another significance when we think of parents whose capacities may be limited, no matter what the reason. They need to feel that they can participate in their children's education in a meaningful way.

And they can! Each parent has something to offer, something unique. Not only that, but by utilizing the parents' gifts and knowledge, the teacher will find that her work is made easier. In the first place, her work is easier because home and school are not engaged in a tug-of-war over the child but are functioning smoothly to reinforce each other. Lessons

---

[1] Bryan, J. Ned, Specialist, Gifted and Talented, U. S. Office of Education. From a speech "Gifts Are For Use" presented before the Williamsburg Student Burgesses on February 10, 1962.

learned in school are appreciated at home; home experiences are enjoyed in school and are used as a basis for building further accomplishments.

Secondly, the parents can actually contribute help and materials to the class to enable it to function in school and to enrich the experiences available to the children.

The first point deserves some consideration because all too often the teacher finds that the parents are so wracked with shame and guilt that they cannot, despite their best intentions, give their special child the help he needs. "Why has this happened to me?" is the common cry. Some parents look into the past for sins they committed or blame earlier sexual escapades or try to find genetic reasons. However, they still must live with the day-to-day care of their child, no matter how they explain this burden to themselves, and they will find their burden lighter if a skillful and tactful teacher shows them how their attitude can help the child care for himself.

But in such matters words mean less than gestures, as Montessori pointed out. It is not enough to give verbal assurance, we must also find a way to demonstrate to parents—and to have parents demonstrate to themselves and their children—that this seeming burden is a way of making a contribution.

A class is liable to contain children from many backgrounds with many reasons for under-achievement, from true retardation to handicaps imposed by physical malfunctioning or socially disadvantageous backgrounds. Therefore, each of the following recommendations will have to be tailored to the particular situation of the child.

(Photo courtesy of Lithuanian Montessori Society of America, Inc., Chicago, Illinois.)

"... parents will find their burden lighter if a skillful and tactful teacher shows them how their attitude can help the child ... "

In assuring that the circuit between home and school remains unbroken, the teacher can begin by explaining to parents how they can maintain a prepared environment at home to reinforce the child's school experiences. The home should be as well prepared as possible to enable the child to function independently.

WHAT DOES THIS MEAN?

In the child's room should be hooks for clothing at his height, a low table with comb and brush and a low mirror, sturdy untippable equipment and furniture, drawers easy to pull open, only a few types of each kind of clothing to make choice possible but not frustrating and clothing easy to get on and off.

Color-coding the child's bathroom equipment, his place at the table, coat hanger, etc. is helpful. Mark everything he uses in common with other members of the family with a strip of tape in a single bright color so that he can remember where to hang his towel, his coat, put his boots and other belongings.

Uncluttered rooms make housekeeping easier for mother, but that is a secondary point! Chaos is profoundly disturbing to the retarded child. Use clean, bright colors, easily-cleaned surfaces, few objects on tabletops, and in his room, *one* picture, *one* plant!

Provide a low bulletin board where he can place his work for family display.

Objects that can be easily damaged should be put away **out of sight.** No temptations to tantrums!

When the child is ready, give him child-sized versions of adult cleaning materials. Perhaps the child's own closet can be arranged with broom, dustpan, mop, cloths and cleaning preparations.

There is also a prepared "mental" environment. This is the attitude of patience and understanding which parents can have. The retarded child can learn, but more slowly. Therefore, time must be given to showing this child how to set a table, how to dust, and so on. But how the joy of accomplishment can light up a once dull face!

This is all very well and good to say, but how can parents overcome feelings of shame and guilt on one hand or—in the case of parents whose own intellectual capacity is limited—be made to see that they are people of worth and dignity so that they can treat their children in the same way?

At the start of the school year the teacher should contact all parents to find out the following information:

      1. Full names, ages, addresses, place of birth of mother and father.
      2. Number and age of siblings in family.
      3. Educational level of parents.
      4. Are parents living together, divorced, is one parent dead? What other adults live in home? Does mother work?
      5. How long has family lived in present home? How many times moved?

6. Space for information about special child's history as seen by parents.
7. Any skills, talents, training parents have. Any special interests. Any work they would like to do.

This information should be supplemented by a personal interview if at all possible. When the teacher has the information in hand she can propose many areas where parents can make a unique contribution, can make their child proud of them and can add to their own self-esteem. The following is only a suggestive list.

For Professional Parents

Operate tape recorder, make tapes, show children how to operate the machines.

Accompany children on trips, review films, film strips, slides, tapes.

Take children to library, read books, make up stories to tell children.

Demonstrate skills—sewing, cooking, experiments with chemistry, biology, electronics, etc.

Prepare illustrated material and lectures on such subjects as wildlife, plants, flowers.

Prepare illustrated booklets to be used for job training in different fields, sex education, reading books, writing handbooks.

Contribute reproductions of paintings, make frames.

Draw maps, charts, graphs.

Act as "resource people," sharing with children their jobs or special knowledge in accordance with Montessori principles of showing, remaining close to concrete knowledge.

For Socially Disadvantaged Parents

Make and repair Montessori equipment, provide sanded blocks, tables, chairs.

Sew aprons, curtains, hem handkerchiefs, squares for folding.

Wash windows and walls, wash and wax floors to prepare classroom.

Paint walls and furniture.

Provide plants.

Assist teacher on snowy days with outdoor clothing, on rainy days with recess games, at snack time.

(Photo courtesy of Montessori Workshop, Natchez, Mississippi.)

"... When the teacher has the information in hand, she can propose many areas where parents can make a unique contribution."

All Parents

Make games and play equipment.

Prepare special foods and show how they are made.

Provide magazines with photographs suitable for cutting out.

Make scrapbooks according to child's needs.

Show girls how to care for hair.

Demonstrate knitting, simple sewing.

Show boys how to use tools, to follow simple wood pattern, to make useful wooden objects—trays, bird houses, toys, etc.

Assist in art lessons, music lessons, dancing lessons.

Assist in field trips.

Use contacts to make arrangements for field trips; i.e., a milkman can bring children to milk company, a grocery clerk to supermarket, postman to post office, doctor to hospital, etc.

Prepare tapes talking about their lives, experience, past—especially good for parents with unusual backgrounds, who may be ashamed of those backgrounds.

Only a Beginning

These suggestions are only a beginning. Parents themselves will come forward with ideas once they understand that they are welcomed, each one for his particular skills. As can be seen from these ideas, however, they are devised to use both fathers and mothers, to reach both boys and girls, to cover the mental and physical development of the children.

The teacher should take pains to assure that each parent can contribute something to foster legitimate pride in his child and that each child can discover an area where he does well. The intelligence of the retarded child may not be acute, but his sensitivities may be very acute and the pattern of success and achievement which Montessori found to be essential to optimum growth will be broken just at the point where it should be most reinforced— relationship between home and school. The circuit will be broken and the light go out.

It is easy to overlook obvious resource people. An experience of my own is pertinent here. At one time I was teaching a special education class in a public school in suburban Maryland and discovered that the school janitor was a fount of information about the local wildlife, that he had the patience to show the children how to observe subtle changes in nature as the seasons changed, how to watch for squirrels and different kinds of birds, how to notice leaf differences. Because his own intellectual ability was not unusually high, he could really communicate with the children, their slowness did not upset him, he did not condescend to them, and they felt his genuine affection for them. At the same time he flowered in the face of so much regard and revealed that he also had the ability to make and repair many of our toys and to provide additional equipment which delighted the children.

One could say that it came as a bonus that, at the same time, some of our boys were learning about a future job role—that of school custodian, a job that some could handle.

If we think of education as a global process, affecting the whole child, this "bonus" becomes another part of an exciting experience in living to the child and to his family. Once again, action speaks louder than words! If a class has children who can be trained for a specific occupation—hospital orderly, janitor, carpenter's assistant—try to utilize community talent by organizing a Career Day and arranging for parents to be present. Then they can *see* the possibility that their child could fill the role of a worker and make a contribution to society. This is the concrete experience which Montessori saw as more valuable than unfounded abstraction.

Another source of fruitful assistance can be grandparents if they live in the child's family or visit. Quite often they have skills they would be glad to share—and they have the patience to work with the slow child. They might be induced to tell stories about long-ago episodes in their childhood, about life in other countries or what it was like to live without electricity or cars. The personal touch makes this information more meaningful to the retarded child. And everyone is learning in another way—without it being brought up consciously—that each person has a unique value in life.

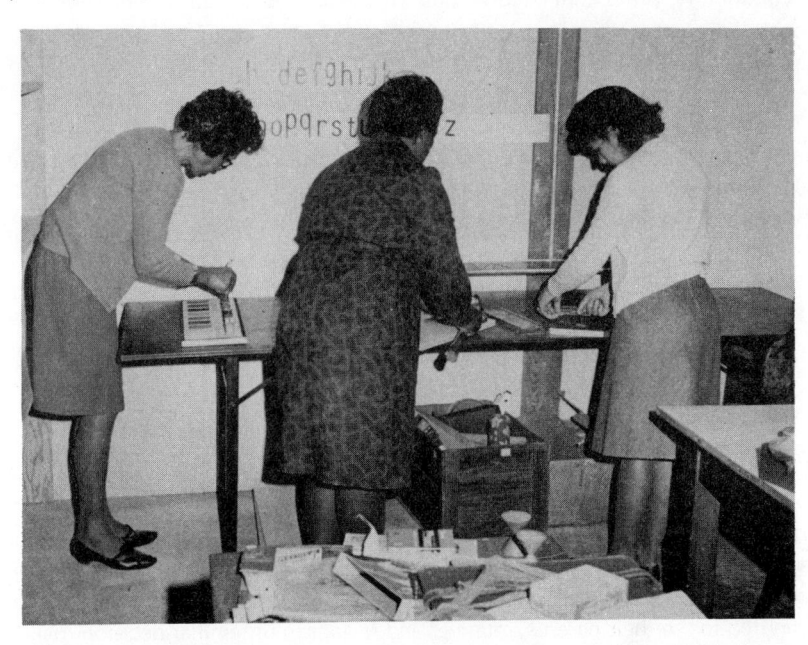

Older retarded children may be ready for direct job preparation. Here also, Montessori principles prove their usefulness. With the assistance of parents, job tasks can be broken down, programmed, as it were, to lead the child from success to success, a step at a time. Many companies produce films designed for training programs and will be pleased to lend such material to educational institutions. If the child cannot grasp the material presented, then parents and teacher can view the film, abstract the essential information and prepare illustrated charts that can be referred to over and over again. The importance of involving the parents lies in the great difference parental attitude can make, by fostering parental involvement and pride in the child's occupation.

The following cases in point summarize impressions, activities, and the outcome of an attempt to introduce the Montessori Method into small and underprivileged communities in Mississippi.

A PARENT PROGRAM FOR THE POOR

Montessori discovered in her first Children's House in the slums of Rome that hitherto apathetic parents could—and did—become involved quickly and completely in the education of their children when they understood that their voices would indeed be heard, their opinions listened to, their experiences respected. Montessori strove to develop an educational method that was free of middle-class bias. This middle-class orientation, this "otherness" of education is most often represented by the teacher, better educated than the parents, of course, speaking differently, wearing different clothes, almost always a visitor to the community who returns after work to her own distant neighborhood.

The summer of 1966, the Child Development Group of Mississippi initiated a program in which sub-professionals would be trained in the theory and practice of Montessori education.

CDGM hoped to find a way of overcoming the difficulty of the "otherness" in education and also of involving the parents closely in their children's education. As long as the parents felt that they simply gave up their children each day to "outsiders," they would not be willing to cooperate fully. In addition, the children would suffer through lack of models in their community; pre-school children pattern themselves on adults they know and love and—hopefully—respect, thus learning to respect themselves also. For Negro children in Mississippi, this is especially difficult, for the adults they see are frequently the humiliated, the rejected, the apathetic.

Considerations of human dignity demand that we respect all people, but the words mean nothing without appropriate actions, and children are particularly keen at spotting the reality behind meaningless words.

A Model Center was set up at Moss Point, Mississippi, which served as a Headstart center for local children as well as a training center to which teacher trainees and resource people could come for observation and discussion. They did not learn from classroom lectures and from textbooks but from the living experiences of working with children in a pre-school situation and from the experience the teacher was able to give them.

Indeed, the response was astonishing. Lacking previous misconceptions about the nature of pre-school education, our trainees brought to their observations a fresh viewpoint and an enormous eagerness to learn. People once hesitant about speaking discovered that they had useful ideas and *that they would be listened to.* Caught up in the excitement of working on *their* programs, the trainees brought other parents in to assist. The children were delighted to see their parents, relatives and friends in unfamiliar decision-making capacities controlling their own centers and began to understand that there were indeed new possibilities opening up for them.

The Riches of Poverty

What could seem more discouraging than the overwhelming impact of poverty one sees in rural Mississippi? Yet, these circumstances are far from discouraging and may, indeed, turn out to be a blessing. More than fifty years ago Maria Montessori opened her first Children's House in the Roman slum of San Lorenzo, and she discovered that the terrible poverty of her children concealed riches that were developed through her educational techniques.

She herself wrote, in EDUCATION FOR A NEW WORLD,[2] the following summary of her discoveries. *The circumstances which favored the first experiment were mainly three:*

> *1. Extreme poverty and a social condition of much difficulty. The child who is very poor may suffer physically from lack of food, but he finds himself in natural conditions, and so has inner wealth.*
>
> *2. The parents of these children were illiterate, so could not give them unwise help.*
>
> *3. The teachers were not professional teachers, so were free from the pedagogic prejudices induced by training on the usual lines. In America, experiments had never succeeded because they looked for the best teachers, and a good teacher meant one who had studied all the things that do not help the child, and was full of ideas which were opposed to the child's freedom. The imposition of the teacher on the child can only hinder him. One must take simple people, and make use of them, and as to poverty, one need not impose it but must not be frightened of it, as it is a highly spiritual condition. If we want an easy experiment with sure success, we should go to work among poor children, offering them an environment which they do not possess. An object scientifically constructed is taken with passionate interest by the child who has had nothing, and it awakens in him mental concentration.*

If we look at the conditions in Mississippi, then, with the eye of Montessori, we see great beauty, richness and possibility in this life. And if we are able to see this beauty, we have taken the first step toward helping the people themselves see their lives in such a way that they can achieve dignity, beauty and fulfillment without having to put on alien manners or to leave their environment for the psychologically displacing conditions of urban poverty and slum life.

Order and Freedom for Learning

Many of the Centers met in church buildings. Our offices were above a dingy funeral parlor. In one Center my desk space was in a tiny baptismal room, its walls painted with

[2]Montessori, Maria, EDUCATION FOR A NEW WORLD. Adyar, Madras, India: Kalakshetra Co., 1959).

religious scenes. All of this is psychologically helpful—surrounded constantly by reminders of life and death, living in scenes of natural beauty—people are forced into an awareness of the few truly important elements that comprise a fulfilled life.

Using the First Baptist Church at Moss Point, Mississippi, as our headquarters, we built a Model Center, utilizing equipment and ideas from the community in an effort to provide a place where people from surrounding communities could discover how to use their own resources—material, mental, psychological—to help themselves and their children.[1]

We began by creating a physical environment of neatness and order, for without order, the child cannot be freed for learning. Rooms and hallways were painted by people from the community, the playground was cleaned up, simple equipment was made by those who had the needed skills. Everyone in the community was drawn into the project; enthusiasm was contagious.

The experience of success far outweighed any verbal instruction. It was clear to all of us that fresh paint, clean buildings, community participation, made *real* differences in the way the people looked at themselves. They were thus prepared for the next steps in learning. Teacher trainees, teacher aides and children were all involved in the learning process, and the discoveries made by them were constantly exciting!

It is well to remember that there is a *distinct advantage in working with subprofessionals and untrained people as teachers for small children.* They respond with genuine freshness and enthusiasm to many of the procedures and results because the experiences are as new to them as to the children. These subprofessionals are under no illusion that they "know it all," nor have they been incorrectly trained by the often routine and deadening curricula of conventional teacher training institutions.

One example must suffice. Feeling the need of books to teach simple object perceptions, our teachers made their own small booklets, and the creative excitement they felt working on this project was immediately communicated to the children, who responded with a great desire to use these booklets and learn from them. They were relatively unsophisticated, but they were a true contribution from the resources of the people themselves, therefore, they were of enormous value as a teaching tool.

Our culture disdains work done with the hands to such an extent that even manual workers themselves feel their inferiority and believe that improvement in status is synonymous with decline in manual work. However, even cursory observation will show that this is not so and that, far from declining, manual work is actually practiced in the form of hobbies by large numbers of middle-class people who feel the psychological necessity of working with their hands. Office workers garden or practice carpentry; college students build their own hi-fi sets; women with every automatic device to make work easier take up sewing or cook elaborate meals. Elderly people turn to activities like painting, ceramics or jewelry making. Home-made bread is increasingly in style. Do-it-yourself kits are in great demand.

At the same time, middle-class people, even if they can afford help in the routine tasks of life, find that such help is not available. College-educated men and women discover that the care of children and running of a house must be done without assistance; someone must make the beds, clean the house, wash the car, paint the storm windows.

There is no longer a life of liberation from manual tasks. And there should not be, for the psychological health of a person depends on his being able to work with his hands, to grasp life, as it were, quite literally in his hands.

To Montessori the exercises of practical life were of great importance in teaching the child to complete a job well, a job that is serving the needs and comfort of others who are dependent on him. To sweep a floor, to wash a table, to polish a window so that the sun may come in—these are not small jobs to be rushed out of the way as hastily as possible, but important parts of the socialization of the child. We learn to do these humble tasks well for two reasons, essentially:

> every job should be done well for its own sake and for the practice it offers in achievement

> these jobs will be necessary throughout our lives as a way of showing our concern and love for others.

The necessity, the dignity, the beauty of humble tasks well-performed must be taught to the trainees and the aides by the example of the resource people, who must not be ashamed to demonstrate their own familiarity with the broom or the mop. Cleanliness and order are the prerequisites for learning, and the creation of this order is a job demanding respect. Resource people should treat cooks, janitors, kitchen aides, with the respect their work earns, not with the contempt that better-educated people all too often show to such manual workers.

There is much beauty and dignity in the rural life. The children may be poor but they are in close contact with nature, that nature for which the city person pines and for which the well-to-do urbanite pays a great deal of money in his brief vacations. The urbanite buys a boat or a summer house so that he may enjoy natural beauty; he travels for hours on jammed highways to get away from the city. Yet this beauty is freely available to our people. Once they learn to see this beauty instead of feeling ashamed of it, they will have gone a long way toward that liberation of spirit which precedes true learning.

Therefore, I suggest that we send fewer people away from their environment for training and choose those that we do send very carefully, picking only those who can profit from verbal instruction and from the more sophisticated atmosphere of a classroom.

Through study of Montessori's philosophy we can guard against the danger of "processing" our children to take their places in a middle-class assembly line devoted to turning out semi-educated college graduates without a sense of self or of vocation. There is room in the Montessori system for the child with intellectual interests or outstanding intelligence, but there is also room for the slow child, the retarded child, the socially disadvantaged child, the quiet child, the average child.

A MONTESSORI WORKSHOP IN NATCHEZ

From January 23, 1967, a Montessori Workshop was conducted in Natchez, Mississippi. This workshop was funded by the Office of Economic Opportunity through the Holy Family Child Development Center.

Rev. William J. Morrissay, S.S.J., Pastor of Holy Family Church, was the Coordinator; Mrs. Marjorie R. Baroni, Community Action Specialist with Star, Incorporated, was Co-ordinating Assistant; Rev. Tupper Drane, Assistant Pastor, aided Father Morrissay. Invaluable help was given by Sister Miryam of the Little Sisters of Jesus, Mamou, Louisiana, a qualified Montessori teacher.

This was the second workshop conducted by the author in Mississippi, and the experience was illuminating and quite moving. Our original plan had been to train perhaps ten women to help Negro retarded children for whom there are no facilities in Natchez. The Holy Family Child Development Center felt that some program was clearly necessary. However, when we opened the doors of the Center on January 23, we found twenty-four women, three of them white, all eager to learn as much as they could. "The three whites had broken the mores of gracious antebellum Natchez to come and learn side by side with those who formerly had been their household help and washerwomen."

"Some of the women could not read or write, but this was no great barrier to the concept of pre-school teaching . . ." We were short of chairs and materials but somehow we managed, as indeed, we knew we had to, for the enthusiasm of these women was not to be believed.

In response to questions, we discovered that some of the trainees had retarded children they wished to help, some had worked in summer Head Start programs and wanted to learn something about the Montessori Method. Through this workshop, some mothers hoped to help their own children, and possibly to find jobs in community organizations to assist Negro children. "These women were 'subprofessionals' in the Montessori plan, housewives and mothers who can be given the rudiments of the method through a workshop."[3]

The general educational level was low, with twelve of the women having less than a high school education. In addition, many of these women had large families and practically all of them had very low incomes. Many traveled as much as 30 miles to reach the workshop and had to make provision for the care of their children. The workshop was from 8:30 A.M. to 2:30 P.M. and therefore meant quite a sacrifice for the mothers. Yet, despite these difficulties, there was no absenteeism and the enthusiasm is a tribute to the pertinence of the Montessori philosophy for these people. Montessori's great understanding of the problems of the poor has given her the reputation of being the first fighter in the War Against Poverty.

We began quite simply with the making of Montessori aprons for children. These aprons are made so that the child may slip them over his head and tie them in front; they are easy to put on and cover the child's clothing.

These aprons utilized one skill almost all of the women had—sewing. Thus they were able to start with a feeling of pride in accomplishment rather than with insecurity because of the lack of verbal skills. When finished, the aprons were tangible evidence of ability to be seen and admired by all. The importance of establishing initial success with those who have known mostly defeat and failure is paramount.

[3]Minor, W. F., MONTESSORI IN NATCHEZ, Special Report to the National Catholic Reporter, March 22, 1967.

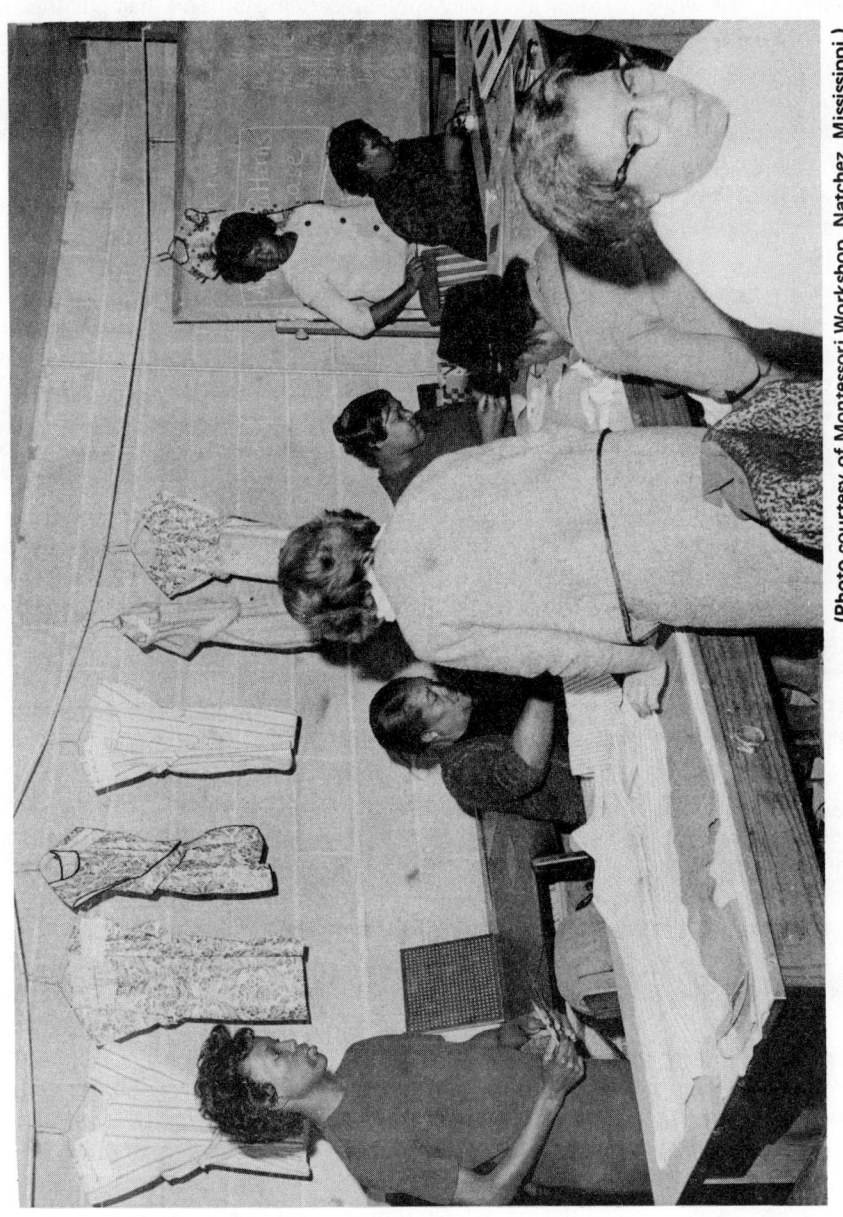

(Photo courtesy of Montessori Workshop, Natchez, Mississippi.)

"We began quite simply with the making of Montessori aprons for children. . . . They utilized one skill almost all of the women had — sewing."

"The Hands Work and the Mind Begins to Work"[4]

When the gay aprons were all hung up to make cheerful spots of color in a dull room, we were able to talk about the reasons for giving the children aprons to wear. These mothers send their children to school dressed in nicely starched dresses and shirts and well-pressed pants, believing, not without reason, that they confer a certain status on their children in this way. At the same time, we know that young children must move freely in order to truly learn. In a conventional school, where movement is often restricted, starched clothes can be worn without too much fear of dirtying them, but we wanted these mothers to understand the need children have for freedom of movement. Yet freedom also includes freedom from fear and guilt over soiling their clothes. And we also knew that these children have limited wardrobes, laundry facilities are often not easily available, and a dirty dress or shirt can be a calamity. This fear can freeze the child into immobility.

The discussions that evolved from the making of aprons thus ranged far and wide. "... women who had found great difficulty in communicating gave splendid little talks about what they had done with their hands, or observed.

"This was an important part of the ... teaching—to draw from these Mississippi mothers who had never had the chance when they were young, their feelings, expressed in their own words, of discovering the tools for bringing a new world of learning to their children."[5]

Every other activity was chosen with the same goals in mind—immediate skill and satisfaction in achieving success, preparation for long-range goals and opportunity for an examination of attitudes. We followed the Montessori ideal of working from the known to the unknown, from verbalization to cognition and then to abstraction.

Next we proceeded to make sandpaper alphabets and the letters of the alphabet from velour paper. Velour paper is especially suited for working with retarded or disturbed children since they are often sensitive to the harsh texture of sandpaper.

Sandpaper and velour alphabets are simply letters carefully cut out and pasted on cardboard, pink for vowels and blue for consonants. The child traces the letter outlined with his fingers until he knows it thoroughly. If he slips, he can feel the difference between the sandpaper and the smooth cardboard. Using these alphabets we gained understanding of another Montessori principle—the control of error and the importance of devising means for such control; in other words, those principles which are built into programmed learning.

In addition to the variety of such activities utilizing Montessori equipment and materials, we spent a great deal of time on language development, since the linguistic poverty of these people is one of the greatest barriers to their over-all improvement. One of the exercises which was very useful was role-playing. The mothers took turns being mother and then child—being the teacher and the one taught. In this way they built a feeling for how to talk to a child or how to teach someone something. These are roles they hadn't before played and for which they began to have a language and an understanding.

[4]Ibid.
[5]Ibid.

(Photo courtesy of Montessori Workshop, Mosspoint, Mississippi.)

"Sub-professionals trained as much as possible in their own communities, trained to deal with their local situations and problems, make ideal pre-school teachers...."

We also used film strips and records as a model of how to tell stories to children, and followed those with Ruth Sawyer's splendid record, WAYS OF A STORY TELLER, Np. WW701 and WW702 produced by Weston Studios, Weston, Connecticut. Miss Sawyer is America's most outstanding authority on story-telling. She describes her adventures as she traveled throughout the world looking for folk tales. Literature is not the province of the sophisticated or literate alone, as we well know. But listening to Miss Sawyer's record, with her vivid tales of traveling through primitive areas of Europe was a revelation to people long accustomed to downgrading themselves and their culture.

We discussed their own folk traditions and tales and how it was possible to pass these on to children. By tapping deep sources of interest and knowledge, we were able to enlarge vocabularies because the need and desire to communicate must precede vocabulary growth.

I discovered that the best in children's literature appealed to these mothers in much the same way it appeals to middle-class mothers.

One of the lessons that I wanted to teach the trainees was the primacy of the mother as teacher for the young child and the primacy of the home as an important environment for the child. Head Start is an absolutely necessary program, there is no doubt of that, but equally necessary is a program to train mothers so that eventually Head Start will be unnecessary. It stands to reason that parents feel inadequate when their children must be given pre-school training by others because they are not equipped to do it themselves, and this feeling of inadequacy is not one we wish to encourage. At the same time, Head Start only reaches a small proportion of children and those not until age three and a half or four. Meanwhile, the first vital years have passed when such a large part of our learning is accomplished. "Subprofessionals, trained as much as possible in their own communities, trained to deal with their local situations and problems, make ideal pre-school teachers.

"They are free of preconceptions that have paralyzed so many of our public school systems, they are receptive to new ideas and procedures, they are willing and able workers."[6]

If we could train mothers from poverty to give their children the support and understanding they need from birth, we could accomplish a great deal in a most economical way and also foster pride in the parents who are able to become resource people for their children. Most mothers will come even though it is difficult, because of the intensity of their desire for improvement.

The aim of a Montessori education for the special child as well as the disadvantaged child is the same as a Montessori education for any child—to arrive at a joyful adult who is utilizing his capacities to their utmost in meaningful work which gives him satisfaction and allows for psychological strength and stability. The "inefficient learner"(as the editors of ACADEMIC THERAPY like to call them) is part of the human continuum—special, yes, but strange, no. And with this realization by parents and teachers, much can be built on these beginning ideas.

[6]Ibid.

EXERCISES OF PRACTICAL LIFE

A Philosophy of Dignity

> *"Make the best of each one's strongest points and compensating aptitudes. The dull child will have failed so often that he will always be expecting to fail again. Give him something at which he can succeed, and keep him happily as well as usefully occupied. Avoid reproaches, and remove the ingrained sense of failure by giving him some special kind of work in which he can quickly achieve a conscious improvement and taste the triumph of a personal success. Never let a child lose heart, for once he has lost heart he has lost everything.*
>
> Sir Cyril Burt, THE BACKWARD CHILD

Actions may speak louder than words, but attitudes speak even louder than actions, especially to the child who is skilled at reading non-verbal communication. There is all the difference in the world between a request given like this: "Mrs. X, would you like to make your wonderful pecan cookies for our school tea? No one can quite make them the way you do." and: "Since you simply can't manage anything more difficult, I guess you'll have to contribute your regular cookies to the program."

Yet, how often do we convey the second attitude to the retarded child through subtle non-verbal indicators?

The exercises that follow should be considered as part of an all-encompassing attitude, a philosophy of dignity, rather than as a set of disparate exercises which will yield wonderful results if they are followed slavishly. No, these exercises are simply the expression of Montessori's profound concern for the development of the whole child. The retarded child is also a whole child. He is more than his handicap. He too craves fulfillment as a complete person to the very limits of his ability.

Montessori felt that the Exercises of Practical Life were an indispensable part of her education for normal and special children alike. If we look closely into her philosophy we can appreciate the many benefits which flow from these exercises when they are seen as the expression of an attitude toward life and toward work which will result in an enhancement of the self-concept and an understanding of the dignity of all useful work.

In the classroom these Exercises may appear, to the untutored eye, to involve a great deal of carrying of dishes and even more energetic scrubbing and sweeping. In a special education classroom, the reaction might well be, "Are the children doing these simple chores because they are incapable of doing more?" But the visitor to a Montessori class for normal children will see the same activities as part of every school day.

Make no mistake about it—these children are *not* simply carrying dishes or washing windows. *They are mastering themselves and their environment!* The classroom is also being cleaned but that is hardly the primary purpose of these Exercises!

What do we mean when we speak of the child mastering himself and his environment? These remarks are applicable to normal children but they apply with special force to socially disadvantaged as well as to mentally retarded or emotionally disturbed children. Such children typically suffer from low self-esteem and come to school after years of rebuffs and lessons in social humiliation. Quite often they are incapable of caring for themselves and their belongings and this inability only reinforces the feelings of self-rejection which they have met in the outside world. They are inclined to believe: "Yes, it is true, how the others see me; I *am* useless, helpless." Within the family they may be the target of derision and anger, they get in the way, they must be helped year after year. Somehow, they never manage to "pull themselves together."

In accordance with Montessori, we begin where these children are. And where they are is in the "slough of despond," seemingly trapped by a low self-esteem that reinforces an initial inability to perform essential tasks, tasks that lead, in turn, to enhancement of the self-concept.

When the child enters the prepared environment of a Montessori classroom, the first step has been taken in his education, for the establishment and maintenance of external order is absolutely essential for the eventual development of internal order. Without order there can be no learning.

NAMES AND POSSESSIONS

The importance of the child's name is vital in another area—that which indicates possession. We do not put his name on his chair, desk, coat rack, etc., solely to familiarize him with his name, but also to show that these things are *his.* In order for the child to achieve respect for the property of others, he must first learn to distinguish what belongs to him from what belongs to others and to cherish his own possessions. Only then can he be brought to understand that the possessions of others are equally cherished by their owners and belong to them.

Just as love of self is basic to love of others, even in the Biblical injunction, because nobody can esteem another person if he does not first esteem himself; so the sense of *mine* precedes the sense of *yours.* All too often we discover that the child who steals is the child who has no possessions distinctively his own, hence no awareness of the differences between mine and yours.

It is part of the prepared environment to have a place for everything and everything in its place. At the same time, each child should have a place of *his* own for *his* possessions with *his* name clearly indicated on it. No one else can touch his possessions without his approval. More than basic security is involved here. The child is being prepared to observe one of society's laws not through imposition of external discipline but through fostering of his growing sense of distinction between *mine* and *yours* and through his understanding of the inviolability of personal possessions.

When this is clearly understood, the child can follow the commandment, "Thou shalt not steal," through the workings of his own conscience.

The Child's Name

All children are very interested in their names—names have an emotional significance for them—and so we recommend that his name be the first word the young child should learn to read and write. Each child should be helped to recognize his name on his first day at school. He should be presented with a label for his clothes rack and shown where to stick it. In the beginning color coding or a picture of an animal, toy, fruit, etc. might be helpful to him. Coats, sweaters, and boots should be marked by parents, so the child's clothes will not be lost. After the child chooses a chair to sit on, a name label should be pasted on his chair. The same type of writing used for his name should be used for a drawer or box to keep his work.

A rubber name stamp of each child's name is desirable in the beginning, so the young child can be taught how to mark his work. The development of his own name and own work helps with the development of respect of ownership. In this context, it is well for the child to avoid learning to write before he is thoroughly familiar with his name.

After the child learns to recognize his name he can begin tracing it. By enclosing the name in plastic he may trace over it with a china marking pencil. A piece of flannel or tissue can serve as an eraser.

There are several games that can be played with the children's names. On a chart write names in color, red for girls, blue for boys, and make matching cards for superimposing on the chart.

A group game can be played with the same chart. The teacher reads the names of the children. As each name is read, the child comes and finds, or is helped to find his own card, until everyone has one. Then she points to various names on her list, and the children whose names are indicated get up and show their cards.

Other games to play with names are matching name with like name, sorting boys and girls names on different piles, building names with movable alphabet letters, or matching a snapshot of each child in the classroom with his name.

These games not only teach the child to recognize and read his own name, but also aid in developing his self concept. It will help the child to independence in labeling his work, and free the teacher from this task.

Identifying names with heroes or great personalities is helpful for development of models for one's self. In addition, where religion is taught, there can be an association of name with a Christian patron saint or with Jewish characters from the Bible.

In a Montessori class, after the Silence game, each child's name is whispered and the child gets up and moves either to another room or another activity. Children wait attentively for their names. In a large class, if the teacher forgets to call a child's name, he is deeply hurt. Montessori recognized the importance a child's name has for him.

We must recall our own emotions to remember vividly the terror of chaos, the dread that comes over us when we cannot understand impressions given to us by our senses, cannot order information into a meaningful pattern. Open a book in a field of advanced mathematics like topology and try to read the signs; then imagine that you *must* read them or face humiliation. Listen to a conversation in a foreign language or try to read a Chinese newspaper, knowing that you *must* understand the language in order to survive. This will give you some faint idea of what the retarded child faces as he struggles to achieve self-mastery and to make sense of the world!

Thus, by the mere establishment of external order we have accomplished much.
The prepared environment is ready to receive the child. In it he can flower. There is nothing in it that he cannot master. But how can we teach him this wonderful knowledge? Through having him care for this environment and be responsible for the maintenance of the order. He learns through doing that *he* can bring order out of chaos and can maintain this order *through his own activities*. He can be truly responsible!

A Case in Point

The therapeutic value of the prepared environment was brought home to me vividly when I taught a special class in a public school in a Washington suburb. Time was needed to prepare the environment in a way to make maximum use of Montessori matrials, so school was in session for six weeks before our class took up its quarters in the refurbished library.

"Each child is provided with a small piece of chalk board for individual work. These slates are invaluable in the development of coordination for writing skill."

(Photo from a Special Class in a public school in Prince George County, Maryland.)

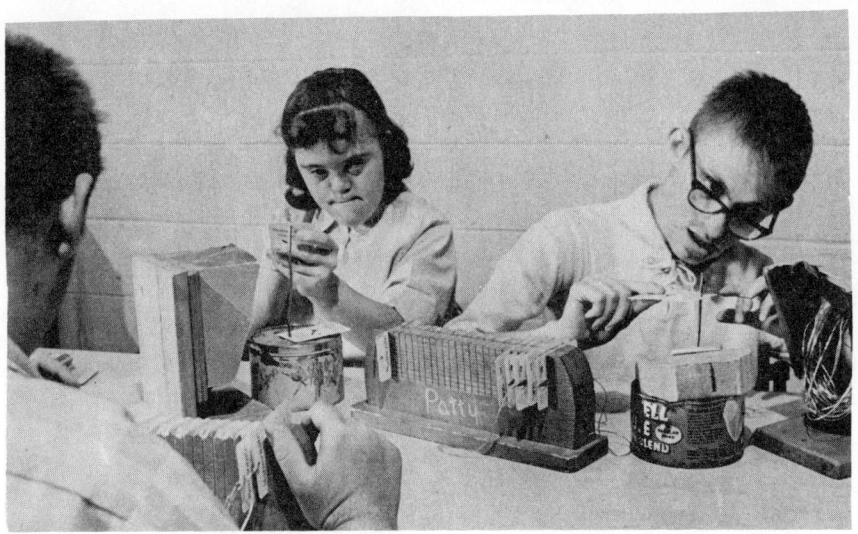

(Photo courtesy of Larendon Hall School for Exceptional Children, Denver, Colorado. Sheltered Workshop.)

"The Dignity of Honest Labor"

Space was carefully utilized; activity centers were geared to create an atmosphere of order so vital to the basic need of approaching learning in ordered surroundings, of finding the environment and keeping it as found; of conquering one's environment and thus being forever freed from slavery to it, freed for independence and self-development.

Selected as the first Montessori pupils were the youngest children in the special education grouping, all with problems, all mentally retarded, ranging in age from 8 to 10 years, with I.Q.'s from 62 to 72.

The immediate positive response of all these children to this prepared environment was astounding. In a very short time they were honoring the rules of law and order and they monitored each other's personal tidiness. Secure in this orderly comfortable setting, their feeling of social responsibility and regard for each other engendered a facilitating emotional climate. Problems heretofore rife were non-existent when each child knew there was a place for everything and he could be a major part of continuing the orderly process of keeping and returning everything to its proper place. Pencils, crayons, scissors, paste, paper—now always available and always where they were expected to be—brought results in their economical and careful use; waste was almost eliminated. Paper was cut in small sizes, for destroying a messy smaller paper produced less guilt than when a small error necessitated destruction of a large piece of paper.

Each child was provided a small piece of chalk board for individual work. These slates were invaluable in the development of coordination for writing skill. Easily erased, readily checked, they were helpful to both teacher and child. The larger chalk board was hung so that every part of it was within the easy reach of the child; everything was within reach.

The practical experiences in the prepared environment started with the responsibility of one's own possessions; the hanging up of one's clothing and new respect for self. For no one can take pride in one's appearance if one's coat has been lying crumpled and wrinkled on the floor. How much better it feels to put on a garment that has been hanging neatly and is clean and pressed in appearance! A new respect and pride for one's own things and for one's self is the outcome.

Caring for this newly set-up environment was the logical next step, and the children responded *en masse* with pride in keeping their classroom clean and bright. The tables were carefully scrubbed to keep them in tip-top condition. Every process in this clean-up was child initiated and followed through with the attendant good feeling of accomplishment—doing each task the "right" way. Also, while sweeping the classroom and keeping their quarters immaculate, the children acquired feelings of responsibility, of pride, and of respect.

To accomplish these tasks properly, it was necessary to have a "resource person." Our custodian graciously met our requests and showed us how. Some of the boys began to identify themselves with the responsible position of custodian in a manner almost of hero worship. This was their first goal for their future role in society, a most necessary occupation which they felt was now within their grasp.

Learning sessions with this "resource" have been invaluable. When paint was spilled on the classroom floor, our custodian held a session, the children spellbound, explaining the use of steel wool and wax for proper cleaning of the spill. The children then went to work on the practical application of what they had just learned—doing; learning by doing—with the attendant success experience.

Hand and Mind Go Together

Montessori philosophy explains that one cannot chop a person in half; hand and mind go together. The hands are put to work as they naturally would be used for tasks that will present themselves as the years unfold. We have basic doing, basic knowledge, natural response, and an environment prepared to meet the child's need to be comfortable and to be a participant in this natural environment and this prepared environment fills his basic needs in life experiences.

All of our culture has been transmitted through the work of hands, and we are fully aware that the developing of the use of hands and attendant development is a unique, an individual reaction. It is not where we walk that leaves our mark for posterity; it is what we do, however minute, with our hands.

Dale is an example of how teaching the hands develops the mind's activity. He was nine years old. Dale couldn't or wouldn't react in previous classroom situations. He was always either late or absent. When he was present, he was pokey, annoyed others, a ten-o'clock scholar in its broadest sense. However, he knew what to do with his hands and used them for shoving and pestering others.

In the new prepared environment, this was all changed. The practical environment gave structure to Dale's need to use his hands, and now Dale was trying to write his name. He used his hands positively, no longer in irresponsible nudging.

One morning, Dale bustled excitedly into class, a small piggy bank clutched in his grimy fist. He purposefully sought out the letter "P" among the sandpaper letters and identified this letter with his very own personal symbol—with his piggy bank. Flushed with success, he wrote "P" with sureness many times on the chalk board. But his day was not yet to his full satisfaction. Success was winging and would not falter. Here was Dale, copying words from the symbol chart and sharing this accomplishment with the teacher who, at his request, read his efforts. Here was the door opening to further reading and writing goals; the recognition that reading is identification of symbols—the first step to reading.

Since there is no competition in a Montessori classroom and no invidious comparisons are made between one child's ability and another's, each child can discover work which he can accomplish and contributions he can make to the harmonious functioning of the class as a whole. In the detailed Exercises of Practical Life in the pages ahead, it is possible to see the varied activities necessary to the maintenance of an orderly environment. It is the teacher's role to assign these exercises in accordance with each child's ability, to present them to children individually so that the children may master them, to endeavor to have each child reach his maximum capacity in performing these exercises, to understand precisely how they can be used not only to enhance self-exteem, but also to teach skills and to aid in the development of muscular coordination.

Programming Each Step

Montessori broke each exercise into steps which could be **demonstrated** in sequence, making them ideal for use in special education. In the beginning the teacher may have to move slowly and carefully and the learning process may take a very long time. But once the exercises are mastered, the children repeat them with an undiminished air of joy and pleasure in their accomplishment.

Let me take just one example to show how much a child can learn from one apparently simple exercise when it is properly structured and presented. Then, if we multiply this one exercise by all the different ones which are performed each day, we can realize the incalculable benefits offered to the child and to the class as a whole by mastery in this area.

We see a child pouring juice into small glasses. A second child is placing those glasses on a tray and serving them to his classmates at snack time. That is what we see. But what is happening underneath? The first child is learning to control those muscles used in pouring—a considerable feat. Hand and lower arm manipulation lead to achievement in many other areas, from tying shoes to writing. It takes great skill to master the art of pouring so that no juice spills over. He is learning visual discrimination—some glasses have juice in them, others are empty. Some glasses may have more juice than others and he is learning to see the difference and to add more juice where it is needed.

The second child is balancing very carefully to carry that tray without spilling. He is beginning the study of counting—one glass to one child. He is discovering the pleasure of serving others with something they want; that is, he is playing his part in a social situation.

All of the children involved are learning by example—not through the teacher's verbalization—an appropriate mode of behavior in a common social situation. There is giving and receiving, there is cooperation.

So it is with similar exercises—cleaning floors, tables, windows, dusting furniture, watering plants, caring for animals, putting away materials, aprons, silverware, washing and drying dishes, cleaning the equipment, and so on. The child learns a specific skill which is an advance in self-mastery, he learns to use hand and mind in a concrete situation, he learns cooperative behavior.

Joy and Dignity in Work

And the child learns something more—something of supreme importance. He learns the joys of honest work. Montessori wrote that work is necessary for the psychic health of man and each one of us on earth has his own work to do. That applies to the retarded person as well. Each of us has a unique contribution to make to the health of society.

But how often the retarded child comes to school unable to perform the simplest task. Either through ignorance or through guilt, parents may do everything for their child without discovering how much the child can do for himself. The realization that many retarded individuals can do a great deal has not yet reached all of those who most need this knowledge.

So in many cases the attitude towards work must be learned in the classroom. This means that the teacher must understand her own attitudes towards work, must appreciate the dignity of all honest labor, must realize that even humble tasks are necessary for the maintenance of society.

Until the advent of mechanization, when all tasks were done by hand, the many repetitive jobs necessary for running a home or farm could be done by retarded people, who were kept at home and welcomed in the family circle for the extra pair of hands they provided, hands much needed in the endless round of domestic tasks—hand-washing, ironing with flatirons, preparing foods without a nearby supermarket, the mending and sewing, the various chores done in barn and garden, and so on.

Since few members of such a society had much schooling and intellectual qualities were not highly valued, the retarded person need not feel inferior in society at large. He may have been clumsier, slower or more silent than his fellow villagers, but they all clearly had their places on a continuum joined by respect for the same standards of work.

It is useless, however, to wish for the return of those days, for we must prepare our children to cope with an entirely different society. It is easy to forget, though, that despite automation, many repetitive tasks must still be performed by people and there will be an increase in the demand for such services as time goes on. Routine clerical and mailing-room jobs, packaging and sorting jobs on an assembly line, all the many jobs needed for the running of laundries, hospitals and other large institutions, will continue to need workers capable of performing routine tasks over the long range without succumbing to boredom and dissatisfaction. Retarded workers make excellent choices for such jobs, as employers in increasing numbers are recognizing.

Beyond learning the skills, however, the retarded person must learn the *attitude* which will make him an effective worker—that there is dignity in all honest labor. He is important, his job is important, he is a person of genuine worth. That is how a useful worker will be developed.

More than four centuries ago Saint Teresa of Avila, herself a woman of surpassing brilliance, rebuked one of her nuns who had left the kitchen work undone because she wished to pray by reminding her that "God can be found among the pots and pans" as well as anywhere else. For the retarded person, too, personal worth can be found among the pots and pans.

Indeed, even before we think of job training as an end result of the exercises of practical life, we can think of their worth in providing a link with the child's home, with the very real pots and pans and beds and dishes he leaves in the morning and returns to after school. Without mutual cooperation and respect between home and school, there will be a tragic waste in our efforts to educate the children who come to us.

The exercises of practical life provide an ideal link between home and school, a link which is reinforced with each success. The child who can come home to demonstrate a helpful skill and win merited praise from his parents is the child who returns to school on the next day better prepared for new learning. And with enhancement in his self-concept, he can learn more which will gain further recognition at home from those whose approval means the most to him, his parents and other members of his family.

PERSONAL EXPERIENCE

Practical Life Exercises: The March of Shines[1]

Every classroom can acquire simple equipment for cleaning and maintenance which can be used with imagination to assist the children in developing a variety of skills. For example, something as simple as shoe shining materials led to an exciting adventure in learning for one of my classes in a suburban Maryland elementary school.

I had taken the chairmanship of a March of Dimes compaign in the school, which motivated our two special classes to earn money to donate to this cause. The way they chose was an outgrowth of a Montessori practical life exercise we had earlier adopted, that of polishing shoes. The children enjoyed doing their own and often asked to polish the teacher's shoes as well. When we showed a film about the March of Dimes and discussed the campaign with our children, they were motivated to assume the responsibility of earning money by setting up a little shoe shine shop.

We advertised the enterprise by making and distributing leaflets to the entire school, using language and art to develop our motto: "A Shine In Time Will Provide A Dime For The March Of Dimes." The children prepared the brushes and various colors of shoe polish on linoleum-covered tables. Older girls made cobbler-type aprons for the boys. Other children became cashiers, learning valuable lessons in handling money and making correct change. A large chart was posted to show the number of shoes that were shined and the amount of money earned each day.

With two special classes, competition was especially lively. Since my class was the younger, comprising educable mentally retarded with ages between 7 and 10, they could not accomplish as much as the older children. However, to compensate, they were able to set up a

---

[1] Gitter, Lena L., "Montessori Exercise of Practical Life and the Development of Citizenship: A Case In Point", reprinted from THE POINTER, Vol. 7, No. 2, Winter, 1963.

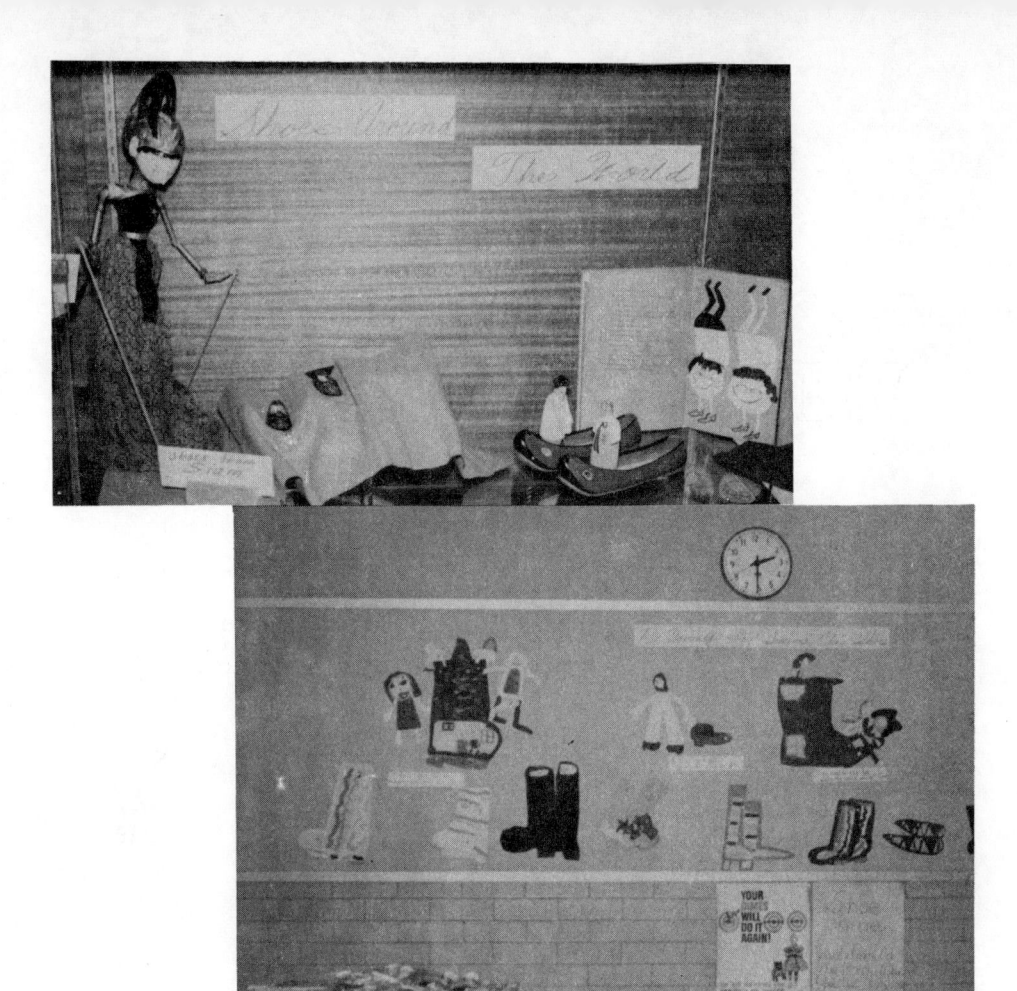

special display consisting of shoes of different colors, types and materials. Indeed, they had not realized there were so many kinds.

This interesting collection drew great attention when it was moved to the public display case in the central hall of the school. Everyone began thinking about the shoes that his father used during military service in different parts of the world, such as Chinese clogs, wooden or fur shoes and Austrian boots. Our special class pupils metaphorically stepped out of their own shoes and into a wider world as they became aware of foreign countries and people, using a map and globe to locate the different countries. Another valuable side effect was the acceptance of our children by the normal children in the school.

We used many stories and poems about shoes while the shoe shine shop was operating. The children especially responded to "The Red Clogs" by Masako Matsuno, about a little Japanese girl who ruins her new red clogs playing in water. There was also a great deal of art work, including slides on art. The children were quite impressed with Van Gogh's painting, "The Old Shoes." The music teacher included songs about shoes, and with her help the class created a little play about shoemakers.

A SHINE IN TIME WILL PROVIDE A DIME

FOR THE MARCH OF DIMES

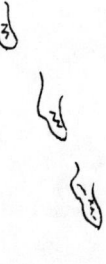

BRING YOUR SHOES TO THE
GREENDALE SHOE SHINE STORE
ROOM 4 AND LIBRARY

HOURS   9:00 - 9:30 A.M.   1:30 - 2:00 P.M.

This was the advertisement used for the Shoe Shine project.

The director of the March of Dimes accepted the money the two classes had earned and quite impressive it was, too—$36.50 in small change, just as it had been received.

This entire project is but one example of the atmosphere that a Montessori-oriented classroom can offer special children. They find themselves in an environment suited to their abilities, with tasks that are both challenging and within their capacity, and confidence-building situations through practical life exercises and similar activities. The special child, often frustrated in the regular academic class through repeated failure, learns that he is not competing with anyone but is only working at *his* own best pace. And the work he is doing does not depend upon sophisticated verbal communication.

Good Habits Work Toward Independence

"A place for everything and everything in its place" is one of the very important principles of Montessori training. It is helpful to set up "in" and "out" boxes, where the children can put their work into the "in" box, and then get it from the "out" box after it has been checked by the teacher. To help the child who is still struggling to learn to write in dating every piece of paper (and it is important to date papers), a date stamp near these "in" and "out" boxes will enable the child to stamp the day's date on his work. He will not only feel grown-up in "stamping" his work with a date stamp, but the necessity for reminding the child to put the date on his work will be eliminated and another step to independence is gained.

A stamp clock (without hands) where the child can stamp it on his paper and then draw the hands in it to designate the time his work is started and completed, has tremendous value in that it enables him to test himself and see the time needed to complete certain jobs. He can compare this with a similar assignment the following day and see how long it took him to complete it. This builds an incentive to repeat certain exercises in order to gain skill and speed. It also prepares the child to accept the necessity of completing jobs within a certain time limit. This will help him later when confronted by the demands of management and/or supervisors—he will already have recognized and developed a good attitude towards the demands of work and have good work habits.

Living in the World

The retarded child lives in the same world with his normal peers and this world begins with the family. This is the first human connection with life, and for the retarded child it remains the primary scene of his experiences long after the normal child has ventured further into the world outside the home.

What is the significance of this knowledge for the teacher? If she sees the child as a total human personality, despite his handicap, then she can recognize that one of her key jobs is to fit him into his home environment, to use his hours in school as preparation for life.

In general, we can say that we encounter two especially difficult situations with the special child where the exercises of practical life provide a strong link between home and school. One is when we are working with the socially disadvantaged child, whose parents may be unable to comprehend his intellectual improvement because of their own limitations but who can respond warmly to the child's performance of household tasks and his ability to care for himself, since they are relieved of a burden.

The other difficult situation occurs when the special child comes from a family which values intellectual attainments; perhaps the parents are college graduates or the siblings may be doing well in school and proud of their scholarly accomplishments. Such a child may suffer greatly from feelings of low self-esteem even if he is loved and knows himself to be loved, for he wishes to *accomplish* and to have his activities praised, not out of kindness but out of genuine pleasure in the work performed.

He wants, not only parental approval, but also the regard of his siblings, and he wants to occupy himself with real work in the midst of a family whose members are all engaged in purposeful activity.

At the same time, if the special child can care for himself and help in the housework, can behave in public and contribute to the family, other family members will be able to harbor good feelings about him, thus relieving themselves of the burden of shame and guilt that all too often accompanies the appearance of a retarded child.

The exercises of practical life are designed to fill the basic human needs. Through them the child learns to care for himself, for example, the dressing frames allow him to practice the many intricate steps necessary for dressing and undressing himself. Provision of child-sized sinks and mirrors allows him to learn grooming in school without the tension of proving himself at once, but this knowledge, when put to use at home, indicates to his family that progress has been made and praise is in order. The child who learns at school the practical life exercises that he will perform at home is like an actor who rehearses without an audience so that he may give a perfect performance when the audience is in the theatre. In this case the theatre is the home and the audience is the family.

Those exercises which develop self-care are the first to engage the attention, of course, since this area seems so urgent but there is yet another part of the practical life exercises that offers a great deal and should be developed as quickly as possible to the extent that each child's ability allows.

Food Preparation

This is the realm of food and food preparation. Food is associated with the primary human satisfaction for all of us, it is a point of immediate sharing, whether the child is normal or retarded, for in this respect, at least, the experience has been the same. Food is important to all of us as a source of emotional nourishment as well as of physical sustenance. Family dinners, holiday feasts, wedding breakfasts or dinners, the banquets which celebrate many basic events in human life from birth to death, all demonstrate the emotional satisfaction we receive from food.

Even today, in the era of prepared and packaged foods, large numbers of women—and men, as well—enjoy the time and attention demanded by the preparation of elaborate meals. Gourmet cooking classes are filled, bread making is popular and the family barbecue is tended by Dad, even though cooking the food indoors would be easier. How many people speak of the calm they find in the kitchen making fancy cakes or putting up their own preserves!

The small child smells cookies baking and is drawn to the kitchen. The older child returning from school immediately senses the warmth when he smells the wonderful scents of a pie in the oven or soup bubbling in the pot.

For small children food has intense emotional identification and we find this same attachment in the special child, quite often to an extraordinary degree. Certain foods are eaten lovingly, obsessively, others are avoided with expressions of utmost horror or emotional disturbance. The special child continues to receive intense emotional satisfaction from food long after the normal child has given this up to some degree.

When we are working with practical life exercises in the realm of food, therefore, we are not only teaching skills to win praise and to provide a solid sense of accomplishment, we are also—quite by the way—providing therapy for many of the children. We are also engaging the child in a complex learning process with many ramifications limited only by each child's capacity.

Cookbooks for children are available (see the Bibliography) which can be used for special classes, sometimes with modifications. It is also possible for the class to make its own cookbooks by engaging in a genuine "research project" quite like those done by normal children. A large supply of magazines is needed, the home-making and women's magazines with their pages of color photographs, perhaps contributed by the mothers as another link between home and school.

The children can find appropriate photographs to illustrate a simple recipe—for example, a box of pudding, a saucepan, a measuring cup, a bottle of milk, then a dish with the finished pudding. Even those who cannot read can memorize the steps with the help of photographs. Small recipe booklets can be prepared for each dish, so that each child in the class can have access to at least one book if he wishes to take it home when he feels confident of his skill. Puddings, gelatin desserts, ice cream parfaits, simple salads, sandwiches, box cakes and cookies, easy-cook cereals, all offer opportunities to demonstrate skill in food preparation on a simple but satisfying level.

(Photo courtesy of Library of Congress and Day Nursery of Okeechobee Migratory Labor Camp.)

"For small children, the retarded, and people with emotional problems, food has intense emotional identification. . . ."

The child is learning the satisfaction of doing for and with other people—his classmates, his family—as well as the profound satisfaction provided by serious work well done. He is serving those he loves with food he has made and which will contribute to their well-being. Small wonder his self-concept is enhanced.

In the best run household there are many occasions when mother will need help in preparing the salad or making the dessert. The child understands that this is not make-work he is being given but a true opportunity to assist just as his siblings are assisting. The mother, seeing her child not as a burden but as a real help, feels better about him and about herself, and this good feeling is transmitted to the child not only through her verbal praise but also through her subtle non-verbal indicators, and reinforcement of self-esteem occurs.

At the same time the child is engaged in a complex learning process as he masters each recipe, no matter how simple. He is learning a sequence of acts which has a beginning, a middle and an end, an orderly progression with predictable results. He is learning manual skills in whipping, beating, folding, stirring. When he scrambles eggs or beats egg whites, he is discovering something about the chemistry of the egg, just as when he makes tea he is learning that the liquid water can turn into a gas, and when he puts ice cubes in that tea to cool it, he is learning that water is also a solid. What better way to teach the three states of matter than to build on such concrete learning, interesting because it has a goal and a purpose which the child can relate to his own immediate life?

MONTESSORI EXERCISES

The Montessori exercises which follow, extensive as they are, offer only a basic structure to be filled in by the teacher according to the background and ability of each child. Exercises can be modified or added to depending on the ability and interest of the child, but it is important to emphasize that the basic Montessori principles are essential to the full realization of these exercises. Any changes made should be in accordance with the concept of working from the concrete to the abstract, from the easy to the difficult, from the known to the unknown. Additional exercises should be added only after the teacher clearly understands how to break each one down into single steps which proceed in logical order to allow for a consistent experience of success.

The same awareness should be present in working with a particular exercise—for example, preparing a salad. Each child should be encouraged to work to his maximum capacity— **but it is of the utmost importance that no child be allowed to fail by being encouraged to work beyond his capacity,** for each exercise is a step into the experience of success.

Keeping all these points in mind need not be difficult if each one is seen, not as a separate step in the child's development, but as a natural outgrowth of the philosophy of dignity we are striving to impart. The exercises themselves are broken down into steps not as an end process but so that they may be recombined as wholes after they are learned. The special child, like his normal counterpart, is more than a collection of attributes; he is a complete individual and each step of his education should serve that whole person. Montessori provides both philosophical framework and practical materials for the "global" concept of education.

For the child who is capable of further work, these exercises provide a basis in immediate sensory and kinesthetic experience, a solid foundation on which additional learning can be build. A concept as difficult as the conservation of matter can be approached through measuring and pouring from different-sized cups. Working with water and its various properties is then the beginning of science. And for those with the ability, reading will take on great meaning when it is associated with a profoundly satisfying, meaningful experience— reading in order to understand recipes.

Other experiences concerned with food provide additional learning experiences. The child who sets the table is learning the left-to-right progression necessary for reading, he is developing his memory as he places the dishes in their proper places (after he has learned how to do this through color-coding in school), he is performing an indispensable daily task which ties him in closely with family life. Stacking and clearing dishes teaches the rudiments of classifying, that essential aspect of mental order and of further learning. Another essential family chore which is valuable in teaching classifying and visual discrimination is the sorting of laundry—folding linens, matching socks, sorting out each person's clothes. With the wide variety of cleaning materials on the market, such chores as scrubbing, dusting and mopping can provide many opportunities for the exercise of choice and judgment so that they become more than routine activities.

Colorful containers and the various types of cleaning materials—granular, spray, liquids which are runny and those which are viscous, foams and paste waxes—can be used to make cleaning interesting and informative to the special child both at home and in school. Since we live, not in a past age of a simpler way of life, but in a time of complexity and abundance of consumer products, we must have the imagination to make use of what our culture provides to give our children a place in this culture.

The Love of Service and the Service of Love

And there *is* a place in this culture for many retarded persons, more than the public believes. True, more and more routine assembly-line jobs are being eliminated by automation, but that is only one side of the technological revolution. The other side is an increase in the demand for services. This demand embraces all services in a continuum, for all of them are increasingly necessary for the functioning of a complex society.

Therefore, if we use these exercises of practical life to their fullest, we will be training many of our students to hold a satisfying job and to fill a demand. If we think of service as a continuum and try to place all students on the track to personal fulfillment, we will be able to take pride in the adult who is an efficient hospital orderly as well as the person who is a surgeon, recognizing that both are necessary to the health of the patient.

Parents will more readily visualize their special child as a success if they have already experienced the child's success in performing practical life exercises at home. Talking is seldom helpful in overcoming deep-seated feelings about a special child's inferiority and inability. The experience of watching the child care for himself and assist in running the house is far more effective in conveying to parents the possibility that their child will grow up to a useful life of service despite his handicap.

In the course of mastering these exercises, the child has mastered himself, has learned bodily control, has come to realize himself as a person of worth and dignity holding his own in the family setting and actually able to provide special services to demonstrate his love for his family. At holiday time, he is the one who frosts the cake or cuts out the special cookies. It is his job, in the midst of a bustle of preparations, to polish the silver trays and candlesticks. He is the one to chop and measure the nuts in the holiday cake, and so on. Patience and imagination are the only limits to providing positive experiences of this kind to help the special child develop a high self-regard so that he may be prepared to seek a job when he leaves school.

The child who has learned that working with food is satisfying is well-prepared for a job as a kitchen helper in a hospital or other large institution. Perhaps he can find employment in one of the nursing homes for the elderly which are growing so rapidly, for he is well-suited to such slow, repetitive tasks as feeding the helpless and he will not display the impatience with the infirmities of age that the normal person often cannot help showing.

Someone must handle all the bed changing, floor scrubbing and dishwashing necessary to the running of a nursing or convalescent home. In the future we will see a rise in day care centers caring for even young children; someone must prepare the children's meals, serve juice and snacks, take a tiny one to the bathroom or supervise handwashing. On snowy days many hands will be needed to cope with snowsuits and boots. Even if we could find sufficient professional help, there is no reason to expect the trained nursery teacher to spend her time at tasks that can be handled by the retarded person working under supervision. Again, the very slowness of the retarded individual can be an asset in dealing with small children, who also move to slow rhythms and delight in repetition.

The special child who remains at home after he has left school needs the skills developed by practical life exercises to fill otherwise empty days and provide the psychological satisfaction he needs quite as much as his normal peers. Here again we can point to the many tasks that can be performed with pleasure and love by the retarded adult—work in the garden, for example, which answers the same deep needs as does working with food. Hoeing, weeding, trimming hedges, cutting flowers, arranging bouquets, working with other members of the family in planting seeds and pruning shrubs—these offer rich experiences to the retarded person.

Other household tasks—polishing shoes, washing windows, waxing floors—can be left in the capable hands of a trained person who wants to do a good job to show his affection for family members. Hours will be spent in the completion of an assigned task and those floors will shine like a mirror! Truly, there is no substitute for the satisfaction that comes from a job well done.

The Language of Life

The possibilities of practical life exercises are still not exhausted, for we now turn to their value in developing vocabulary and communication skills. The normal child learns the social customs of his society and the appropriate daily vocabulary from the environment around him. He does not need special schooling. This is not the case with the retarded or the socially disadvantaged child. But we come upon a paradoxical situation with these children—while they need vocabulary development far more than the normal child, teaching them is far more difficult.

If we follow Montessori's principles of beginning with the concrete, however, we can overcome to a considerable extent the difficulties of teaching communication skills to the special child. And the practical life exercises offer abundant opportunity to talk about concrete situations, to approach the child with new material to be learned when he is feeling good about himself, to provide him with a subject about which he wants to communicate.

This last is important—why should anyone talk when he has nothing to talk about? All too often the special child does not speak because he can find no words which refer to a felt reality in his life and the words used by others are literally meaningless to him because he has not experienced the situations or the emotions they describe. But the many steps involved in one single practical life exercise involve many activities for which appropriate vocabulary can be introduced, and the wide scope of all these exercises thus allow for the discovery of many hundreds of words tied to an appropriate action.

In addition, the desire to communicate is also developed by providing the children with a subject to talk about. They want to tell their parents what they have learned at school, they want to explain the difference between the **boiled** egg they prepared last week and the **fried** egg they made today, between **washing** and **waxing** because these differences have become significant through realization by themselves. He can speak of addition and subtraction through knowing what these concepts refer to in his concrete activities—add one teaspoon of salt to a mixture, subtract two tablespoons from a stick of butter.

In connection with teaching communication through the practical life exercises, it is helpful to have the instructions taped for permanent use. Quite often, as with autistic children, a man's voice will reach the child more effectively than a woman's. Therefore, the teacher might arrange to have tapes prepared by fathers of the students.

These tapes can be played while the child is actually performing the exercise, thus conveying to him in dramatic form the intertwining of word and action, the way in which certain words refer to particular acts and take their meaning from these acts. The tapes can be played again and again; they can be used to revive fading memories and they can be played by the children themselves after they have mastered an exercise for reinforcement learning. Those children capable of operating a tape recorder are also taking another step toward controlling their environment when they feel themselves in charge of this complicated machine and know they are free to play appropriate tapes when they want to hear them. A little time taken at the start in showing children how to operate these machines will prove valuable throughout the school year. Here again, fathers interested in making tapes—and there are many—might be interested in coming to school and providing the instruction themselves. No opportunity for providing a link between home and school should be overlooked.

The language thus learned is a basic language. Even people with great intellectual ability use the basic words for daily activities as they go about their ordinary businesses. Words associated with domestic tasks and shopping form the basic language of life, closely tied to emotional needs. With such a vocabulary, there is less need for the frustrated child to express himself through tantrums and screaming, for he has learned the superior value of communication through language.

Here again it is important to see language development through practical life exercises as part of the development of the whole person through the philosophy of dignity. The aim is not to produce children with a miraculous vocabulary, quite as if they were talking dolls, but to give these children the means they need to live in society and to hold their own in social situations.

The retarded person needs to foster psychological strength and stability to the extent his limitations allow, and this psychological health is built upon thousands of tiny incidents which enable him to enhance his self-respect. To be able to join his family for dinner in a restaurant, make his food wishes known, handle the implements properly, join in the discussion from time to time with appropriate remarks, have the language to make comments on the food or the furnishings of the restaurant—these are no small achievements for the retarded person and accomplishing them gives him a great sense of dignity and self-regard.

From these remarks it is possible to see that the exercises which follow are conceived as part of a harmonious program for the growth of the entire child, each exercise to play its part in providing a skill, an emotional satisfaction, which will help him utilize his capacities to the maximum. The aim should not be to produce children whose achievements advertise the teacher's superiority but to develop children redolent of that peace and joy which comes from performing useful work well and receiving from the eyes of others the regard we all look for and come to cherish.

Color Coding

Many classes in special education receive children who have been discouraged by the competition of academic learning and who consequently lack the rudiments of a positive self-concept. Here is a wonderful place to begin! Color coding is valuable here. We help the child to help himself by assuring that all the needed tools are placed neatly on open low shelves and that tools required for a particular job are marked with the same color. A broom has a pink stripe pasted on the handle; the closet where the broom belongs has a similar pink stripe pasted just below the proper hook. Spoons are marked with blue tape and so is the spoon drawer and perhaps the place at each table setting where the spoon should go. Paper place mats are yellow, there is a yellow stripe over the shelf that holds them and a yellow outline on the table where each place mat should go. Color coding is so useful that it is being used in hospitals and other institutions to make categories clear at a glance. Different kinds of prewrapped sandwiches are marked with a colored strip; a bulletin board identifies the code, and customers can see without poking which sandwich they want. In hospitals colored strips on charts identify types of illness and matching strips mark diet trays, special equipment, etc. Because color coding aids mental order it will be increasingly used.

This prepared environment helps the individual to feel the enormous sense of achievement which results from the performance of an important and useful task with a minimum of supervision and with a maximum of dependence on himself and his hitherto derided powers of memory.

These exercises are also lessons in socialization, a process which is frequently difficult to achieve in the retarded, not only because they lack so many of the spontaneous qualities of curiosity and judgment which the normal child applies to his tentative efforts at socialization, but also because many retarded children are kept in isolation in their homes.

Psychology Behind Exercises of Practical Life

It is important to consider the individual rhythm of the child and his individual purpose for working in order to instill a sense of achievement, a liberation of the spirit, a subconscious drive for movement and rhythmic activity, or to fulfill his desire for muscular control. At his own norm the child works with a vital activating force. Through consistently patient work with a child and an introduction to meaningful activities, unbridled activity becomes constructive, deviations disappear and inner discipline develops. Abundant sense impressions are formed into a working pattern which facilitates intellectual growth. When the person is in unity with brain and muscles functioning together, there is a need to develop muscular coordination through movement. Muscles carry out the command of the will, and thought is externally expressed in art, crafts, and so on. Muscular control, gained through movement, strengthens the will. Muscular control is essential. Therefore education must be integral—a duel, simultaneous development of both physical powers and mental powers.

Personality development is fostered through concentration—careful demonstration of the ideas to be stressed and frequent repetition of the demonstration with imperceptible emphasis upon any corrections.

The teacher, in the preparation of work materials, must isolate difficulties and analyze each step of the process to be presented. The children will demonstrate the results of her efforts by their increased concentration, fascination, coordination, self-reliance, consideration, responsibility, precision, foresight, and independence.

SUGGESTIONS FOR MATERIALS FOR PRACTICAL LIFE EXERCISES

Attractive and colorful materials will challenge the child so that he works to the utmost of his ability. Montessori believed that limited amounts of materials creates the lure for learning. A red broom for **each** child in the class would soon lose popularity; it would also not give the child the lesson in waiting his turn. In addition, a broom for each one in the classroom would not be in accord with reality. The Practical Life Exercises must be based on real experiences, according to Montessori principle, and thus keep the child in the world of reality. A carpet sweeper must really sweep, an iron heat, and a glass break.

A teacher who attempts to use these ideas will have to assess her classroom and the background of the children to understand what they will need for the mastery of the environment. Before attempting to teach any of these Practical Life Exercises, the teacher should be sure of all the equipment necessary to carry out a project. The equipment may be purchased locally to conform to criteria of size, functionality and beauty—pitchers, trays, baskets, buckets, brooms, glasses, pans, etc. The exception might be the Montessori dressing frames. (See pages 100, 101.)

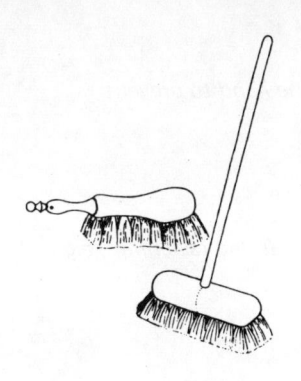

The Exercises in Practical Life are the most important part of a Montessori class in its beginning stages. These activities are the only way toward settling of disturbed and disorderly children. They are the only necessary part of the classroom. Without them we can do nothing, for they lay a foundation of order. Order is both the basis of exactness, and the basis of communication. Through activity the child orders and augments his intelligence. He learns self-control and develops thoughtfulness and a conscious respect for the other people.

SUGGESTED EXERCISES OF PRACTICAL LIFE

Exercises with Water.

With very little children, start with pouring rice from one vessel to another, then go on to the water exercise.
Pouring water from one vessel into another.
Filling a jug.
Pouring water into a cup.
Washing hands.
Washing the top of a table.
Washing and drying glasses.
Washing and drying plates.
Washing and drying silver and cutlery.
Cleaning the glass of windows and pictures.
Washing house linen, wringing and hanging to dry.
Washing little towels and dusters.
Changing water in flower vases.
Watering flowers in flower pots, either carrying them outside or spreading oilcloth underneath.

Exercises in Carrying.

Carrying chairs.
Carrying packets.
Carrying flower pots and putting them out of doors.
Carrying cups, saucers, cutlery, glass, etc. for meals.
Carrying newly-ironed linen in baskets.
Carrying objects and placing them correctly in cupboards.
Hanging dusters on rails and clothing on pegs or hangers.
Putting away hats and shoes in their places.

Exercises in Polishing.

Polishing tables.
Polishing brass.
Polishing shoes.

Exercises in Opening and Shutting.

Opening and shutting room doors silently, holding them with one hand to prevent their banging.
Opening and shutting cupboard doors.
Opening and shutting windows.
Opening and shutting drawers.
Opening and shutting boxes and trunks, with different kinds of lids and fastenings, e.g., latches, bolts, keys, padlocks.
Opening boxes with secret springs and adjustments.
Fastening window shutters.

Care of the Environment Indoors.

Setting chairs, tables, etc. in order after use.
Putting away objects after use.
Sweeping floors.
Sweeping mats.
Dusting.
Laying the table.
Clearing the table.
Washing up.
Washing and polishing furniture.
Washing and polishing floors.
Cleaning silver.
Cleaning brass.
Cleaning windows and pictures.
Washing and ironing house linen.

Care of the Environment Outdoors.

Weeding.
Picking dead leaves from plants.
Sweeping up fallen leaves.
Raking.
Watering.
Digging.
Hoeing.
Protecting delicate plants.
Tying muslin over fruit to protect it from insects, etc.
Gathering fruit in small baskets.
Laying fruit or vegetables in the sun to dry.
Gathering wood in bundles and carrying it in.
Tying up herbaceous plants.
Collecting vegetables.
Fetching eggs from the hen house.
Feeding poultry, pigeons, and other animals.

Care of the Person.

Washing hands.
Cleaning teeth.
Taking a bath or shower bath.
Washing hair.
Brushing and combing hair.
Rinsing the mouth and gargling.
Manicuring the nails.
Brushing clothes.
Cleaning spots from clothes.
Cleaning boots and shoes.
Folding clothes.
Washing and ironing clothes.
Dressing and undressing.

Exercises in Folding and Packing.

Folding with care and exactness, tableclothes, napkins, dusters, etc.
Ironing, with small irons.

Exercises in Cutting.

Cutting with scissors with rounded points.
Cutting string on parcels.
Cutting flower stalks.
Cutting dry twigs from faded plants and flowers.
Cutting mats to lay on plates and trays, the designs having been outlined on attractive papers.
Cutting with knives, which should be blunt and with rounded points.
Peeling potatoes and other vegetables and fruit.
Cutting bread.

Social Relations.

Bowing, shaking hands and other forms of greeting.
Offering something to someone.
How to invite someone to come in, to be seated.
Making way for someone to pass.
Picking up what someone has let fall.
Setting right what someone has done wrong by mistake.
Accompanying someone.
Begging pardon.
How to avoid disturbing other people, by passing behind.
How to blow one's nose.
Seeing one is clean and tidy before presenting oneself.
Washing before and after meals.

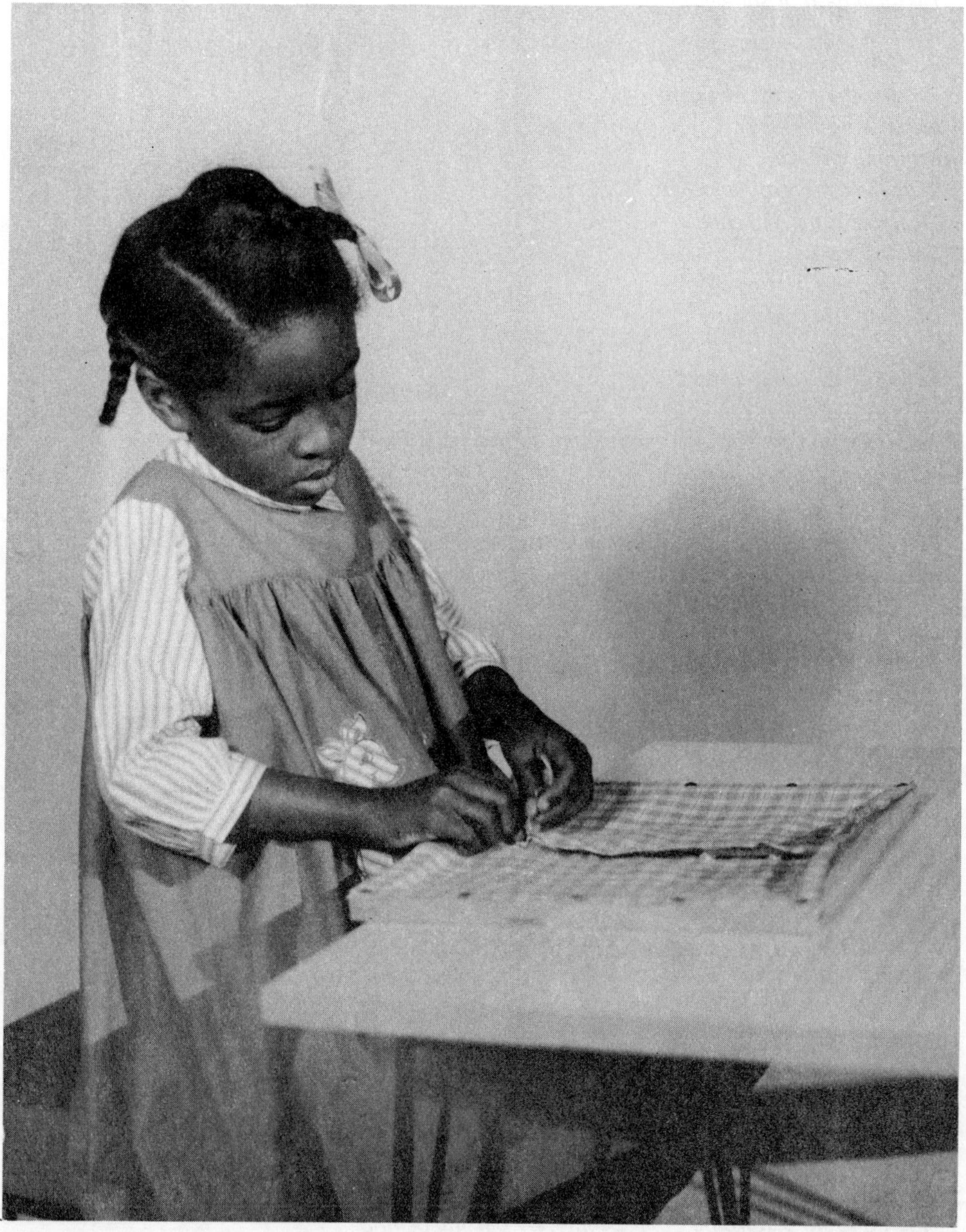

PAPER-CUTTING AND USE OF SCISSORS

Pre-drawn lines, on stiff paper, help guide the scissors.

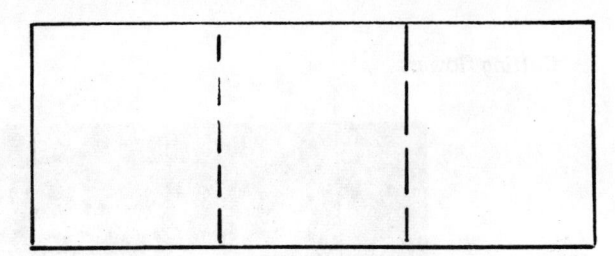

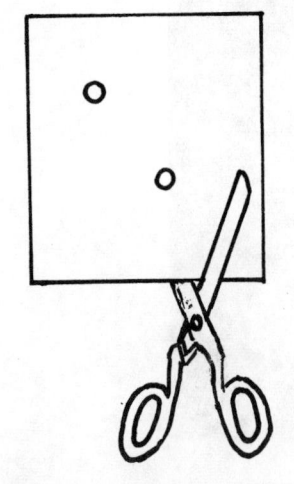

Cutting a curve is simplified with pre-punched holes.

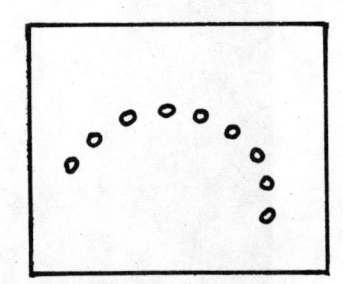

Punched holes or pre-drawn circles give direction for the child to follow.

DRESSING FRAMES

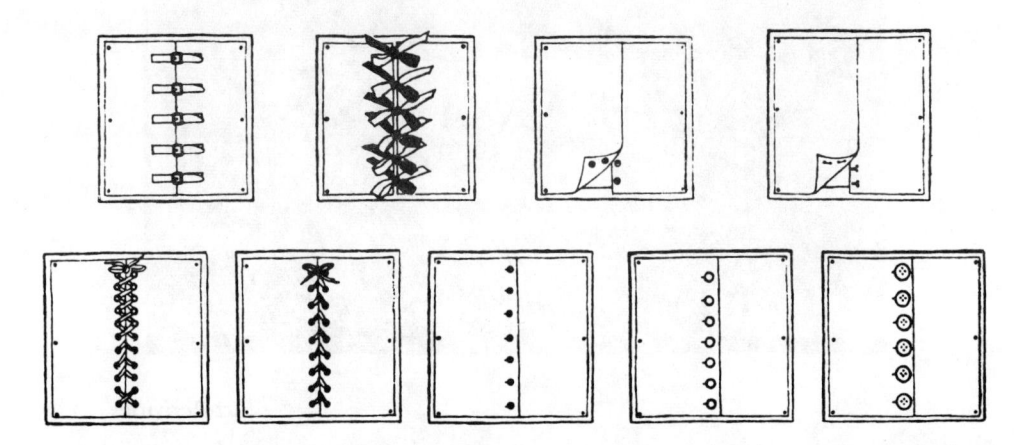

101

EXERCISES OF PRACTICAL LIFE

Cutting flowers . . .

leads to . . .

Art Activities.

EXERCISES IN FOLDING

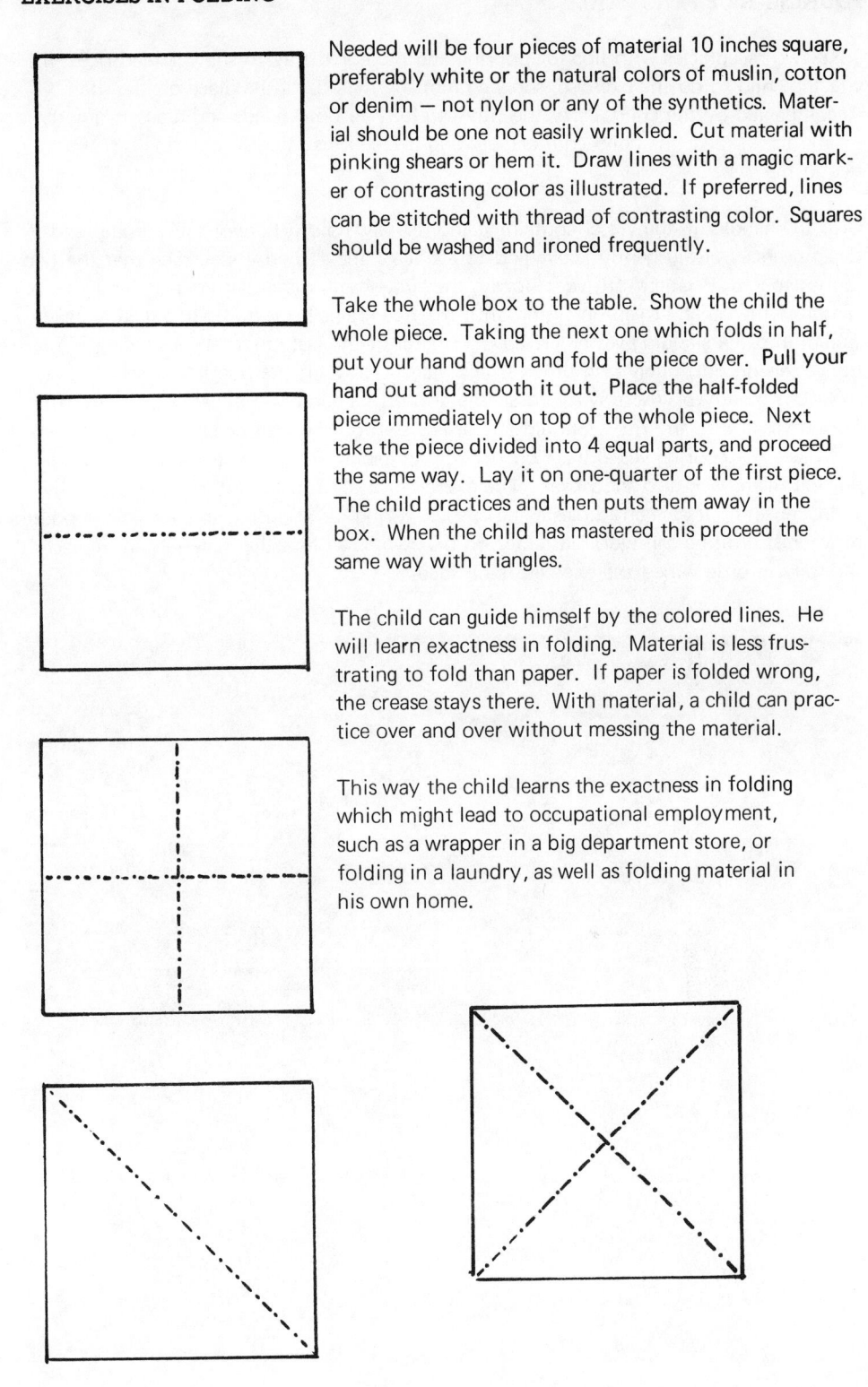

Needed will be four pieces of material 10 inches square, preferably white or the natural colors of muslin, cotton or denim — not nylon or any of the synthetics. Material should be one not easily wrinkled. Cut material with pinking shears or hem it. Draw lines with a magic marker of contrasting color as illustrated. If preferred, lines can be stitched with thread of contrasting color. Squares should be washed and ironed frequently.

Take the whole box to the table. Show the child the whole piece. Taking the next one which folds in half, put your hand down and fold the piece over. **Pull your hand out and smooth it out.** Place the half-folded piece immediately on top of the whole piece. Next take the piece divided into 4 equal parts, and proceed the same way. Lay it on one-quarter of the first piece. The child practices and then puts them away in the box. When the child has mastered this proceed the same way with triangles.

The child can guide himself by the colored lines. He will learn exactness in folding. Material is less frustrating to fold than paper. If paper is folded wrong, the crease stays there. With material, a child can practice over and over without messing the material.

This way the child learns the exactness in folding which might lead to occupational employment, such as a wrapper in a big department store, or folding in a laundry, as well as folding material in his own home.

POURING RICE

Take two receptacles with lips for pouring and a colored tray to show spilled rice. Invite the child to do the exercise, showing him the material in its place on the shelf. Accompanied by the child, carry the tray carefully in both hands and place it quietly on the table. Seat the child comfortably and awaken his interest, pointing out the rice in the vessel.

Grip the handle of the vessel containing the rice and hold it between the thumb and two fingers. Raise it gently above and to a side of the second vessel. See that the two do not touch. Begin to tilt, very slowly, the first vessel, directing its lip toward the center of the other. Keep on tilting until the rice grains begin to pour out in a steady stream into the standing vessel. Keep pouring until the last grain falls in, seeing that the vessels do not touch each other at any stage. Now tilt the pouring vessel back and replace it quietly on the tray. Loosen the grip on its handle. Repeat pouring from the second vessel into the first. Should any grains spill on the tray or table, stop pouring and place the pouring vessel back on the tray or table. Pick up the grains, one by one, putting them back into the vessel. The exercise can be carried out in this manner by the child, repeating it as many times as he wishes. Bring his attention to each of the points of interest until he can work correctly on his own. See that the materials are replaced carefully in order when the exercise is finished.

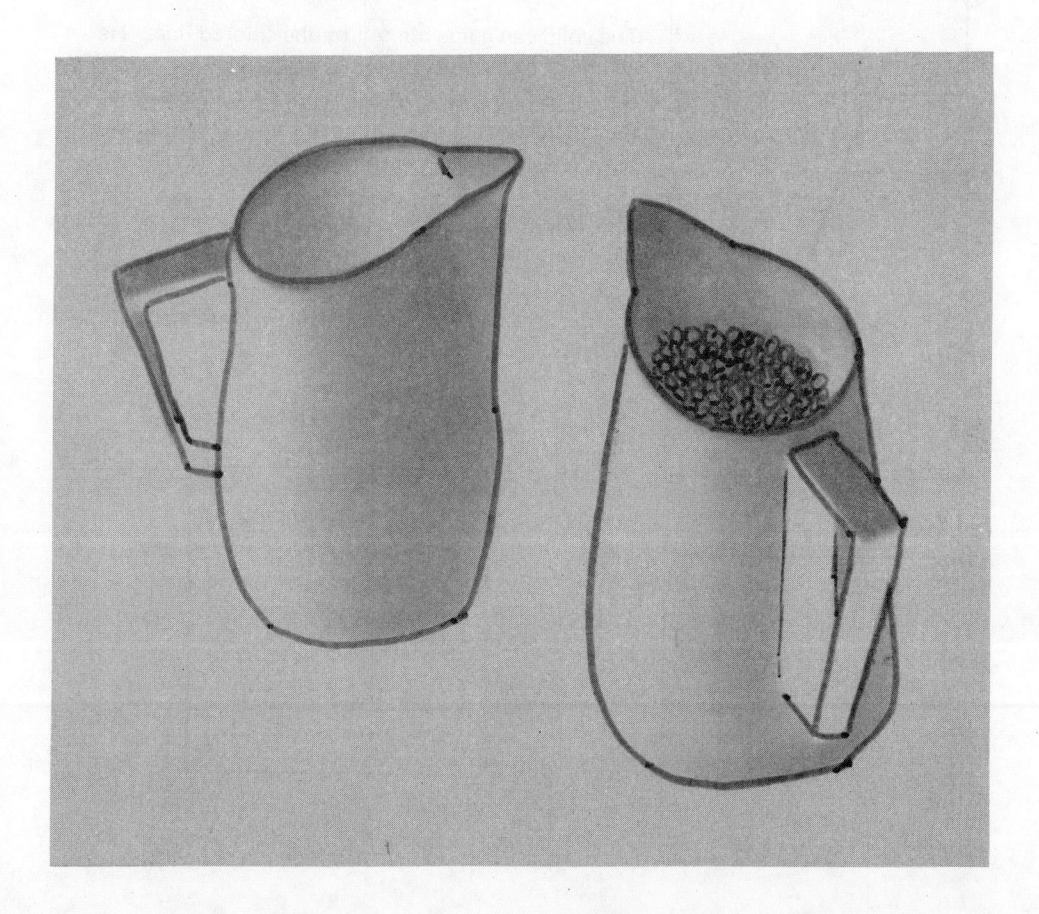

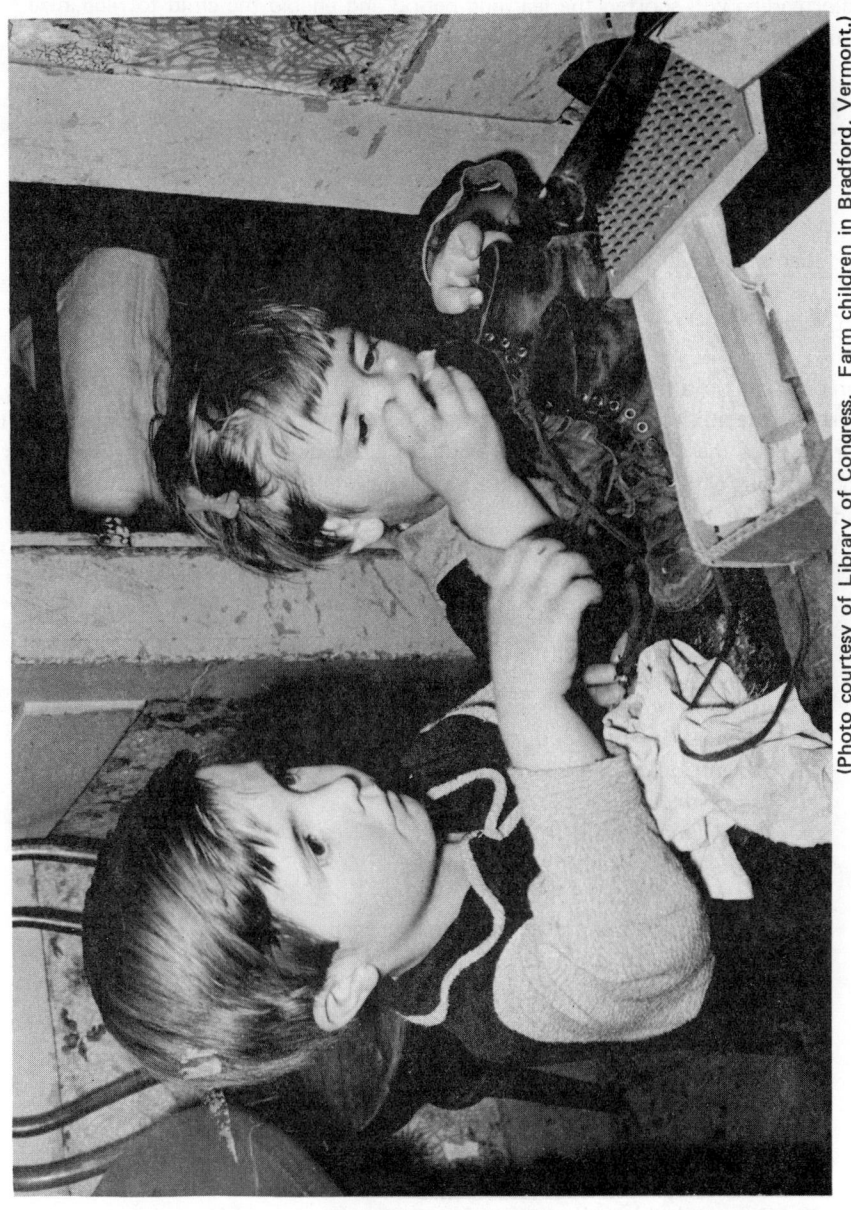

(Photo courtesy of Library of Congress. Farm children in Bradford, Vermont.)

"Acceptance of self and development of self-esteem are fostered by the ability to care for one's own body and immediate possessions."

SELF CARE

Personal Routine

Mastery of this information is necessary for the child to feel secure in school. Extensive use of color coding will shorten the learning period and enable the child to recognize familiar surroundings as quickly as possible.

> *Familiar with his bus driver and attendant*
> *Finds his classroom*
> *Finds his own desk and seat*
> *Recognizes his own belongings*
> *Keeps his desk and belongings tidy*
> *Cares for belongings.*

Personal Grooming

This is preparation for a lifetime. Acceptance of self and development of self-esteem are fostered by the ability to care for one's own body and imeediate possessions. Montessori apparatus, like the dressing frames, provide the groundwork for the exercises in personal grooming but actual practice should not be overlooked, especially when working with trainable children.

1. *Passively cooperates when being dressed.*
2. *Removes mittens, socks, and hat.*
3. *Unfastens zippers, snaps, and buttons.*
4. *Tells an adult his clothes are soiled.*
5. *Assists in dressing, rather than just cooperating.*
6. *Removes his shoes and galoshes.*
7. *Can put on a simple article of clothing.*
8. *Can distinguish front from back.*
9. *Can distinguish top from bottom.*
10. *Distinguishes his left from his right.*
11. *Can remove some of his clothing with some assistance.*
12. *Can handle his clothes if given the proper equipment.*
13. *Can button, snap, and zip.*
14. *Can tie laces with assistance.*
15. *Can dress only needing help with complicated fasteners and tying shoelaces.*
16. *Can put on shoes and galoshes.*
17. *Can tie his shoes.*
18. *Can tie her head scarf.*
19. *Can dress and undress quite independently.*
20. *Selects clothing appropriate for weather.*
21. *Selects clothing appropriate for occasion.*
22. *Respects property of other children.*
23. *Buys own clothing accessories.*
24. *Can polish his own shoes.*

(Photo courtesy of Library of Congress. Farm children in Bradford, Vermont.)

"Acceptance of self and development of self-esteem are fostered by the ability to care for one's own body and immediate possessions."

SELF CARE

Personal Routine

Mastery of this information is necessary for the child to feel secure in school. Extensive use of color coding will shorten the learning period and enable the child to recognize familiar surroundings as quickly as possible.

> *Familiar with his bus driver and attendant*
> *Finds his classroom*
> *Finds his own desk and seat*
> *Recognizes his own belongings*
> *Keeps his desk and belongings tidy*
> *Cares for belongings.*

Personal Grooming

This is preparation for a lifetime. Acceptance of self and development of self-esteem are fostered by the ability to care for one's own body and imeediate possessions. Montessori apparatus, like the dressing frames, provide the groundwork for the exercises in personal grooming but actual practice should not be overlooked, especially when working with trainable children.

1. *Passively cooperates when being dressed.*
2. *Removes mittens, socks, and hat.*
3. *Unfastens zippers, snaps, and buttons.*
4. *Tells an adult his clothes are soiled.*
5. *Assists in dressing, rather than just cooperating.*
6. *Removes his shoes and galoshes.*
7. *Can put on a simple article of clothing.*
8. *Can distinguish front from back.*
9. *Can distinguish top from bottom.*
10. *Distinguishes his left from his right.*
11. *Can remove some of his clothing with some assistance.*
12. *Can handle his clothes if given the proper equipment.*
13. *Can button, snap, and zip.*
14. *Can tie laces with assistance.*
15. *Can dress only needing help with complicated fasteners and tying shoelaces.*
16. *Can put on shoes and galoshes.*
17. *Can tie his shoes.*
18. *Can tie her head scarf.*
19. *Can dress and undress quite independently.*
20. *Selects clothing appropriate for weather.*
21. *Selects clothing appropriate for occasion.*
22. *Respects property of other children.*
23. *Buys own clothing accessories.*
24. *Can polish his own shoes.*

25. Can fold and store clothing.
26. Can wash his own clothing.
27. Can iron his own clothing.

Health Routines

The importance of the following routines is that mastery of them protects the child from the shame that follows upon catastrophe in many of these areas. Human dignity is fostered by the child's ability to care for himself in these essential areas.

1. Recognizes when hands are dirty.
2. Tries to wash his hands.
3. Rarely has a bathroom accident.
4. Can wash and dry his hands with some assistance.
5. Washes his hands after toileting and before eating.
6. Usually asks someone to take him to the bathroom, but may go himself.
7. Keeps his fingers out of his nose and mouth.
8. Covers sneezes and coughs.
9. Can blow his nose without help.
10. Can wash and dry hands without help.
11. Uses a washcloth properly.
12. Knows proper way to blow nose.
13. Carries a clean Kleenex.
14. Can wash his face and brush his teeth.
15. May need assistance in wiping himself adequately after a bowel movement.
16. Helps bathe himself.
17. Is more conscious of his body and wants privacy.
18. Knows the importance of the rest period.
19. Is able to take care of needs alone in the bathroom.
20. Boys can brush their hair.
21. Girls need assistance in combing their hair.
22. Has overcome nervous habits like nail-biting, tongue-sucking, scratching, pulling at ear.
23. Bathes himself adequately.
24. Uses a deodorant.
25. Combs and brushes hair.
26. Can shampoo own hair.
27. Keeps comb and brush clean.
28. Girls take proper care during menses.
29. Boys can shave own self.
30. Changes undergarments regularly.
31. Trims nails.
32. Uses nail brush, clipper, and cuticle remover.

Lunchroom Routines

Mastery of these routines will prepare the child to function in the world at large in situations where he will eat out in a restaurant or a cafeteria. The retarded person who has a job will need this knowledge to get through his day comfortably.

These routines can be broken down according to Montessori methods to allow isolation of difficulties. For example, in the classroom the child can practice carrying a tray with blocks on it, then with empty unbreakable containers, then with containers filled with water, before he is given a tray with actual food on it.

1. Can place food and milk on tray.
2. Carries his tray to the table.
3. Empties and returns tray properly.
4. Unwraps lunch.
5. Usually uses both hands in holding his glass.
6. Drinks without much spilling.
7. Is able to use a spoon with some spilling.
8. Drinks from a straw.
9. Uses napkin properly.
10. Chews his food.
11. Can hold a small glass with one hand.
12. Discriminates food from other objects.
13. Unwraps a piece of candy before eating it.
14. Learns difference between foods.
15. Can use a fork.
16. Eats food served to him.
17. Tastes and learns to eat strange foods.
18. Can get a drink without help.
19. Can pour from a small pitcher.
20. Can wipe up spilled liquids.
21. Can serve himself and others.
22. Likes to choose the foods he will eat.
23. Can set the table.
24. Can eat at the table without demanding too much attention.
25. Passes food adequately.
26. Social during the meal.
27. Uses a table knife for spreading.
28. Uses table knife for cutting.
29. Helps prepare food.
30. Has good table manners.
31. Can clear the table.
32. Can clean up and wash dishes.
33. Can dry dishes and put them away.

Safety Routine

The following routines, once they are learned, will allow the child to cope with today's environment — crowded streets, rushing cars, close proximity to other people, small apartments and houses. These conditions demand special preparation which can be obtained in the classroom.

1. Can figure out ways of overcoming some obstacles.
2. Runs simple errands.
3. Cautious about common dangers such as unprotected places, strange animals, sharp utensils.

4. Gets around the neighborhood independently.
5. Adequate ability to see.
6. Adequate ability to hear.
7. Controls his personal conduct.
8. Uses toys and play equipment properly.
9. Uses materials and tools properly.
10. Picks up and stores toys after play.
11. Follows simple safety rules in work and play.
12. Reports injuries promptly.
13. Does not pick or scratch sores.
14. Carries sharp articles properly.
15. Recognizes fire alarms.
16. Recognizes air raid warning.
17. Knows traffic precautions.
18. Knows how to handle keys, latches, chains.
19. Knows how to light matches.
20. Knows how to light candles.
21. Knows how to extinguish candles.
22. Knows how to plug and unplug electric appliances correctly.
23. Uses electric appliances only with dry hands and shoes.

(Photo courtesy of Library of Congress.)

A LESSON IN HAND WASHING

For the child to learn to wash his hands properly and develop control and coordination of movement, use a low sink, preferably in the classroom, soap and a soap dish, a towel and apron. The teacher may choose anytime to show a child or group of children the organized movements of hand washing.

Push sleeves up to avoid getting wet. Turn the cold then hot taps until water is of a comfortable temperature. Wet hands first, then shake them slightly before taking soap. Rub soap on the palm of each hand and replace soap in the soapdish. Rub hands together and each finger in turn. Rinse hands under the running water, shake them slightly and wipe them with a towel.

As points of interest note wetting the hands first, lathering the soap, watching the water discolor if the hands are really dirty, and shaking the excess water off before wiping.

Later the child may be shown how to use a nail brush.

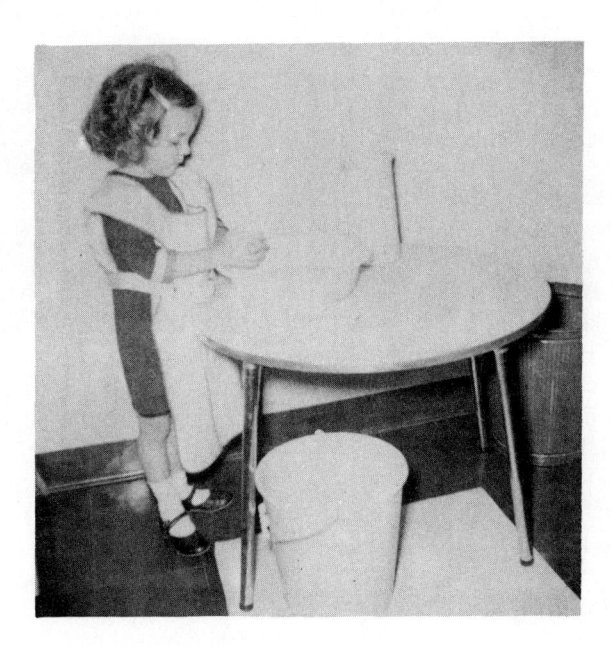

A Case History

It is clear why such Montessori devices as the clothing frames are useful for the child with learning problems. But why use them for the child who could learn how to fasten his clothes by simply fastening his clothes? Why bother with this special equipment? Can't the normal child observe and practice on his own?

What we tend to overlook is that a child can be quite intelligent and still suffer from poor motor coordination, so that he can know how to fasten without having the capacity to make his hand follow his mind. When he is trying to dress himself in the morning there is the tyranny of the clock; he must admit failure and ask for assistance. With the dressing frames, there is no pressure; he can practice as long as he will.

Some years ago I was teaching a second grade class of very gifted children. One of these children, a boy named Ken, could read and understand material on the highest level but he was plagued by such poor motor coordination that he could not write down the remarkable compositions he was capable of composing. It was clear that he had to balance his extraordinary mental activity by some manual activity.

I led him to the dressing frames indirectly, by suggesting that he research information for a paper on clothing fasteners through the ages. This intelligent boy responded with great interest and prepared an excellent report. At the same time this interest drew him to the dressing frames and he began to work with them. Slowly he became independent of help in zipping his pants or buttoning his coat and his pride in being able to do this for himself was very great, indeed.

Ken went further. He discovered the pleasure of working with his hands, even though he was still far from skillful. One day he came to school with some wood to make a bookcase for his books. He could measure and calculate quite easily, but what a job he had with the manual work. He hit his thumb with the hammer and cut his fingers as he sawed the wood. Yet, each day he found time to work on his bookcase and when it was finished at last, he carried it home proudly.

Ken's family moved. Many years later I received a call from his parents. They told me that Ken had graduated from college *summa cum laude* and had received a Rhodes scholarship. When he heard that they were visiting near my home, he asked them to call on me so that they could tell me that, through all his school years and college years, his bookcase had held his books and now it would be going to England with him.

Through all the years of academic accomplishment, he had cherished the homemade bookcase because it represented for him a much more difficult accomplishment and an achievement he could well be proud of, for working with his hands had never been easy for him. But it was necessary, as a balance for the work of the mind, and he knew it and wanted to let me understand that he knew it.

So we can see that the value of such devices as the dressing frames is not limited to their immediate value but extends further into the life of the child. For the bright child, it is helpful to develop his interest in using and practicing on the dressing frames by interesting him in the history of clothes and fasteners.

CLOTHING FASTENERS THROUGH THE AGES: Brief Suggestions on Their History To Be Used with the Dressing Frames

Buttons

Buttons first became popular in the 13th century. Women used them to fasten their long, fitted tunics.

During Queen Victoria's reign, in the 19th century, buttons achieved their greatest popularity. Rows and rows of buttons were used by both men and women for fastening and for trimming. They were made of a wide variety of materials — pearl, ivory, bone, horn, etc.

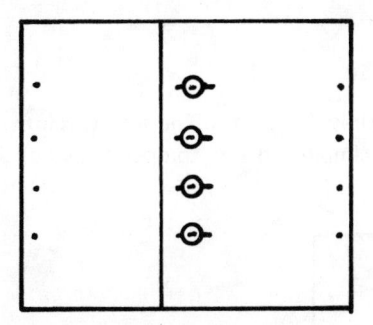

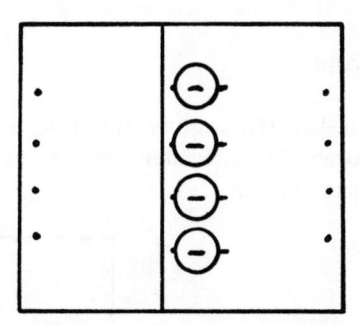

Hooks and Eyes

The Roman warrior of 100 A.D. fastened his leather breast armor with metal prongs resembling our hooks and eyes.

During the 16th century, the hook and eye, as we know it today, was first used. The ladies of that day wore tight-waisted garments, and the hooks and eyes helped to hold their waistlines in.

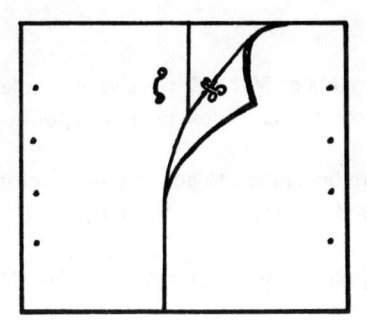

Zippers

The idea for the first slide fastener was conceived in 1891 by an inventor named Whitcomb L. Judson. It was very cumbersome — a metallic chain of flat, curved metal hooks were joined together by running a slider over the chain and turning the hooks into eyes.

In 1913 the first zipper as we know it was made.

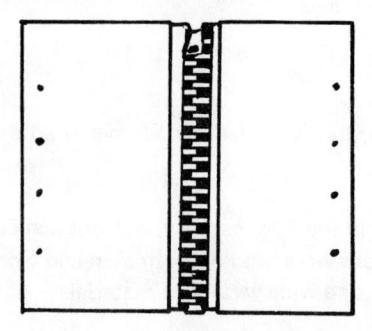

Snaps

The late 19th century was the age of invention in dress fastenings. The snap was introduced and immediately became popular for it was simple and easy to operate as well as inconspicuous.

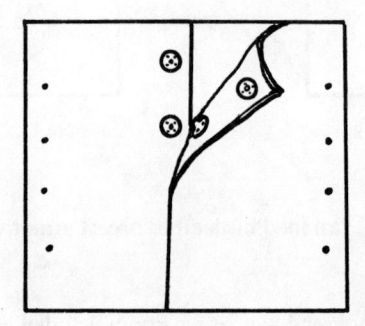

Buckles

Although the Greek garments of 500 B.C. were very simple, the people often added large buckles to their sandals and boots. These were only for decoration.

By 300 B.C. buckles were being used to actually fasten clothing. Etruscan men fastened their tunics with a ring and pin device much like the buckle we use today.

In the 13th century buckles became huge and very elaborate. They were often made of gold and studded with jewels.

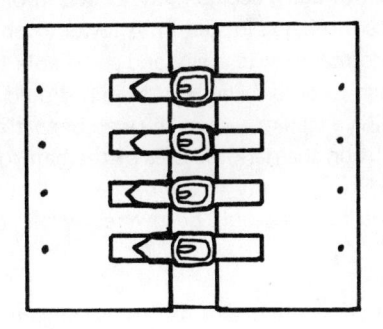

Lacings

In the 13th century, both men and women used lacings to fasten their tunics. No record of lacings having been used earlier can be found.

Laces were used to supplement hooks and eyes in the 16th century.

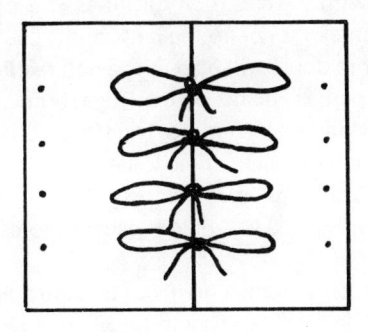

EXTENDING THE PREPARED ENVIRONMENT TO THE LAVATORY

It is important, as important as is the prepared environment, that lavatory facilities be adapted to the needs of the children. Locks should be removed or jambed so they no longer constitute a threat—the threat of being accidentally locked in or recalling a situation where the child has been exposed to being locked in. A lower knob or handle can be affixed to most doors for the child to manipulate easily and so be able to attend to his toilet needs alone when mature enough to do so. The light switch should be adjusted to be within his reach—perhaps by installing a step or two at the wall beneath the switch for the child to climb upon to shed light on the dark recesses of the bathroom. Steps, too, can be built around the toilet bowl fitting tightly to the fixture so that the child can securely use this facility. Toilet paper and towels should be lowered within easy reach of even the smallest child.

The Montessori directress knows how important it is to learn from the parents the vocabulary the child uses for his different toilet needs, and any habits peculiar to his or her upbringing. In interviewing the parents and child, she will point out how important a part the clothing plays in this regard. Sunsuits that the child cannot manipulate quickly because of elaborate and unreachable fastenings can be most frustrating to the young child. Buttons and zippers are often a great challenge to the very young or the motor-handicapped boy, particularly at a moment of stress. It may be noted that pants with elasticized waists are obtainable and so easy to handle by the child.

In familiarizing the new recruit with the classroom facilities, it is of equal importance to include a visit—en masse(parents in tow)—to the bathroom. The designating pictures on the entrance or inner bathroom doors will help in the non-reading child's orientation. The attractiveness of the room, perhaps plants on the ledge, bright mirrors, colorful walls, will add to his feeling of security and make him less frightened. The teacher or assistant should learn from the parents the particulars of his toilet training experience to help her to understand the attitude of the child to adjustments in class. The teacher, and assistant if there is one, must both be aware of the vocabulary peculiar to each child in this regard.

The child cannot be depended upon to remember from this introductory trip where the bathroom is, and in his first few days in class should be taken at regular intervals to help prevent untoward incidents. The child must not be left at the door and neither should the teacher or assistant walk away, but remain as escort in the room with the child especially in the first few days when he needs this feeling of security.

Despite the most careful supervision and preparation, there will still be accidents. The changing of the soiled garments must not be considered a major tragedy. The situation must be taken as a matter of course without any remarks such as "bad boy" or "why didn't you tell me?" Even if the teacher is very matter of fact, many children will still burst into tears and have guilt conflict, the result of practices at home where the child may be scolded or laughed at (perhaps by elder siblings), or chided for not being a "big" boy. This child needs extra tender loving care. One special note—panties should not be hung up like flags to dry—in public display. They should be disposed of discreetly.

In an article in PEDIATRICS (Jan. 1962, Vol. 29 #1), Dr. T. Berry Brazelton divides toilet training into three separate phases and advocates mastery of one phase before the second one is introduced. His comments also apply to the training of retarded children of any age.

> *Phase 1* - Early discussion and study of the theory before it is put into practice.
>
> *Phase 2* - Appraisal of the child's physical and psychological readiness to train.
>
> *Phase 3* - Guidance, encouragement and opportunities offered but not urged on the child.

Dr. Brazelton makes a special point of insisting: "The importance of allowing a child freedom to master each of the steps at his or her own pace cannot be over-emphasized. Encouragement and reminders are useful unless they are so constant they amount to coercion."

Mother Isabella Eugene, Training Director of the Ravenhill Academy in Philadelphia, Pennsylvania, insists on divided facilities, different facilities for boys and girls, complete privacy at an early age to insure a healthy attitude to sex and moral behavior. Separate facilities develop a natural respect for the sex organs and a sense of delicacy and modesty in this area. If it is at all possible in the setting up of classroom facilities, separate but equal bathroom facilities should be provided. This is not only for the purpose of a child's identification with his own sex but to help achieve such identification.

Bathroom Cleaning

Experience in keeping the bathroom spotlessly clean should be given before any major catastrophe makes it necessary to do a "special" on it. How do we keep our bathroom clean?

1. Using a mop for the floor.

2. Blood stains are best removed with cold water.

3. Feces are best removed from floor and seat with cold water.

4. Urine is best removed from floor with wet mop.

5. Vomit is best removed from bowl with running cold water. And from floor with wet mop.

6. To teach cleaning the toilet bowl a brush with long handle and a bucket of a lighter weight than that used by the custodian should be supplied. Scouring powder too should be supplied.

7. For cleaning the sink a sponge and scouring powder will be sufficient.

8. If facilities get stuffed up the custodian will be called by the children.

9. Paper towels must be put into the refuse can after use, and sanitary napkins must be rolled in tissue before being disposed of in the trash can.

10. Mops and brushes and buckets used must be washed thoroughly before being put away in their proper places.

GRACE AND COURTESY

Manners are the external sign which reveal we are able to conduct ourselves in accordance with the social norms of a given society. They bind together members of the same social group and provide a cushion against the abrasions of society. Manners are a way of recognizing the individuality of each person with whom we come into contact.

Children from certain homes may find that not knowing acceptable manners limits their effectiveness in society at large. These children should be given the opportunity in the classroom to learn proper social relations. There are practical reasons for observing proper modes of conduct. The classroom is, in itself, a group situation in which a number of children must function in harmony with each other.[2]

Grace and courtesy exercises, upon which Dr. Montessori placed such emphasis, can be prepared and taped in question/answer form and played back either to the class as a whole or to individuals. Since tapes can be erased, trial and error is possible, and a successful tape can be preserved in a tape library. Parent involvement is very important, and should be especially encouraged for the retarded child. Why couldn't parents read books onto tape for later replay? The child whose parent's voice is heard in class has an occasion for pride. And the parents themselves will understand better what is being done if they are drawn into the work of the class with full explanations from the teacher.

As you can see, there are no limitations to what can be done with the tape recorder in making learning individualized and programmed for success. The difficulties of each learner can be considered if the teacher gives careful thought to preparing tapes to enhance success and to create a good feeling about himself and about learning.

Preparation for Group Living

Social relations will also govern the behavior of the children with each other. Again working through example and patient repetition, the children will be taught to greet each other, to wait patiently while another child is speaking, to seat themselves quietly and to rise without disturbing the class. One child may bring a glass of water to another, offer it politely and be thanked in return. A child may offer to help a classmate button his coat or tie his hat. Each action can be performed so that mutual recognition of individuality is strengthened and the often precarious self-image of the special child is enhanced in the process.

If milk is served, the children can prepare the table by cleaning it, then setting it with small mats or napkins. They can take turns serving the milk and cookies, offering the food to

[2]Reference: "Direction for Headstart" by Lena L. Gitter. R. C. Orem, Editor, MONTESSORI FOR THE DISADVANTAGED. Putnam, New York, 1967.

(Photo courtesy of Lithuanian Montessori Society of America, Chicago, Illinois.)

"Sharing food in common is one of the primal human social experiences and even a small snack can become a tranquil and enjoyable occasion."

each child and receiving thanks for it. Sharing food in common is one of the primal human social experiences, and even a small snack can become a tranquil and enjoyable occasion. The teacher will show by her own actions that we eat and drink without rushing or spilling, that we wait for others to be served, that we receive the food with thanks and eat in a relaxed manner.

At the end of the snack, the teacher offers once again the vital clue to help the special child learn the requirements of social relations. "That was a very good vanilla cookie, wasn't it? And how fresh the milk tasted!"

The children rise quietly, clear the table in an orderly way and are thanked for their assistance.

The classroom offers countless situations for the practice of mutual courtesy and it is an essential function of the teacher to set the tone for this practice by the children as well as to demonstrate by example how harmonious social relations serve to create a pleasant atmosphere in the classroom group and in the larger society which the child will someday enter.

One of the most crucial ways in which a teacher can fulfill her role as a model or exemplar is in setting the tone of the entire school day through her conduct in the very first minutes of class.

Opening Exercises

Each morning should begin with the teacher greeting each child personally with a hand shake and a few pleasant words. "Good morning, Michael, how are you? My, what a nice green sweater you are wearing!" This brief exchange does many things. It gives the teacher time to observe the child; does he seem tired, unusually disturbed, upset in some way? The child hears his name and has another opportunity to associate his name with himself. He feels good when he hears an appreciative comment about *his* clothes or *his* hair. The pleasant tone of the greeting creates a good atmosphere for the rest of the day, even if the teacher should not have much time to spend with the child. It gives the child a chance to tell the teacher anything that is on his mind; perhaps a grandmother has come to visit or his mother is ill or he has received a new toy. Such happenings may affect his behavior for the day and the teacher can be of assistance if she understands the reason for his unusual excitement.

The child, of course, is learning day by day, through this example, how to behave with others when he is meeting them, how to shake hands, how to make the appropriate polite remark. Through the teacher's carefully chosen words he is adding to his vocabulary and also to his understanding of the correct context in which to use particular words.

Finally, in this brief moment when the child is looked at directly and can return this look, when eyes meet and acknowledge the existence of another person, the child is experiencing a vital human exchange. In the life of a special child, such moments may be tragically few. The teacher should not neglect the chance of increasing them.

SOCIAL SITUATIONS THE CHILD SHOULD BE PREPARED TO MEET[3]

1. Morning greetings. Relationship of children to each other. Relationship to teacher and other adults. Importance of fixing through repetition standard expected greetings of weather, etc.

2. Attaching person's name to the greeting.

3. Show through example that all people are treated with courtesy — cook, custodian as well as teacher, policeman.

4. How to ask permission: *excuse me, I beg your pardon, may I.*

5. Show through constant example politeness in listening, not interrupting another's conversation.

6. Table manners to be learned through serving of snacks, lunches, special feasts in classroom.

7. Holding a door open for an older person; or a boy holding the door open for a girl.

8. Waiting in line; waiting your turn.

9. Social behavior and greetings expected on various holidays — birthdays, Christmas, New Year's.

10. Showing appreciation by appropriate use of *thank you* with specific act or gift named.

11. Teacher should introduce visitors in classroom to children as a group. Children learn how to respond when similar situation arises in home.

12. Etiquette of gift-giving. Whom to give gifts to, on what occasions, appropriate gifts, making one's own gifts.

13. Social behavior in public places — restaurants, museums, trains, airplanes. Speaking softly, not calling attention to oneself, not pointing.

14. Bathroom etiquette. How to leave public or private bathrooms in good order without messiness.

15. Early morning behavior. Not waking other members of the family if child arises first.

16. Proper deference to older people — rising to offer seats, treating with respect.

17. Behavior in shops — waiting one's turn, asking politely for service.

[3] WHITE GLOVES AND PARTY MANNERS by Marjabelle Young and Ann Buchwald. R.B. Luce, Washington, D. C. 1965.

THE RATIONALE OF THE EXERCISES OF PRACTICAL LIFE

Unfortunately, this rationale for the practical life exercises is not understood and is criticized by large numbers of people on the basis of either faulty presentation or faulty understanding. A paper written by a group of faculty members of the early childhood education department of Newark State College sums up the criticisms that are frequently leveled at these exercises. The authors feel that practical life exercises do not have meaning for the child of today who does not come from a home where clothes are washed on a scrubbing board or whose mother uses a vacuum cleaner rather than a broom. Over and over again similar criticisms are voiced—in this age of electricity, all we need to do is turn a switch and our appliances take over, so why should the child learn the "old-fashioned" ways of housekeeping?

If the purpose of the practical life exercises were merely to prepare a child to be a good housekeeper, such criticism would be perfectly just. But there is no evidence that Montessori had such a purpose in mind. The fact that boys as well as girls are encouraged to master these exercises would prove that Montessori's purpose was a different one, for in Italian culture men do not help with household chores and there would be no reason for boys to master these exercises if the purpose was to prepare adults able to keep house.

Rather, the exercises serve more profound needs in the child's development and I would like to spell these purposes out quite clearly and specifically to avoid the danger of misunderstanding. This is what Nancy Rambusch has to say in her Introduction to the Montessori TEACHER'S MANUAL,[3] when she speaks of these exercises:

> *At first glance, they appear to be a series of ritual gestures centering around table washing and the carrying of full tureens of hot soup.*
>
> *Upon closer examination, they prove to be ways in which the child, by coping with extensions of his physical self through manipulative activities like pouring, becomes more self-aware and self-confident.*
>
> *The world is the child's environment and no gesture which will help him master it should be inappropriate in a school setting.*
>
> *All the gestures of civilized society, from shaking hands to dialing a telephone, are grist for his mill of self-mastery.*
>
> *The gestures of the culture are learned by him through example more often than precept. The rapidity and success with which he learns to perform simple tasks enables him to forget that they are learned and build complex tasks upon them . . . .*
>
> *An obvious relationship exists between the mastery of one's self and the mastery over one's environment. The activities of practical life lead naturally to the exploration of many media and it is no surprise to designers of child en-*

---

[3] Rambusch, Nancy. MONTESSORI TEACHER'S MANUAL. New York: American Montessori Society, 1968.

> *vironments that the obvious place to put art activities is in the practical life area. If, as Piaget suggests, the child knows himself in knowing the world and the world in knowing himself, the manipulation of art media becomes easily seen as central to his early explorations.*

Let me schematize what Mrs. Rambusch is saying and elaborate on some points.

The purpose of practical life activities is to aid the child in mastering his environment *now*, not in the future. They are not preparation for adult housekeeping but a way of allowing the child to attain independence *now* through being able to do things for himself.

Since the purpose is present self-mastery, it is irrelevant that mother uses a washing machine and vacuum cleaner because such equipment is beyond the reach of the child. Shall we do for him until he is old enough to use electrical equipment? Shall we assume the child will be completely dependent upon such equipment?

That question leads to a most important point. We hear more and more the lament that one of the reasons for man's alienation from himself is his sense of being dominated by the machine instead of feeling himself in control. This is a genuine dislocation of vital feeling. A person can control a broom and make it go where he wishes. But unless he is an electrician, a broken vacuum cleaner must be repaired by someone else. For practical reasons as well as for reasons of psychological wholeness, it is important to learn to work with simple equipment lest the child and the adult become so dependent upon complicated equipment that they cannot function without a protective electric cushion.

So, in addition to various practical elements involved in making children experience the pleasures of independence and of self-care now, we find there is a need for these exercises to produce a person who is psychologically whole. I would like to call on a few witnesses here who are not associated with Montessori at all and who testify, each of them, from a different perspective entirely.

In CHILDHOOD AND SOCIETY, Erik Erikson quotes Sigmund Freud replying to the question, "What should a normal person be able to do well?" as "To love and to work." (Norton, New York, 1963, pp. 264-265). Work, in other words, is one of the indispensable elements of the psychic life. For a person to achieve full satisfaction in his life's work he must first develop an attitude towards work in general that will encourage the discovery of satisfaction in this activity. Only then is he in a position to approach his work, whatever that may be, in such a way that he can use it in a meaningful way. Some people are fortunate; they can choose their work and they have capabilities great enough to permit them to succeed in work of their choice. But the fact that such choice is possible for large numbers of people, especially in America, must not blind us to the fact that for most people such choice is not possible. Circumstances, abilities, accident or hazard determine their work. Those with average intelligence or less, those from poor families, those who grow up in certain areas of the country, those with emotional problems, those with family responsibilities, those with limited ambitions due to upbringing—all will probably find themselves in situations where they must "make the best of" jobs they did not choose but cannot abandon.

However, if children are brought to see the satisfaction inherent in any job well-done, they will become adults who can choose their attitude toward work and thus gain as much as possible from their jobs. Since they must work and since work is a necessity for a healthy psychic life, part of our concern with education should be in the developing of a healthy attitude toward **work in itself.** The practical life exercises are arranged so that the child may accomplish a job by himself and may see the completion of the task and its visible results. That is certainly one reason for the relatively simple nature of the equipment and the basic tasks the child assumes. He will go on to learn more complicated activities, but the attitude governing his subsequent mastery will be based on the earliest, simplest tasks of all.

This is not a "Montessori" attitude unshared by others in the field of early childhood education. In the September 1967 issue of YOUNG CHILDREN, The Journal of the National Association for the Education of Young Children, Joanne Hendrick makes the same points in her article, "The Pleasures of Meaningful Work for Young Children." Mrs. Hendrick is Director of the Parent-Child Workshop at San Marcos High School in Santa Barbara, California, a nursery school workshop which is a laboratory school for high school students and also a cooperative sponsored by the Adult Education Division of Santa Barbara City College. Let us listen to Mrs. Hendrick.

After listing the various ways in which we can quickly encourage children to develop negative attitudes toward work (criticizing, hurrying, assuming that work must be unpleasant), Mrs. Hendrick points to the positive advantages of providing young children with meaningful work experiences.

First, she discusses work as a way of helping the child's passion for identifying with adults and their roles in life and for facilitating sexual identification, a problem for children in one-parent families. Since children develop this passion to imitate adults, why thwart it by telling them they are too young, too small, to do adult work when in fact they can do a great deal of similar work?

Mrs. Hendrick then speaks of the value of work as an ego strengthener. "Every time a child accomplishes something tangible and sees the results turn out reasonably well, his image of himself as being a positive, capable person is strengthened. This is particularly valuable for very retiring or very aggressive children."

Then Mrs. Hendrick introduces another valuable thought when she writes about using work to reduce guilt feelings if a child has broken or spilled something. ". . . I believe it is valuable for a child to experience the actual consequence of his action through repairing the result and . . . because I think it's a good way for him to learn that doing something **wrong** is not the end of the world, that one can often make amends."

Most fascinating of all is Mrs. Hendrick's list of jobs that the children of San Marcos Nursery School like to do because these favored activities coincide at virtually every point with Montessori exercises.

    Washing dishes after really cooking with them.

Loading sand in small wheelbarrows, carting it to the swing area and shoveling it under the swings after a rainy day.

Planting, weeding, fertilizing and watering the garden.

Cutting flowers and arranging them.

Cleaning the aquarium.

Setting up rabbit cage, feeding rabbit, cleaning cage.

Mixing paint.

Washing the fingerpainting tables.

Cutting up fruits and vegetables for snacks.

Helping set up snack baskets.

Fetching juice for snack table.

Doing all kinds of cooking.

Sanding and waxing blocks.

Sawing, nailing, hammering, puttying.

Mopping the housekeeping corner.

Oiling tricycles when they squeak.

Washing easel brushes.

In the exercises which follow there are practical life exercises which correspond almost exactly to the items on this list!

Mrs. Hendrick makes other points which are familiar to anyone who know Montessori's work: "The goal should basically be pleasure in accomplishment....work must be scaled to reality and the possible. Children need real tools to do work....Dull, tinny tools breed frustration and encourage children to give up in disgust."

Finally, Mrs. Hendrick gives three fundamental axioms about work:

Anything involving food is fun!
Anything involving earth is fun!
Anything involving water is the most fun!

Perhaps we can see in this independent testimony why Montessori children spend so much time absorbed in chores like scrubbing tables or washing clothes that are already clean, although some observers are horrified at the repetition and the seemingly simple nature of these favored chores.

Beyond all of this, there is yet another purpose served by the practical life exercises. One might ask—isn't this quite enough? Yes, if we are interested in developing the child into a partial human being, one who functions well as we observe him. But the completed person has an inner life which we can reach only indirectly and it is this inner life which modern education is increasingly unable to reach. Thus we witness the phenomenon of the "empty" man, such as is depicted in Camus's novel THE STRANGER, a phenomenon discussed in newspapers and magazines everywhere.

Montessori was concerned with the development of the whole person. And an *essential element* in this development is the hand. Hand and mind working together form a whole; one without the other is only partial. The exercises of practical life are designed to train the hand in accomplishment. And here I would like to summon as witness a very great scholar in a field far removed from early childhood education. The Frenchman Henri Focillon was a world-renowned specialist in art history, particularly in the period of medieval history which saw the great cathedrals rise, living monuments to the artistic abilities of entire communities, communities of peasants almost entirely illiterate but able to express their conception of life through the work of their hands.

In his THE LIFE OF FORMS IN ART (Oxford University Press, New York, 1948), Focillon published an essay "In Praise of Hands." The entire essay should be quoted but I am contenting myself with bringing to notice only a very few of his profound remarks which directly relate to the work of a Montessori classroom and provide a wholly independent rationale not only for the practical life exercises but also for the sensorial materials.

> *Surface, volume, density and weight are not optical phenomena. Man first learned about them between his fingers and in the hollow of his palm.*
>
> *Without hands there is no geometry, for we need straight lines and circles to speculate on the properties of extension. . . . Man's hands set before his eyes the evidence of variable numbers, greater or smaller, according to the folding and unfolding of the fingers.*
>
> *Whatever the receptive and inventive powers of the mind may be, they produce only internal chaos if deprived of the hand's assistance. . . . What distinguishes dream from reality is that the dreamer cannot engender art, for his hands are asleep. Art is made by the hands. They are the instruments of creation, but even before that they are an organ of knowledge.*
>
> *Above all, the hand touches the world itself, feels it, lays hold of it and transforms it. The hand contrives astonishing adventures in matter. It not only grasps what exists, but it has to work in what does not exist; it adds yet another realm to the realms of nature. . . . Centuries have passed over man without changing his inner life, without making him renounce his old ways of discovering and creating the world. For him, nature continues to be a repository of secrets and marvels.*

If we change *man* in the last quotation to **children**, we can see the relationship between these remarks of a philosopher of art and a classroom of young children. The exercises of practical life, like those using sensorial materials, are a bridge between the world of childhood and the world of art, thought and wonder which should be the natural home of all people but which have been limited to only a fortunate few at the present. It is this bridge which Montessori believed could be crossed through education and with this philosophy in mind, she devised her materials and exercises. No educational method is immune from criticism and many Montessori critics have offered valuable suggestions and improvements. But the criticism of practical life exercises which is based on surface observation only and does not understand the many values fostered by these tasks is beside the point, for it criticizes what does not exist unless the teacher herself has misunderstood the purpose of practical life exercises.

The Practical Life exercises can certainly be performed for themselves alone; some value will be derived from them. But a true estimate of their function must consider them on many levels and place them in a total educational pattern, the end result of which is the harmonious adult personality.

FORMATION OF CONCEPTS

Montessori placed great emphasis upon education of the senses. The senses as routes to intelligence require training if they are to become most effective in helping the individual to acquire even further education. Sensorial materials are the vehicles for educating the senses.

According to R. R. Tomlinson:[1]

> *The world's great educationists have from the time of ancient Greece— and probably before that time—recognized the value of coordinating sensory and mental training. Plato and Aristotle, both of whom dominated the intellectual world until the Middle Ages, stressed the importance of training the hand as a preliminary to the formation of right habits of mind. Plato, furthermore, recognized also the paramount importance of esthetic laws in their application to education.*
>
> *Their teaching was furthered by such great thinkers as Rabelais, Montaigne, and Comenius—particularly the last. In the 17th Century, the English philosopher John Locke advocated the training of the senses and by doing so inspired Rousseau. Contributions to the cause were made by Salzmann, Hervart, and Froebel. All these great educationists recognized and stressed the value of development of sense perception as against the time-honored formal study of grammar. They revolted against the theory that education is a purely intellectual discipline. They maintained that the essential thing in education is the development of all human powers—physical, mental and spiritual, and that hand and eye training is as important as the study of Latin and Greek. These theories at last influenced progressive educators and ultimately the state itself.*

Montessori was among those influenced by these thinkers, as were Drs. Itard and Seguin, whose work she found stimulating. Also the "Bauhaus" in Weimar, Germany, established after the First World War as an art center of very progressive people, was a place where sensory training was important. In his book, THE NEW VISION AND ABSTRACT OF AN ARTIST, Laszlo Moholy-Nagy says:[2]

---

[1]Tomlinson, R. R., CHILDREN AS ARTISTS; Harmondsworth, England and New York: Penguin Books Ltd., 1947.

[2]Moholy-Nagy, Laszlo, THE NEW VISION AND ABSTRACT OF AN ARTIST; New York: George Wittenborn, Inc., 4th ed., 1947.

Sensory training. Systematic work toward "mass production" starts in the institute (the Bauhaus) with a non-art approach. By experience with material, impressions are amassed, some often at first appearing unimportant. There is a further aim: knowledge of materials, of the possibilities in plastic handling, in tectonic application, in work with tools and machines — such as is never attained through book knowledge and traditional verbal instruction.

Basic sensory experiences — gained by these exercises — undergo development and intellectual transformation, and later are brought into relation to other experiences. It is not possible to skip any stage in experience, though it may sometimes appear desirable. From the first inarticulate experience, the whole of life is one continual growth. Therefore it is indispensable, in human development, to pass through all the stages of elementary experience in every field of sensory activity. Little by little man attains his own way of expression, and finds his forms.

Since the majority of people build up their world at second hand, removed from their own experience, the Institute must often fall back upon the most primitive sources in order to guarantee an individual approach.

All students in this art school (the Bauhaus) had to undergo a study period in sensory training before they creatively applied the knowledge they had gained.

When we speak of sensorial education, many people object that children do not have to attend school to learn this. They consider the sensorial impressions received in school very poor compared with those obtained outside. That is quite true, but the objection to sensorial education is based upon a complete misunderstanding. Sensorial *impressions* are not the same thing as sensorial *education.* It is possible for an individual to receive any amount of sense impressions and be "none the wiser." We know that there are adults who can travel around the world and afterwards be unable to recall anything of interest. Sense impressions alone are not enough; the mind needs some education to discriminate and appreciate. Otherwise it is a case of "eyes that see not, and ears that hear not." What is needed is not more and more impressions which only cause weariness, but education. This education can come about only through the activity of the hand, and that is why the sensorial material is provided.

The cardinal importance of manual activity in intellectual development is Dr. Montessori's great discovery. This could never have been arrived at by preconceived theory; it could only be discovered by unprejudiced observation under rather special circumstances. For it is something completely foreign to the adult mind that has become familiar with the use of language and abstractions. Moreover, a fact of this sort, even after it has been conclusively demonstrated and generally admitted, always tends to be ignored and forgotten in actual practice. Educators may say vaguely that they understand the importance of the hand in education and yet make practically no use of it in their methods.

SENSORIAL EXPERIENCES AND LANGUAGE DEVELOPMENT

Since, as adults, we have had many experiences with our senses and can remember them abstractly, it is easy to forget that a child is dependent upon his senses to provide information for his mind and cannot rely on an abstraction. Ruth M. Bilenker, in an article in the NEA JOURNAL (Oct. 1967, Vol. 56, #7) points this out when she writes: " 'Please hand me the *frobish*.' You won't understand this request. Since you have never had any experience with a frobish, you can't bring any meaning to the word." Then she goes on to discuss the various ways in which we can learn about a frobish—pictorial, which is good but limited, as only the sense of sight is involved in the learning experience, or a multi-sensory experience involving touch, smell, and sound. Give a child a frobish; let him feel it, smell it, absorb it through all his senses. Then he will know what a frobish is!

Mrs. Bilenker then relates this sensory experience to the development of language, just as Montessori did, and points out the importance of such experiences to the child with learning problems who does not absorb language from his everyday environment.

> *A word—whether spoken or written—has no intrinsic meaning; it is we who assign meaning to it. And the only meaning we can bring to a word is that which we first learn through experience.*
>
> *This underlying principle of language learning is reflected in speech—that beginning medium of communication that seems to just emerge with the growing child. But—careful! It will see to "just emerge" only when the child has someone who cares enough to nourish his environment with many experiences—and with the words that label them. The disadvantaged child lacks those experiences and consequently those labels. If ever the schools had a mission, it is to provide meaningful experiences and teach the words that go with them.*
>
> *The schools can do this best by getting to the roots of human experience: by engaging the child's five senses in continuous and conscious involvement and by supplying him with words to express as much of his experience as possible in speech. It seems to be that the school's greatest potential for supplying these sensory experiences lies in the arts.*
>
> *The various art experiences—visual, musical, and physical—can sharpen children's sense perceptions in steady progression from the very real and concrete to the increasingly abstract.*

The basic aim of sensory education is the whole development of man. Through understanding of one's environment comes self-attainment and self-mastery.

Specifically, sensory development forms the basis for intellectual development by refining the senses on both the concrete to abstract level as well as the unconscious to conscious level. It leads to self-discipline which liberates the child from the confusion of his disorganization. It develops self-awareness and an appreciation for oneself which leads to an appreciation of others. The child's power of observation is developed by refinement of the senses. Man's inner life is connected with the physical world. His pleasure is increased.

These materials for education of the senses were designed to help the child's mind focus on some particular quality, and by active manipulation lead to a comparison of the objects used for each phase.

Each one begins with an emphasis on the concrete and leads to an emphasis on the abstract. They feature points of interest. There is isolation of difficulties and control of error. Concepts are taught rather than specific facts. They are graded to assure the child of a reasonable chance of success and challenge. They encourage auto-education.

PRACTICE FOR THE TEACHER

It is recommended for those who wish to instruct children in sensory exercises to begin by working with the didactic materials themselves. The experience will give them some idea of what the children must feel, of the difficulties which they must overcome, and, up to a certain point, it will give them some conception of the interest which these exercises can arouse in children. Anyone making such experiments himself will be most struck by the fact that, when blindfolded, he finds that all the sensations of touch and hearing appear more acute and more easily recognized. The interest of the experimenter will be aroused by this alone.

To concentrate the attention of the child upon the sensory stimulus which is acting upon him at a particular moment, it is well, as far as possible, to *isolate* the sense; for instance, to obtain silence in the room for all the exercises and to blindfold the eyes for those particular exercises which do not relate to the education of the sense of sight.

A general rule in the order of procedure for the direction of the education of the senses should be:

> Recognition of *identities* (the pairing of similar objects and the insertion of solid forms into places which fit them).
>
> Recognition of *contrasts* (the presentation of the extremes of a series of objects).
>
> Discrimination between objects very *similar* to one another.

Do-It-Yourself Montessori

The sensory materials and exercises which follow show with what careful precision Montessori designed materials to provide experiences which lead to language and concept development. I have chosen a representative selection with special emphasis on materials which can be constructed easily or which can be adapted from commercial games. In addition, I have included exercises which can be used by the teacher who does not have actual Montessori training.

Developing sensorial materials provides an excellent opportunity for parent and community involvement to assist the teacher. Willing and skillful hands are needed to make the materials and many a parent who feels intellectually inadequate will shine at working with his hands.

The home-made materials have several advantages. First, of course, it does save money and time. More important, it is in the spirit of Montessori, who always advocated simplicity and dependence on one's own resources rather than on easily-purchased assistance. Working together to create the materials brings parents, children and teachers closer to each other and to the essential work of the school. Work with the hands fills a genuine need among today's highly educated headworkers and also allows parents with scant formal education to produce work which allows them and their children a feeling of self-worth. The children who see their parents happily engaged in making pieces of equipment will enter the Montessori class with healthy attitudes and a clearer understanding of the importance of handling the materials carefully.

Carrying Out the Exercise

Have all the objects needed to carry out any particular exercise. Show the child where the material is kept on the shelf, and how to carry it to his place of work. The table should be clear of materials. If a rug is needed, go to get one. Carry it so as not to bump anything. Place it out of the way of traffic.

Interest the child in the main point of the exercise, either in the point which will keep him from disaster(breaking the material or cutting himself)or the salient feature to be taught (the contrasts, the function of one of the mathematical operations, etc.). Show the child the exercise, pausing at the important points so that he can see and understand the emphasis. Be sure the child is watching. If he loses interest, wait for a better moment.

Invite the child to do the exercise, remaining nearby to observe his first attempt. When he has repeated the exercise as often as he wishes, all materials are to be returned to their place on the shelf in the order in which they were found.

The first presentation is not the time to discuss all the interesting variations inherent in the material. Its purpose is to show the child what to do with the apparatus so that he can work by himself. Conversation is appropriate to bring his attention initially and later to reinforce his interest, but it should not distract him from the demonstration. Let the child discover as much as he can for himself, as long as he is generating interest. If he is not sufficiently interested, show him points to renew his interest and to carry him to new levels of accomplishment. Most normal children, if working on something suited to their age and interest, do not need to have their attention recalled and will repeat their exercise many times, correcting their own errors and disliking interference or help.

Get up from the chair at the table and replace the chair quietly. Put the material back on the shelf in the correct place with all the parts of the material in the order in which it was found.

The Child Begins

As usual, the teacher, by doing the exercises herself, first shows the child how the pieces of each set should be arranged, but it will often happen that the child learns, not directly from her, but by watching his companions. She will, however, always continue to watch the children, never losing sight of their efforts, and any correction of hers will be directed more towards preventing rough or disorderly use of the material than towards any *error* which the child may make in placing the rods in their order of gradation. The reason is that the mistakes which the child makes, by placing, for example, a small cube beneath one that is larger, are caused by his own lack of education, and it is the ***repetition of the exercise*** which, by refining his powers of observation, will lead him sooner or later to *correct himself*. Sometimes it happens that a child working with the long rods makes the most glaring mistakes. As the aim of the exercise, however, is not that the rods be arranged in the right order of gradation, but that the child *should practice by himself,* there is no need to intervene.

One day the child will arrange all the rods in their right order, and then, full of joy, he will call the teacher to come and admire them. The object of the exercise will thus be achieved.

These three sets, the cubes, the prisms, and the rods, cause the child to move about and to handle and carry objects which are difficult for him to grasp with his little hand. Again, by their use, he repeats the *training by the eye* to the recognition of differences of size between similar objects. The exercise would seem easier, from the sensory point of view, than the other with the cylinders described above.

As a matter of fact, it is more difficult, as there is *no control of the error in the material itself.* It is the child's eye alone which can furnish the control.

(Photo courtesy of Lithuanian Montessori Society of America, Chicago, Illinois.)

Discrimination of Form

The discrimination of form is developed through the use of the geometrical form cards, which are arranged in series of circles, rectangles and a square, triangles, and so on. Within each series the dimensions differ. One card from each series may be used for gross comparison of rectangle with square, circle with oval, and so on, and also for learning of nomenclature. These geometrical shapes can be used in a number of ways. The child can first place each shape in its proper inset form. Observing the exact matching of shapes, he can trace the outline of the shape with his hands, **feeling** the contours and the differences between one form and another, and, when he is ready to use a pencil, he can lay the form on paper and follow the outline with a pencil, making his own geometrical forms which he can compare with the original. The teacher has a wide choice available to her in using the form insets and cards, from the simplest exercises to the most sophisticated.

THE PINK TOWER

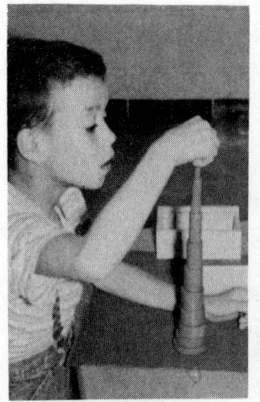

The Pink Tower is made from ten pink wooden cubes varying in size, from one cubic centimeter to one cubic decimeter and gloss painted. Spread a mat on the floor. Scatter the cubes over the mat. Build a tower beginning with the largest cube. Choose with deliberation. Grasp cubes from above with one hand to get the muscular impression of size. The child may not be able to grasp the largest with one hand, but let him grasp all the others in this way. Place each cube concentrically on the previous one in one movement.

When the child can do the exercise well, he can be shown how to build a tower with one corner exactly above the other all the way up and the two edges exactly even. The smallest cube can then be fitted around the two ledges left on each cube in turn. This demonstrates the relationship in size between the cubes.

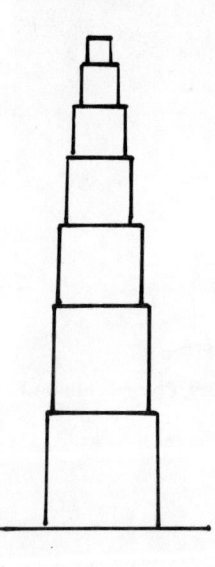

Child building Pink Tower

Visual and muscular perception of dimensions, an awareness of dimension leading to observation, and an understanding of dimension are fostered by this exercise, as well as coordination of movement.

As an indirect approach to mathematics the ten cubes act as a preparation for the decimal system and for cube root. The cubes represent the cubes of numbers 1-10. Eight of the smallest cube make the second cube, 27 of the smallest cube make the third cube, 64 of the smallest cube make the fourth cube etc., and 1,000 of the smallest cube make the tenth cube. The largest cube would hold a liter.

If very badly built, the tower topples over. With trainable children, give every other cube at first. The child will then have more chance of succeeding—he will build a tower. When he can do this well, he can be given all cubes to work with.

THE GEOMETRY CABINET

Visual Perception of Form

A polished wood cabinet of six drawers, each containing six wooden frames with geometric insets of various shapes—squares, rhomboids, rectangles, circles, triangles, polygons, ellipses, etc.—make up the Geometry Cabinet.

These insets are fitted into position by the child, the frames acting as a control. By passing the fingers around the outlines, the child, through the tactile muscular sense, receives the perception of the form of each shape, and at the same time is taught the names of the various geometrical forms.

The geometry cabinet shown here is quite an expensive piece of apparatus to use in the classroom, but Montessori felt it was of great importance because it helps to develop an understanding of plane geometry. Using this geometry cabinet, the child sees triangles, rectangles and other geometric shapes in tables and other objects around him. He learns to be more observant of his environment and learns the geometric shapes at the same time. It is usually thought useless to teach geometry to mentally retarded children, but in this automated and industrialized world of today, a knowledge of geometric shapes is mandatory. Architects use geometric shapes to make necessary buildings beautiful. The child, in learning the geometric shapes, also learns to appreciate the beauty of the buildings and other objects made by man around him. The apparatus is also used as a puzzle and as a vocabulary builder. Later, what is learned can be used in learning geometry.

The vocabulary of the Geometry Cabinet taught using the three-period lesson, is listed below:

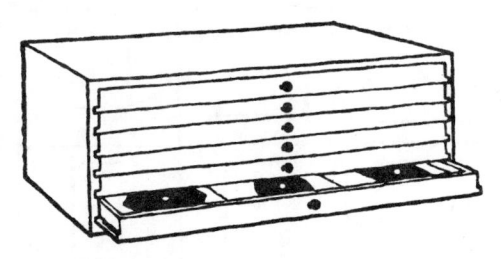

circle	pentagon
curvilinear triangle	polygon
decagon	quadrilateral
ellipse	quatrefoil
heptagon	rectangle
hexagon	rhombus
nonagon	square
octagon	trapezoid
oval	trapezium
parallelogram	triangle

Polished wooden cabinet of six drawers, containing 36 wooden geometrical insets and frames.

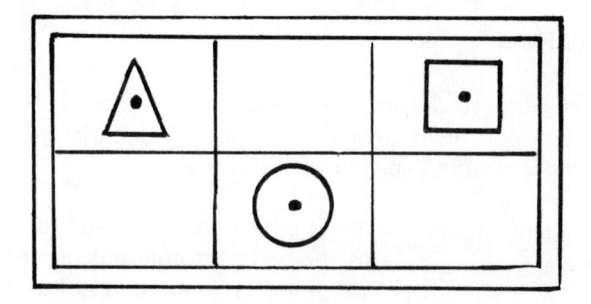

A Demonstration Tray

This tray consists of a circle, a square and a triangle. The three remaining squares are filled with plain squares of wood. The circle, triangle and the square should be taught first because they are the most contrasting figures, and are of the greatest importance in the study of geometry.

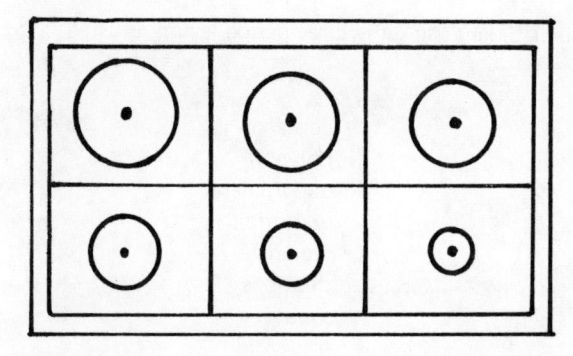

The First Drawer

This tray contains 6 circles varying in diameter from 10 centimeters to 5 centimeters.

The Second Drawer

This tray contains 6 rectangles beginning with a square. Each one is a little smaller than the previous one.

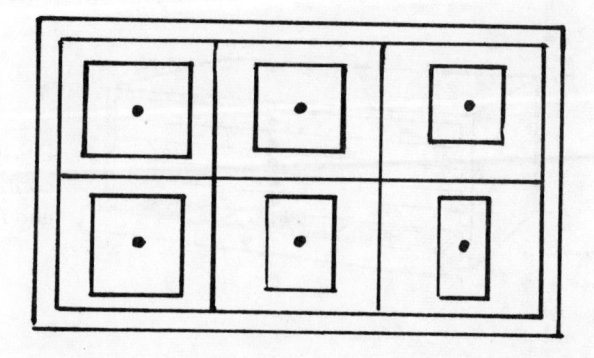

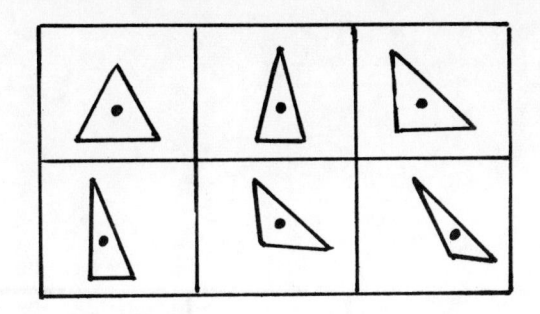

The Third Drawer

Six kinds of triangles are contained in this tray.

The Fourth Drawer

This tray contains 6 polygons, the pentagon to the decagon.

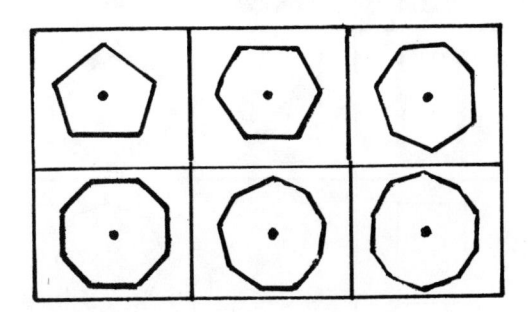

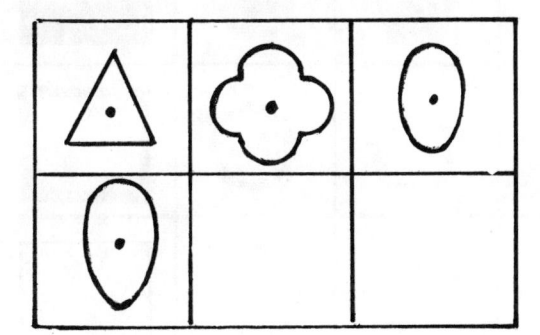

The Fifth Drawer

This tray has curvilinear figures, oval, triangle(curvilinear), flower shape and ellipse.

The Sixth Drawer

This tray contains four-sided figures.

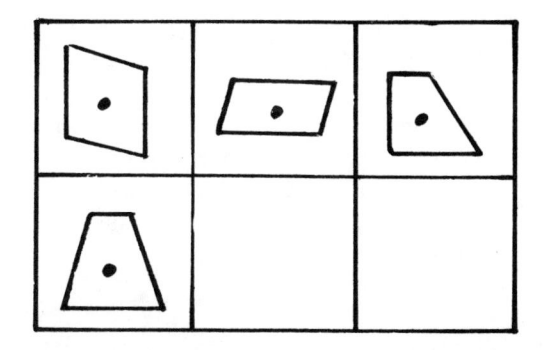

GEOMETRY CARDS

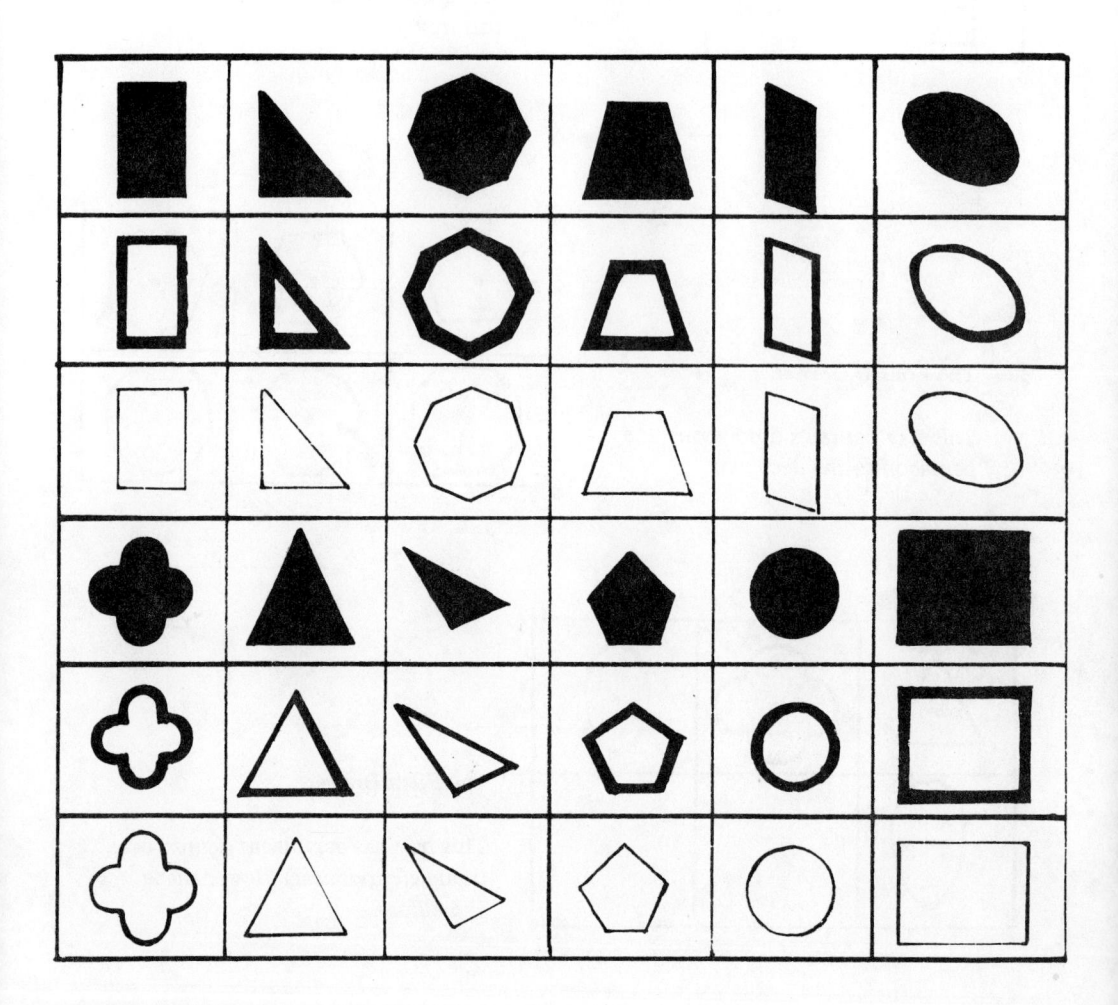

Three Series of Cards

In the first series the cards represent the same geometrical forms in the same size as the wooden insets, and are printed in solid blue. In the second series the same geometrical forms are depicted by a thick blue contour about a quarter of an inch wide. In the third series the geometrical forms appear in thin outline. Thus the child passes by easy stages from the concrete form of the wooden shape to the abstract outline.

VISUAL PERCEPTION OF DIMENSION

For the discrimination of dimension Montessori prepared various kinds of cylinders, some with knobs and some without. One set varies in height and diameter, going from small and thin to tall and thick; another set progresses from small and thick to tall and thin. A third set simply varies in diameter while remaining the same height and the fourth set varies in height but not in diameter. There is another matching group of sets of cylinders with knobs, which fit into the appropriate hold in wooden blocks. Use of these cylinders prepares those muscles which are necessary for writing. At the same time, the child is learning correct use of nomenclature to designate comparison: tall-short, for example, or thin-thinner-thinnest. He is developing the concept of dimension sensorially, as well as intellectually.

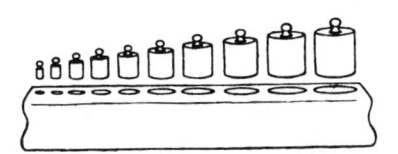

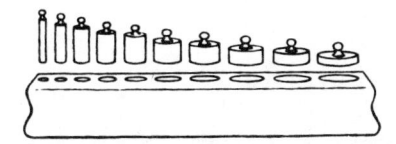

Cylinders vary in height and diameter.

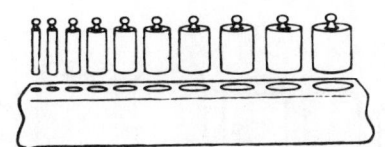

Cylinders vary in diameter.

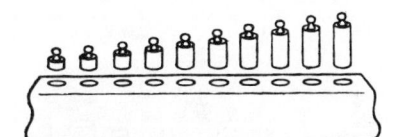

Cylinders vary in height.

The knobbed cylinders teach visual discrimination of size and dimensions. This is indirect preparation for writing through manipulation of the cylinders.

(Photo courtesy of Montessori Workshop, Natchez, Mississippi.)

Boy practicing with knobless cylinders.

Knobless Cylinders

Four boxes, in color, with the same dimensions as cylinders with knobs but without blocks to fit into.. Allows for more imaginative arranging.

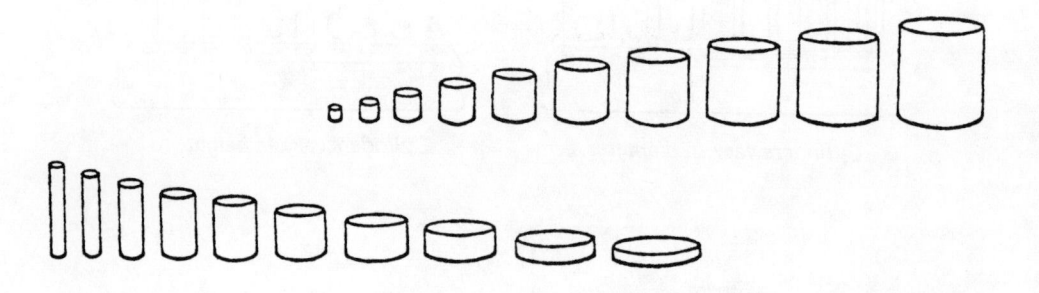

Cylinders vary in height and diameter.

Cylinders vary in height.

Cylinders vary in diameter.

CONSTRUCTIVE TRIANGLES

In working with the Constructive Triangles, the child learns that the triangle is the basic "constructive" plane figure, and he learns to construct different geometric shapes himself. At first this learning is a concrete, sensory, manipulative experience, and not a verbal, symbolic or abstract one. Later the child learns the geometric vocabulary.

In the conventional classroom, the child is taught that an acute angle is like a wedge of pie as an introduction to geometric shapes. In the Montessori classroom, the child is first taught the terms and definitions of the geometric shapes and when he is sure of these, he is shown the resemblance of things in the real world to the geometric shapes to increase his appreciation and recognition.

An acute angle is an angle smaller or less than a right angle. A little piece of pie makes an acute angle.

This is an example of the conventional definition.

THE BINOMIAL CUBE

The binomial cube consists of wooden cubes and rectangular prisms painted red, blue and black. It is kept in a specially built box with two hinged sides which open down to reveal two sides of the cube. The base of the cube is painted on the lid.

Exercises with the binomial cube help in preparation for the mathematical concepts involved in the binomial theorem.

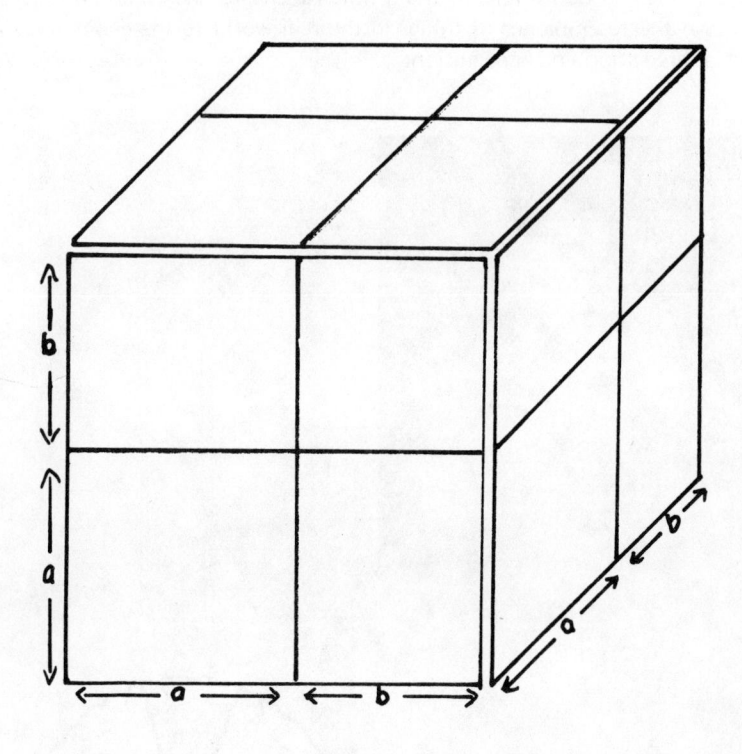

Formula: $(a + b)^3 = a^3 + 3a^2b + ab^2 + b^3$

THE TRINOMIAL CUBE

The trinomial cube consists of wooden cubes and rectangular prisms painted various combinations of red, blue, yellow and black. It is kept in a specially built wooden box with two hinged sides which open down to reveal two sides of the cube. The base of the cube is painted on the lid.

Exercises with the trinomial cube help in indirect preparation for the mathematical concepts involved in the trinomial theorem.

Formula: $(a + b + c)^3 =$
$a^3 + 3a^2b + 3a^2c + 3b^2a + 3c^2a + b^3 + 3b^2a + 3c^2b + c^3 + babc$

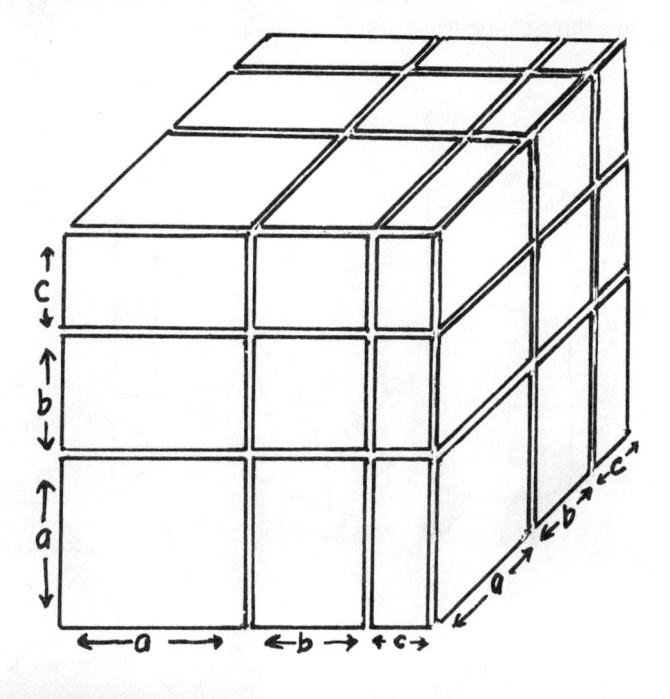

(Photo courtesy of Lithuanian Montessori Society of America, Chicago, Illinois.)

THE GEOMETRIC SOLIDS

The Geometrical Solids are smooth wooden figures which fit on bases for matching. The child learns their names, identifies them by feel with his eyes closed or blindfolded. After an exercise of this kind the child observes the forms when his eyes are open with a much more lively interest. Another way of interesting him in the solid geometrical forms is to make them *move.* The sphere rolls in every direction; the cylinder rolls in one direction only; the cone rolls round itself; the prism and the pyramid, however, stand still, but the prism falls over move easily than the pyramid. The vocabulary for the geometric solids is taught in a three-period lesson.

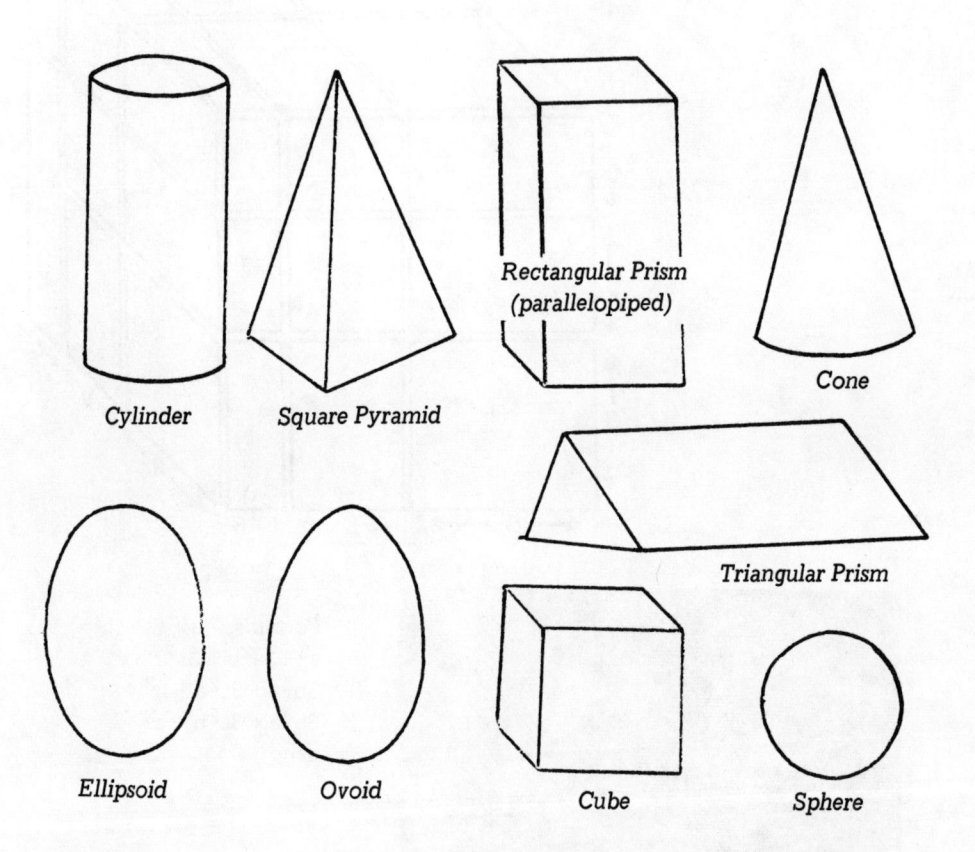

Cylinder   Square Pyramid   Rectangular Prism (parallelopiped)   Cone

Triangular Prism

Ellipsoid   Ovoid   Cube   Sphere

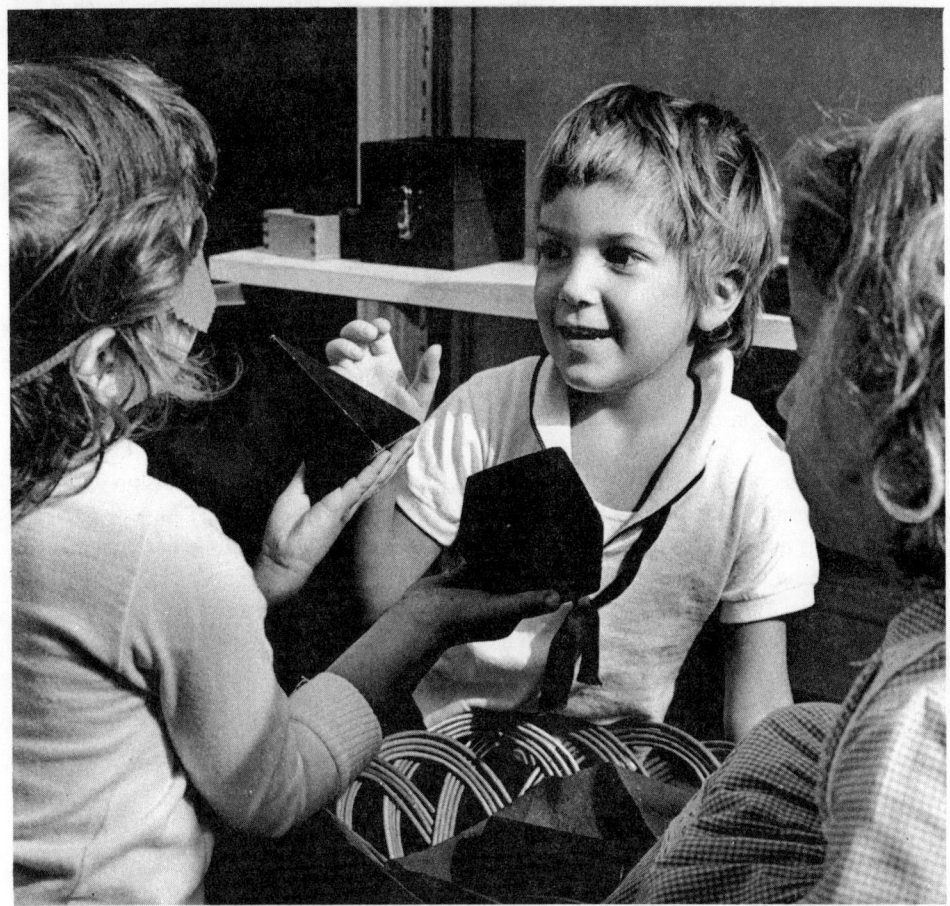

(Photo Courtesy of Sunday Sun Magazine, The Baltimore Sun, Maryland, and Montessori Children's House, Baltimore, Maryland.)

"One way of teaching a child to recognize the geometric solids is for him to touch them with closed eyes and guess their names."

ACCURACY IN SPEECH

The sense of hearing has great importance because it is the sense necessary for speech. Therefore, to train the child's attention to follow sounds and noises which are produced in the environment, to recognize them and to discriminate between them, is to prepare his attention to follow more accurately the sounds of articulate language. The teacher must be careful to pronounce clearly and completely the sounds of the word when she speaks to a child, even though she may be speaking in a low voice, almost as if telling him a secret. The children's songs are also a good means of obtaining exact pronunciation. The teacher, when she teaches them, pronounces clearly, separating the component sounds of the word pronounced.

A special opportunity for training in clear and exact speech occurs when the lessons are given in the nomenclature relating to the sensory exercises. In every exercise, when the child has *recognized* the differences between the qualities of the objects, the teacher fixes the idea of this quality with a word. Thus, when the child has many times built and rebuilt the tower of the pink cubes, at an opportune moment the teacher draws near him, and taking the two extreme cubes, the largest and the smallest, and showing them to him, says, "This is large," "This is small."

The two words only, *large* and *small*, are pronounced several times in succession with strong emphasis and with a very clear pronunciation, "This is *large*, large, large"; after which there is a moment's pause. Then the teacher, to see if the child has understood, verifies with the following tests: "Give me the large one. Give me the small one." Again, "The large one." "Now the small one." "Give me the large one." Then there is another pause. Finally, the teacher, pointing to the objects in turn asks, "What is this?" The child, if he has learned, replies rightly, "Large," "Small." The teacher then urges the child to repeat the words always more clearly and as accurately as possible. "What is it?" "Large." "What?" "Large." "Tell me nicely, what is it?" "Large."

Large and small objects are those which differ only in size and not in form; that is, all three dimensions change more or less proportionally. We should say that a house is "Large" and a hut is "Small." When two pictures represent the same objects in different dimensions one can be said to be an enlargement of the other.

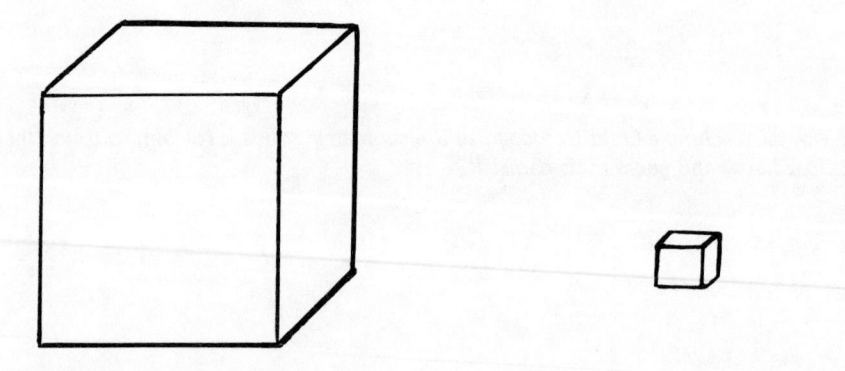

This is the largest cube.   *This is the smallest cube.*

When, however, only the dimensions referring to the section of the object change, while the length remains the same, the objects are respectively **thick** and **thin**. We should say of two posts of equal height, but different cross-section, that one is thick and the other is thin. The teacher, therefore, gives a lesson on the brown prisms similar to that with the cubes in the three periods which I have described:

> Period I. **Naming.** "This is thick. This is thin."
>
> Period 2. **Recognition.** "Give me the thick. Give me the thin."
>
> Period 3. **The Pronunciation of the Word.** "What is this?"

There is a way of helping the child to recognize differences in dimension and to place the objects in correct gradation. After the lesson which I have described, the teacher scatters the brown prisms, for instance, on a carpet, says to the child, "Give me the thickest one of all," and lays the object on a table. Then again, she invites the child to look for the thickest piece among those scattered on the floor, and every time the piece chosen is laid in its order on the table next to the piece previously chosen. In this way the child accustoms himself always to look either for the **thickest** or the **thinnest** among the rest, and so has a guide to help him to lay the pieces in gradation.

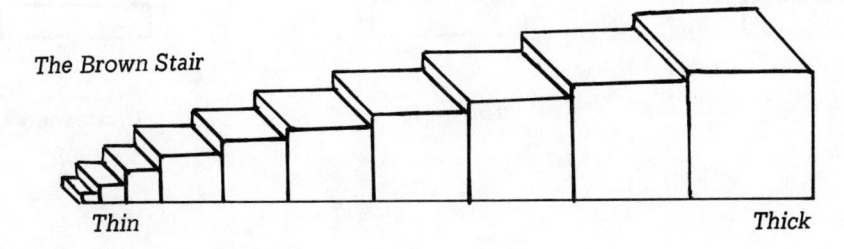

The Brown Stair

Thin   Thick

When there is one dimension only which varies, as in the case of the rods, the objects are said to be **long** and **short**, the varying dimension **short**; when the breadth varies, they are **broad** and **narrow**.

Of these three varieties we offer the child as a fundamental lesson only that in which the **length** varies, and we teach the differences by means of the usual "three periods," and by asking him to select from the pile at one time always the **longest**, at another always the **shortest**.

The child in this way acquires great accuracy in the use of words. One day the teacher had ruled the blackboard with very fine lines. A child said, "What small lines!" "They are not small," corrected another; "they are **thin**."

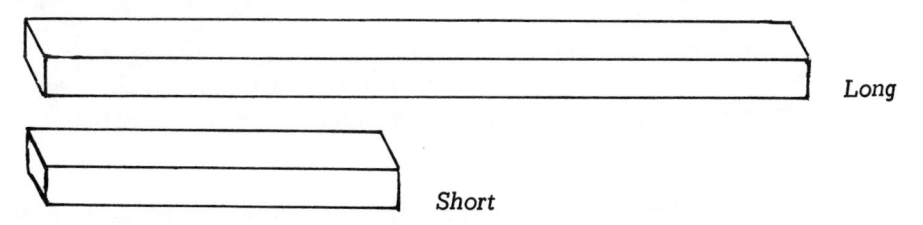

Long

Short

COLOR AND FORM

When the names to be taught are those of colors or of forms, so that it is not necessary to emphasize contrast between extremes, the teacher can give more than two names at the same time, as, for instance, "This is red." "This is blue." "This is yellow." or, again, "This is a square." "This is a triangle." "This is a circle." In the case of a gradation, however, the teacher will select (if she is teaching the colors) the two extremes **dark** and **light,** then making a choice always of the **darkest** and the **lightest.**

The child's powers of observation and of recognition have greatly increased. Further, the mental images which he has succeeded in establishing are not a confused medley; they are all classified—forms are distinct from dimensions, and dimensions are classed according to the qualities which result from the combinations of varying dimensions.

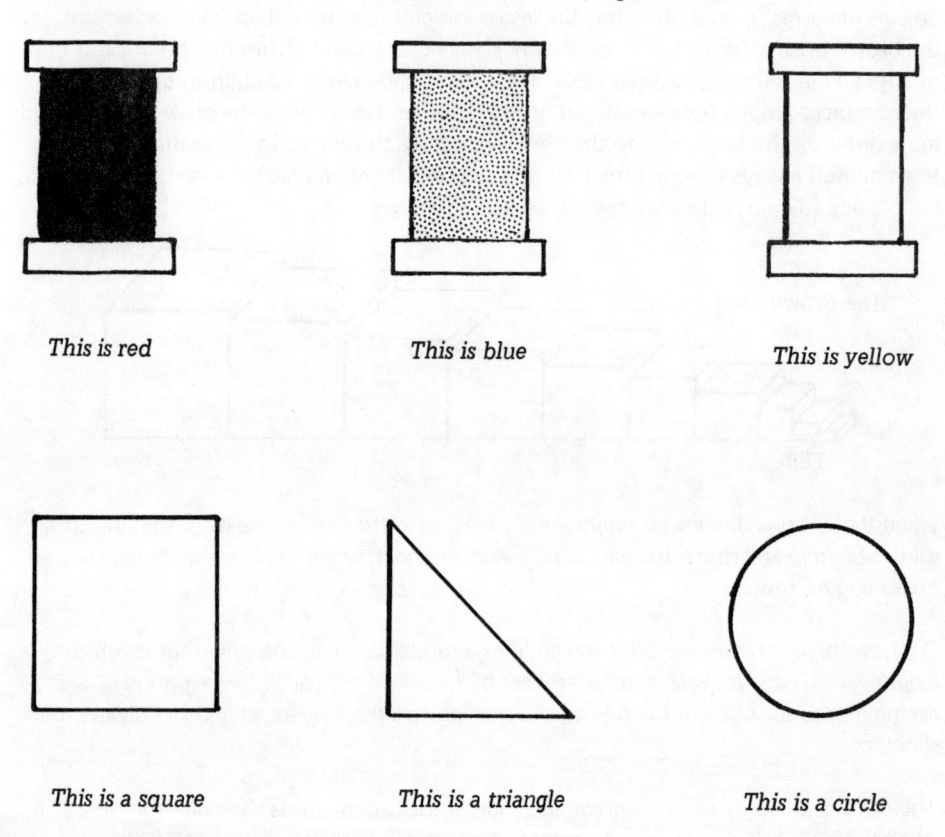

This is red   *This is blue*   *This is yellow*

This is a square   *This is a triangle*   *This is a circle*

All these are quite distinct from **gradations.** Colors are divided according to tint and to richness of tone, silence is distinct from non-silence, noises from sounds, and everything has its own exact and appropriate name. The child then has not only developed in himself special qualities of observation and of judgment, but the objects which he observes may be said to go into their place, according to the order established in his mind, and they are placed under their appropriate name in an exact classification.

The first exercise for the child is that of **pairing the colors**; that is, he selects from a mixed heap of colors the two tablets which are alike, and lays them out, one beside the other.

The teacher naturally does not offer the child all the one hundred and twenty-eight tablets in a heap, but chooses only a few of the brighter colors, for example, red, blue, and yellow, and prepares and mixes up three or four pair. Then, taking one tablet—perhaps the red one—she indicates to the child that he is to choose its counterpart from the heap. This done, the teacher lays the pair together on the table. Then she takes perhaps the blue and the child selects the tablet to form another pair. The teacher then mixes the tablets again for the child to repeat the exercise by himself, i.e., to select the two red tablets, the two blue, the two yellow, etc., and to place the two members of each pair next to one another.

Then the couples will be increased to four or five, and little children of three years old end by pairing of their own accord ten or a dozen couples of mixed tablets.

When the child has given his eye sufficient practice in recognizing the identity of the pairs of colors, he is offered the shades of one color only, and he exercises himself in the perception of the slightest difference of shade in every color. Take, for example, the blue series. There are eight tablets in gradated shades. The teacher places them one beside another, beginning with the darkest, with the sole object of making the child understand "what is to be done."

She then leaves him alone to the interesting attempts which he spontaneously makes. It often happens that the child makes a mistake. If he has understood the idea and makes a mistake, it is a sign that **he has not yet reached the stage** of perceiving the differences between the gradations of one color. It is practice which perfects in the child that capacity for distinguishing the fine differences, and so we leave him alone to his attempts!

There are two suggestions that we can make to help him. The first is that he should always select the darkest color from the pile. This suggestion greatly facilitates his choice by giving it a constant direction.

Secondly, we can lead him to observe from time to time any two colors that stand next to each other in order to compare them directly and apart from the others. In this way the child does not place a tablet without a particular and careful comparison with its neighbor.

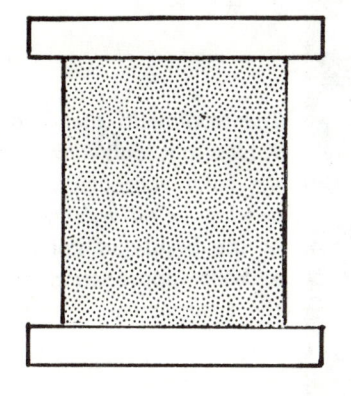

Actual size

Finally, the child himself will love to mix the sixty-four colors and then to arrange them in eight rows of pretty shades of color with really surprising skill. In this exercise also the child's hand is educated to perform fine and delicate movements and his mind is afforded special training in attention. He must take hold of the tablets in a particular way, he must avoid touching the colored silk, and must handle the tablets instead by the pieces of wood at the top and bottom. To arrange the tablets next to one another in a straight line at exactly the same level, so that the series looks like a beautiful shaded ribbon, is an act which demands a manual skill obtained only after considerable practice.

These exercises of the chromatic sense lead, in the case of the older children, to the development of the "color memory." A child having looked carefully at a color is then invited to look for its companion in a mixed group of colors, without, of course, keeping the color he has observed under his eye to guide him. It is, therefore, by his memory that he recognizes the color, which he no longer compares with a reality but with an image impressed upon his mind.

The children are very fond of this exercise in "color memory"; it makes a lively digression for them, as they run with the image of a color in their minds and look for its corresponding reality in their surroundings. It is a real triumph for them to identify the idea with the corresponding reality and to **hold in their hands** the proof of the mental power they have acquired.

Exercises with the Color Tablets

The materials needed for the three color tablets are as follows:

> Box 1—Three pairs of wooden tablets painted in the primary colors, red, blue, yellow.
>
> Box 2—Eleven pairs of tablets in the following colors: red, yellow, blue, orange, green, purple, pink, grey, brown, black, white.
>
> Box 3—Sixty-three tablets in seven shades of each of nine different colors in a box with a partition for each color. Blue, red, rellow, green, orange, purple, grey, brown, crimson.

The work with the Color Tablets not only develops the color vocabulary, but develops a refined awareness of the beauty of colors and a deeper appreciation of the environment.

(Photo courtesy of Montessori Workshop, Natchez, Mississippi.)

Choose a table of neutral coloring or spread a neutral colored mat. Take Box 1 to the table. Take the colors out of the box and mix them on the table in front of the child. Pick up one of the tablets. Show it to the child and ask, "Can you find another one like this?" When he does so, place the two tablets together and repeat with the others. Mix the tablets and repeat. Do not mention the names at first as a child can recognize colors before he knows their names.

When the child can do Box 1, he may be given a few more pairs from Box 2. It is not necessary to give a second lesson. Just add more pairs as he is ready for them, until he can pair them all.

Take a set of tablets from Box 3, arrange them in gradation beginning with the lightest or darkest. Arrange them so that the colored edges are together in a row. The child often mixes the different colors in Box 3, and proceeds to sort and grade all 63 tablets.

AUDITORY SENSE: THE SOUND BOXES

There is a series of six cardboard cylinders, either closed entirely or with wooden covers. When these cases are shaken they produce sounds varying in intensity from loud to almost imperceptible sounds, according to the nature of the objects inside the cylinder.

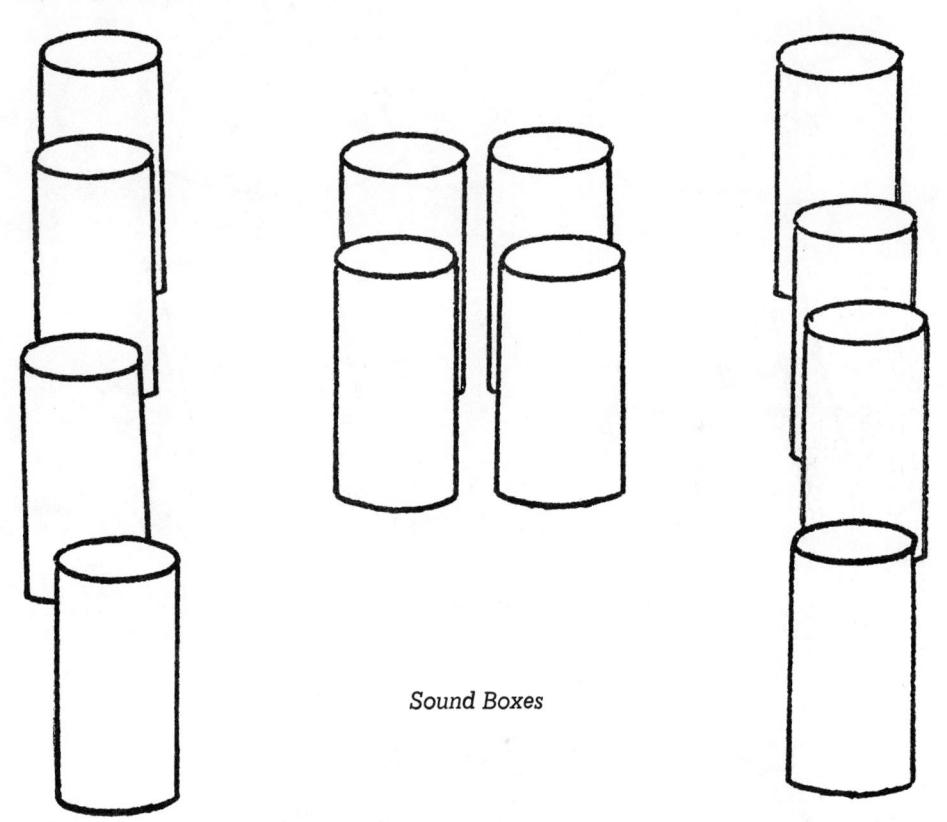

Sound Boxes

There is a double set of these, and the exercise consists, first, in the recognition of sounds of equal intensity, arranging the cylinders in pairs. The next exercise consists of the comparison of one sound with another; that is, the child arranges the six cylinders in a series according to the loudness of sound which they produce. The exercise is analogous to that with the color spools, which also are paired, and then arranged in gradation. In this case also the child performs the exercise seated comfortably at a table. After a preliminary explanation from the teacher he repeats the exercise by himself, his eyes being blindfolded that he may better concentrate his attention.

MUSICAL BELLS

The auditory sense is developed through the use of bells whose sounds correspond to the notes of the diatonic scale so that the child may progress from distinguishing the different sounds to recognizing and naming them when they are associated with the names of the notes. In addition, the Silence Game is valuable in developing sensitivity to the softest sounds and to discriminating among various sounds which are masked by the normal noise of our extremely noisy society. The children learn that one level of silence—when they are all absolutely silent in the room—only allows for the revelation of another, hidden level of sounds which they may well have ignored.

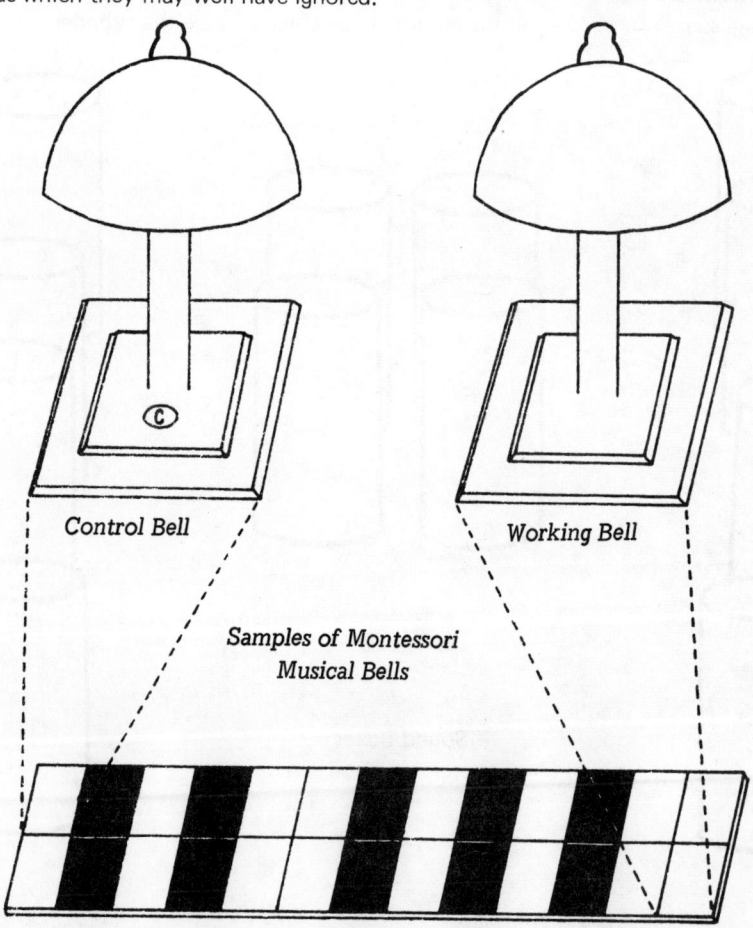

Control Bell

Working Bell

Samples of Montessori Musical Bells

SENSE OF TOUCH

When initiating the child into the education of the sense of touch, the teacher must always take an active part the first time; not only must she show the child "how it is done," Her interference is a little more definite still, for she takes hold of his hand and guides it to touch the surfaces with the fingertips in the lightest possible way. She will make no explanations; her words will be rather to encourage the child with his hand to perceive the different sensations. When he has perceived them, it is then that he repeats the act by himself in the delicate way which he has been taught.

After the board with the two contrasting surfaces, the child is offered another board on which are gummed strips of paper which are rough or smooth in different degrees. Graduated series of sandpaper cards are also given. The child perfects himself by exercises in touching these surfaces, not only refining his capacity for perceiving tactile differences which are always growing more similar, but also perfecting the movement of which he is ever gaining greater mastery.

Following these is a series of fabrics of every kind: velvets, satins, silks, woolens, cottons, coarse and fine linens. There are two similar pieces of each kind of fabric, and they are of bright and vivid colors.

The child is now taught a new movement. Where before he had to **touch**, he must now **feel** the fabric, which, according to the degree of fineness or coarseness from coarse cotton to fine silk, are felt with movements correspondingly decisive or delicate. The child whose hand is already practiced finds the greatest pleasure in feeling the fabrics, and, almost instinctively, in order to enhance his appreciation of the tactile sensation he closes his eyes. Then, to spare himself the exertion, he blindfolds himself with a clean handkerchief, and as he feels the fabrics, he arranges the similar pieces in pairs, one upon the other, then, taking off the handkerchief, he ascertains for himself whether he has made any mistakes.

This exercise in **touching** and **feeling** is peculiarly attractive to the child, and induces him to seek similar experiences in his surroundings. A little one, attracted by the pretty fabric of a visitor's dress, will be seen to go and wash his hands, then to come and touch the fabric of the garment again and again with infinite delicacy, his face meanwhile expressing his pleasure and interest.

ROUGH AND SMOOTH BOARD

Four wooden rectangular hardboard boards, 12 x 6½ inches, mounted with strips of paper with smooth and rough surfaces are used for this exercise. One should be mounted half with a very smooth paper and half with a fine sandpaper; the second with alternate strips of the very smooth paper and fine sandpaper, each strip about 1½ inches wide. The third should be mounted with five strips of sandpaper graded in smoothness from very smooth to rather rough, and the fourth mounted with five strips of paper which have different surfaces.

To begin the child washes his hands in warm water, gently rubbing the tips when drying in order to increase sensitivity. Show the child how to feel the first board very lightly from top to bottom, first one half and then the other, with the finger tips. If the child presses heavily, show him how to keep his wrists up and touch gently with the tips of the fingers. When the child understands the exercise, get him to do it with his eyes shut, then encourage him to use a blindfold. Do not ever insist on the blindfold. Some children like to use them at once; others do not want to for a long time.

The child may practice this light touching alone over a period of time until he reaches the point when to touch a shade more lightly would be not to touch at all. Boards 2, 3 and 4 are added at intervals as the child is ready for them. As with all the apparatus, do not hurry the stages.

This exercise gains a refinement of the tactile senses, awakens a conscious awareness of the texture of surfaces and is an education of the hand. A hand which can touch lightly is able to write later without pressing into the paper.

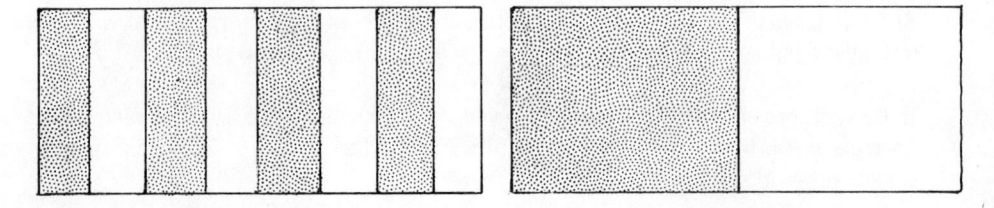

TOUCH: THE FABRICS

Here is needed a box containing two each of a variety of material cut into the same sized squares. A pair of each of the basic materials—silk, linen, nylon, cotton, etc.,—should be in the box. Each pair of materials is a different color.

Start with the three most contrasting materials from the point of view of touch. Linen and cotton, for example, are too alike and therefore would be too difficult to begin with.

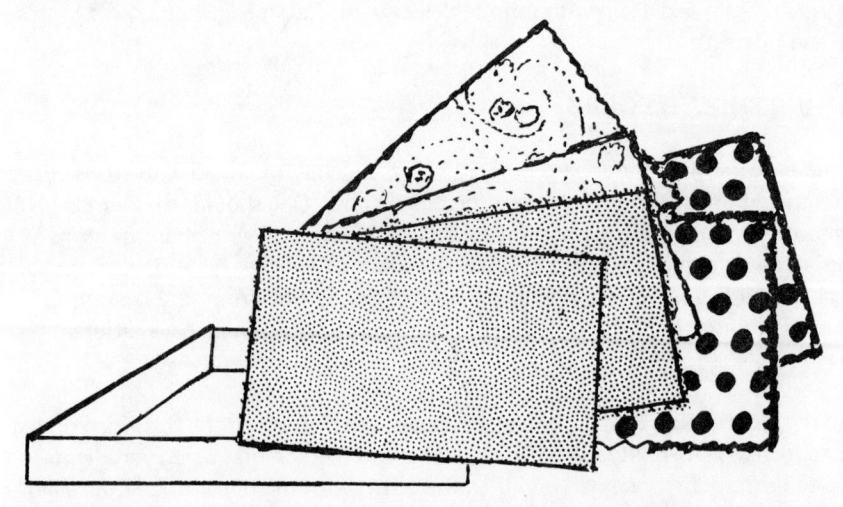

Take the three pairs to the child's table; leave the other pairs in the cupboard. Do not show them to the child. Mix the three chosen pairs on the table, show the child how to feel them with his fingertips, and between his finger and thumb (as one usually feels materials). Let him pair them by feel. Then encourage him to feel and pair them with his eyes shut or with a blindfold over his eyes. When the child has paired the materials, he takes off the blindfold. He can see by the color whether or not he has matched the pairs correctly, as two of the same color are always the same material.

Here again he is developing and refining the tactile sense as well as learning discrimination of materials.

WEIGHT: THE BARIC TABLETS

A little later we shall see the children interest themselves in a much more difficult exercise. There are three sets of wooden tablets, uniform in size but varying in weight from the qualities of the wood. Each set is of a slightly different colored wood and is kept in a box with a sliding lid.

Take the lightest set and the heaviest set. Sit facing the child. Ask him to hold his hands off the table, palms upwards, with the fingertips spread out and slightly bent. Balance one tablet from each set on his fingertips. Ask him to say which tablet is the heavier. Show him how to put the heavier in one pile and the lighter in another. Repeat until the child understands the exercise. When the child understands the exercise (not necessarily the first day) get him to do it with his eyes shut, then give him a blindfold. The child mixes the two sets and does the exercise blindfolded, or the child is blindfolded and the teacher (or another child who knows the exercise) places the tablets on his fingertips.

The hand must move up and down as though to weigh the object, but the movement must be as imperceptible as possible. These little movements should diminish as the capacity and attention for perceiving the weight of the object becomes more acute and the exercise will be perfectly performed when the child comes to perceive the weight almost without any movement of the hands. It is only by the repetition of the attempts that such a result can be obtained.

When the child can tell the difference in weight between the lighter and heavier tablets, he can have the lighter and medium tablets, the heavier and medium tablets, and finally all three sets, light, heavy and medium, to mix and sort into three piles by weight.

When the blindfold is taken off on completion of the exercise, the different colors of the sets show up any mistakes he may have made, and the child can correct himself.

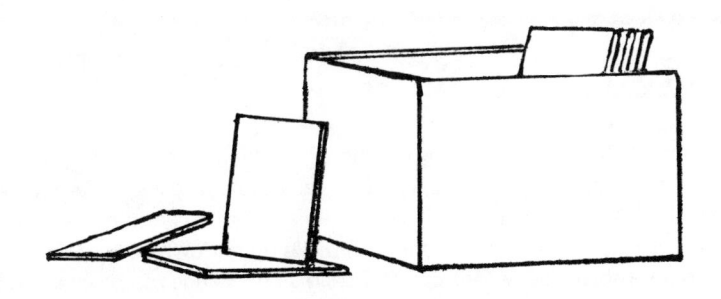

The exercise stresses perception of small differences in weight and the awareness of the weight of things which leads to intelligent observation.

THERMIC TABLETS

Thermic tablets are in pairs of different materials which have a different temperature to the touch, e.g., china tiles, cork, cardboard, metal, leather, etc. All the tablets are the same size.

Take two or more contrasting pairs to the child's table. Mix them. Show the child how to pair them by putting his hand lightly on each in turn to feel the temperature. More pairs are added as the child is able to do them. The child works alone as soon as he understands the exercise.

The materials vary in color and therefore mistakes can be seen when the blindfold is removed. Discrimination of slight differences in temperature are realized by this exercise.

TEACHING THE VOCABULARY OF COMMON AND EXOTIC WOODS

To learn the vocabulary of wood in a concrete situation, we follow the same procedure, by preparing pairs of different woods in matching exercises. Boys show a particular interest for this exercise, and this vocabulary may be a good preparation for later work in woodworking or an interest in trees or geography.

The teacher may make up her own list of common and exotic woods and continue to add to it to develop the children's knowledge of woods.

Actual size recommended for hardwood and fabric. Make two for each sample.

TEACHING THE VOCABULARY OF FABRICS

Use the different fabrics from the matching exercises. Working with the child with poor motor coordination or with the very young child it is advisable to paste different swatches of material on cardboard or Masonite. A duplicate of each fabric is included so the child can match the two identical ones. The teacher can make up her own list and add to it to develop the children's knowledge of fabrics. The child's knowledge can be checked by the three-period lesson.

Following is a list of suggested fabrics:

acetate	linen
brocade	nylon
corduroy	organdy
cotton	orlon
crepe	rayon
dacron	satin
denim	silk
felt	suede
flannel	taffeta
jersey	velvet
	wool

The retarded child can learn to associate the fabric name with the correct fabric through hearing the name repeated when he is actually touching the fabric. This can be done when he matches two pieces of the same fabric.

OLFACTORY: THE SMELLING BOTTLES

Doctors, by the sense of smell, can diagnose an illness very often. The development of the sense of smell has a preventive use also, like smelling gas in the home, burning foods, certain acids that are dangerous, such as Clorox or ammonia. It helps us identify the content of a bottle without knowing all about it, or if the label is lost. The sense of smell helps if the bearing of our car burns out—it can be detected through its smell. The refining of the senses is an immeasurable safety valve which is of great importance to many retarded who are unable to learn to read all signs and labels, or even to know about certain things. The retarded is protected like the primitive man in many instances by the sense of smell.

Two sets of bottles comprise the materials. The first set of 6 to 8 pairs of similar, opaque bottles should contain liquid substances with distinctive smells e.g., eau-de-cologne, dettol, vanilla flavoring, peppermint flavoring, coffee, lavender water, etc.

The second set of 6 to 8 pairs of similar, small opaque jars with air-tight stoppers should be filled with dry substances which have distinctive smells e.g., dried lavender, dried herbs, coffee, cloves, other spices, etc. Mark the top and bottom of each pair of bottles or jars with a colored disc.— each pair marked in a different color. The child is shown how to put the right stopper on each bottle or jar according to the color of the disc. This prevents the smells from becoming mixed. The dry substances in Set 2 are best sewn into muslin bags and the bags rammed tightly into the jars to prevent spilling.

Take two or more contrasting pairs from either set to the child's table. Remove the stoppers. Mix the containers and show the child how to **pair them** by smell. More pairs are included as he becomes proficient at the exercises. Each pair, when the exercise is completed, should have the same color discs on the bottom of the jars.

The **Smelling Bottles** can educate the sense of smell and bring the child's attention to various smells in the environment. The environment should contain other opportunities for exercising the sense of smell. Aromatic herbs and scented flowers should be grown in the garden or in pots or window boxes. Sachets containing lavender, rosemary, etc., can also be in the room.

SENSE OF TASTE

The sense of taste cannot always be separated from the sense of smell. The teacher can develop the sense of taste with the practical exercises below. The teacher can also request catalogues from large food companies for her classroom.

Cooking

These lists can be used as exercises in taste as well as in smell, and in many cases can be incorporated into juice or lunchtime. Don't miss the opportunity to show the children the botanical aspects of these products, to explain where and how they are grown; the various ways that we use them and the various means of preparing them (fermentation, drying, extraction of essences). Some of the herbs or flowers could be grown in the school. Point out those that the child can find in his own locality. Ask the children if they can tell what is cooking by the smell, so that they can begin to make observations on other cooking smells and combinations of smells in their kitchen at home.

Fruits

Use real fruits as well as juices. Children can help in preparation as practical life exercise. Language exercises can also be used here. Consider asking a fruiterer for a catalogue.

lemon	apricot
lime	prunes
orange	raisins
grapefruit	grapes
pineapple	currants
tomato	strawberry
apple	raspberry
peach	blackberry
pear	blueberry
plum	cantaloupe

Cheeses

If a cheese specialty store is in the vicinity, a wide variety, including gradations of cheese could be obtained. Comment on fermentation, places they come from. Children could be offered cubes to smell and taste at eating time.

Roquefort
Cheddar (mild, sharp, extra sharp, etc.)
Port Salut
Camembert
Limburger
Swiss
Monterey Jack
Muenster

THE ROLE OF THE MASS MEDIA IN A MONTESSORI CLASSROOM

When Montessori devised her teaching apparatus, the various mass media were unknown. However, she was always so open to new possibilities that we can be certain she would have welcomed the wonderful teaching tools now available to every classroom through the use of the mass media.

Since the Montessori method is not a rigid, closed-end system but a flexible way of educating children by cooperating with their own development, it can be easily adapted to use with the mass media. The teacher has only to remember and apply the basic Montessori principles to this new material.

Jerome Bruner notes (ON KNOWING)[3] that the human being can receive only six or seven inputs at the most; after that, our circuits become overloaded and we do not understand. The retarded child, of course, cannot even handle that number, so we must reduce the sensory inputs to one or two at a time. The temptation with the mass media is to use them without careful planning.

What is to be taught? How can we isolate this material from the background? How much time should a lesson take? How many repetitions are needed? Quite often, the same material can be used for several different lessons; then it must be presented at different times. Above all, mass media must not be overused so that the children become mere passive spectators to the images flashing before them, but it should be used as a supplement, as a way of presenting information, as an active cooperator with the child in his own educational activity.

Montessori sounded a note of warning in one of her references to the new media (THE FORMATION OF MAN).

> *Culture can be transmitted by means of the spoken word, also by the radio and photographic records. It can be given by the help of projections and films. Above all, however, it has to be taken in through activity with the help of an apparatus which permits the child to acquire culture by himself, urged onwards by the nature of his mind which seeks and is guided by the laws of his development. These laws prove that culture is absorbed by the child by means of individual experience, by the repetition of interesting exercises which always require the contribution of the activity of the hand, the organ which co-operates with the development of the intelligence.*

The following suggestions are just that—suggestions. There is no end to the possibilities of these media. Even some slight acquaintance with the work of Marshall McLuhan will show how our entire range of perception is being affected by these electronic marvels; the retarded child also participates in his society and is affected by these changes.

Camera

The box camera is one of the simplest tools for a child to operate. The children who are capable of it can also be taught to load the film. A pictorial record of class activity can be made by the children. The advantages of this are:

[3]Bruner, Jerome, ON KNOWING, Cambridge: Belknap Press of Harvard University, 1962, p. 7.

Photographs can be taken home to provide a graphic record of class work and to supplement the reports of a child with communication difficulties.

Stories can be built around the photographs in different arrangements.

There is enhancement of the child's self-concept as he views himself.

They can be used for comparison purposes at the beginning and end of the term.

Home Movies

If the equipment is available and if the teacher or parent can operate it, a movie record can be made of a class activity—a picnic, an assembly program, etc. The film can be played again and again. An excellent way to develop vocabulary and memory as children talk about that great event once more.

The Tape Recorder

The tape recorder allows for individual instruction. The teacher can prepare material suitable for each pupil and arrange time for listening on an individual basis. If there are pupils in a class who are capable of operating the equipment, they can be taught to do so—time spent now will result, not only in time saved later, but also in the acquisition of a skill leading to an improved self-concept in those students who can perform the job.

The tape recorder can be used in the area of language development with great effectiveness since tapes can be individualized within each learner's range of comprehension to assure success. Intimations of failure so often associated with books are eliminated. Making certain that she is a model of good speech patterns, the teacher can make tapes that begin with simple questions with time for the listener to repeat, then to respond. The child then can play back the tape with his own responses registered on it. Suddenly he hears his own voice, is aware of himself as a person with a unique voice, a recognizable speech pattern. Also he can hear his own improvement from tape to tape and be encouraged to continue his work.

Lessons in many different subjects can be taped. Manners, for example. With the teacher putting one side of a conversation on the tape, the child can practice making the appropriate responses, then play the tape again and again. Since tapes can be erased, trial and error is possible, and a successful tape can be preserved in a tape library.

Parent involvement is very important and should be encouraged in this area. Why couldn't parents read books onto tape for later replay? Or tell simple stories? The child whose parent's voice is heard in class has an occasion for pride. And the parents themselves will understand better what is being done if they are drawn into the work of the class with full explanations from the teacher.

The tape recorder can also function as an "electronic pencil" for those children who have writing difficulty. They can speak their compositions or thoughts into a recorder for later typing, then can keep the typed copies of their work just as if they had been able to write by themselves. Much can be done in this area, especially with older retarded children.

Phonograph Records

Stories and poems for children have been recorded and are excellent as supplementary work but should not be used too often because the child is in an essentially passive position in relation to them. However, quite often they can be used to entertain one group of children while the teacher is working with another group. Music such as rhythm records are useful for dancing and free movement or work, quiet music is useful for soothing an agitated class or for accompanying an exercise like painting or the silence game. Folk songs can acquaint a child with his cultural heritage and teaching history.

Our Great Museums as the "Book of the People"

Our great museums—the Smithsonian, the National Gallery of Art, the Metropolitan Museum, the Cleveland Museum, for example—almost all offer educational services, generally free upon request. Films, film strips and slides are available, in sets to be used at the teacher's discretion, often with accompanying tests and teaching manuals.

What many of us absorb almost unconsciously through awareness of the complexities of daily life, must be taught in structured situations to the retarded. Here the world of art can provide ample opportunities for question and answer discussion designed to evoke new words. Simple history can be taught through discussion of differing styles of dress, for example, and we can use portraits of certain presidents to focus on a discussion of history that remains on a level easily grasped by the retarded child. Pictorial information on architectural styles can be utilized for the same purposes.

The great advantage of pictures and film material is that they are concrete and thus serve the educational needs of those whose limitations tie them to the concrete. They can be used in many ways and the same material will frequently serve many purposes. The imagination of the teacher and the reaction of the pupils will suggest many possibilities. Among the subjects that can be taught through films and film strips are language(vocabulary especially), history, geography, arts and crafts.

Other governmental agencies (Dept. of Agriculture, for example) and many, many commercial firms produce films which are available for educational purposes either free or at a nominal cost. They can be used to teach about industry, agriculture, growth of America and such essential subjects as hygiene, dress, behavior at job interviews, or care and treatment of pets.

A Bibliography of audiovisual material is included at the end of the book.

Suggested List of Equipment for Extending the Senses

The following list is from David Holbrook's book, ENGLISH FOR THE REJECTED. David Holbrook, Fellow of King's College, Cambridge, England, is the author of books in poetry, fiction, criticism, and education. Teachers working with inefficient learners will find a wealth of helpful ideas in his books on education.

The list of Mr. Holbrook's is convenient but the teacher in America should not stop with it. She should be constantly aware of the new teaching aids being developed by technological research every day. A teacher working with backward children particularly, must always have a forward look.

> *Tape recorder and tapes*
> *Typewriters and duplicating machine*
> *Puppet theatre and glove puppets*
> *Percussion instruments*
> *Television set*
> *16 mm film projector*
> *Loud amplifier*
> *Mobile floodlights and spots for dramatic work*
> *Simple sets of switches and lights for setting up "broadcasting studios"*
> *Materials for simple drama sets*
> *Record player and records*
> *Radio*
> *Machinery for showing films, film strips, slides*[4]

These exercises are only a sampling, of course, of the various activities. Some of them require special apparatus but many more do not; they require, rather, an attitude on the part of the Montessori teacher, a receptivity to the children and an awareness of the ways in which they are learning. A teacher who is not alert to the possibilities of the special equipment will not use it fruitfully, and conversely, good results can be achieved with the simplest equipment, such as art materials that are available in every classroom, whether or not it is equipped with other Montessori materials. For the teacher who would like to go into the exercises more deeply, the list of books below would be interesting and helpful.

Montessori, Maria, Dr. Montessori's Own Handbook, New York: Schocken Books, 1965.

Montessori, Maria, The Advanced Montessori Method, New York: Frederick A. Stokes Co., 1917.

Carinato, Sister Mary Matthew, et al., Montessori Matters, Cincinnati: Ohio Province, 1967.

Gitter, Lena L., A Strategy for Fighting the War on Poverty, Washington, D.C.: Homer Fagan Press, 1968.

A LAST WORD ABOUT SENSORIAL MATERIALS

Although the sensorial materials and exercises are not always understood, they are the part of Montessori which should be most accessible to those who observe and reflect upon the learning process, not only in children but also in adults. For example, think of the difficulty faced by an adult in learning a foreign language and how much easier it is for him to speak and understand this language when he is actually in the country where it is spoken. Instead of being faced with words on a page which he cannot relate to any experience of his own but which he must learn through memorization and a conscious effort of

---

[4] Holbrook, David, ENGLISH FOR THE REJECTED: TRAINING LITERACY IN THE LOWER STREAMS OF THE SECONDARY SCHOOL. Cambridge: Univ. Press, 1964.

the will, he discovers words and grammatical forms linked to people and vivid experiences. Thus language learning becomes an ongoing process rather than an activity rigidly limited to so many hours a day and utilizing only a few aspects of the intelligence.

This difficulty is even more acute for the child learning his own language because he is too young to be able to handle abstractions at all; he must pass through the stage of concrete learning first. Also he does not have any background in language at all. Considerable research is being conducted in the area of language development as a means of teaching socially disadvantaged children, and results to date push the stage of language formation far back into the infant's life, long before he begins to speak. Infants and young children store language up, as it were, for several years; then they bring it out in speech. By the time the child enters school, it is too late to restore fully the range of vocabulary and experience he has lost. Since reading is, in a sense, an abstraction of speech—sounds are transformed into black marks on a page to which an arbitrary meaning has been assigned—retarded language development means reading retardation and the whole tragic story of school failure.

The child's speech begins with nouns—words for specific, concrete things which are within the range of his experience—and only then broadens to take in other forms of speech, especially the simple action verbs. The comination of a few simple action verbs with a vocabulary of nouns enables the child to make his wishes known with great success.

The sensorial materials and the exercises which use them provide a deliberately enriched atmosphere of experience which enables the child to develop a sophisticated vocabulary with ease, since the words he learns are tied to specific operations and to concrete objects which he is free to manipulate and to master through his senses. If these materials did nothing else, their role in language development would make them outstanding learning tools.

Even for the normal child whose home provides ample opportunity for language development, they extend the range of his experiences. For the child with learning problems they are invaluable, for they provide what he will probably not receive elsewhere, they provide it in concentrated, pure form, they allow for the necessary repetition which is essential for language development and they provide it in an atmosphere removed from failure and from the tensions which often are present at home. With the sensorial materials the child is freed to learn to speak, to comprehend and to express his growing comprehension in language.

The sensorial experience with Montessori apparatus cannot be separated from language development. The child is helped through his work with concrete, sensorial objects to develop his abstract thinking and language abilities. Thus, in this book, although there are separate chapters for sensorial exercises and language development, there is much overlapping. If certain exercises or apparatus are not explained or demonstrated in one of the two chapters, it will most likely be shown in the other. A division of the apparatus and techniques into those belonging to sensorial and those belonging to language skills was necessary for this book, but it is not the true state of affairs. In all good teaching, the inter-relationship of all the knowledge of the world must be shown. Language skills and sensorial skills have a **basic** inter-relationship and *must*, if the sensorial exercises are to achieve their goal.

THE DEVELOPMENT OF LANGUAGE SKILLS

The ability to communicate in language and to pass on the achievement of our ancestors to each succeeding generation belongs solely to man.

Language, reading, and writing power develop in the same way as the child learns to speak. We talk of writing before reading, sounds before words, reading of slips of paper before books and above all, much, much conversation before anything else. This is how Montessori observed that a child naturally developed.

Therefore, vocabulary building is the first requirement. In a Montessori class, vocabulary is developed in all areas: practical life, sensorial and cultural. The teacher functions as the language model for the children, just as she is the model in other areas. She must use speech correctly but not overwhelm the child with too much speech at one time. In addition to being aware of her own speech, she should know what she can reasonably expect from each child in the way of speech patterns and vocabulary level.

In his book, LANGUAGE LEARNING AND LANGUAGE DEVIATIONS, G. L. Wyatt gives two general rules for all types of language behavior which are pertinent here:

> *1. Language patterns in all categories change with age of child.*
>
> *2. Stress interferes with the child's word finding capacity, word variety decreases and repetitions increase.*

The following list (also from Wyatt), although it refers more to the disturbed child than to the retardate or disadvantaged, is nevertheless helpful in providing a descriptive base line for diagnostic purposes.

> *A. Normal Language Behavior: Appropriate for child's age and cultural background.*

B. Severely Defective Articulation (without organic deficiency): Auditory discrimination of speech sounds and patterns of articulation underlearned.

B1. Def. Articulation and Secondary Stuttering: Child reacts with anger to difficulties in communication, caused by B.

C. Groping Speech: Patterns of grammar and syntax underlearned.

D. Stuttering: Normal language development interrupted by separation from mother. Disruption of customary reciprocal feed-back pattern. Child reacts with anger and anxiety, later with feeling of guilt, fears of disaster and defense mechanisms.

E. Cerebral Dysfunction Speech: Various forms of language difficulties as part aspects of general motor expressive disorder. (Difficulties with word finding, articulation, "cluttering" speech.)

Regardless of the level of communication, it is important to begin at the child's level, taking him from where he is. "Children's comfortable language is the starting point in a school language program." (Bill Martin, Jr., "Language and Literature," NEA.)

In that same pamphlet, Mr. Martin goes on to say that it is with abundant oral activity that new language patterns are firmly fixed in children's minds. Later on, children can transpose those patterns into their own thinking and verbal activity.

An excellent source of speech models are poems and stories that children can imitate in exploring new language patterns and in learning about the structure of language (see listing in bibliography). Wherever possible field trips should be arranged to assist vocabulary development through concrete experience.

Montessori did not believe in over-verbalization or in all instruction being made through language. Children will develop linguistic responses to experiences in music, dancing and painting; often, words will come after a period of intense silence has brought feelings the child wishes to communicate, to the surface.

"The goal of language," Mr. Martin concludes, "is not to develop language skill in and of itself, but to help children claim their humanity through the use of language."

The following exercises show the many ways in which language can be developed. It is important to remember that Montessori always taught vocabulary through the three-period lesson, since this is the best means of isolating difficulties and "programming" for success. In addition to formal language lessons, Montessori devised language games. These also follow in this chapter.

Diagnostic Studies in Reading Problems

In studying children we will want to think of these points. Is the child an educational or a reading case only? Into what category does he belong?

Non-reader—one who recognizes less than 25 words, but has been exposed to reading a year or more.

Delayed reader—mentally capable, but handicapped by immaturity, etc., so does not progress normally during first year.

Defective reader—one whose reading falls considerably below mental age.

Retarded reader—one whose reading falls about one year below mental age.

Fair reader—one not up to capacity, but up to grade level.

Excellent reader—one whose reading age exceeds mental age by one or more years.

What is causing the reading disability?

Physical—defective vision, hearing, speech, general physical condition, etc.

Educational—changes in schools, excessive absence, improper school placement, inexperienced teachers.

Environmental—low cultural background, broken home, low socio-economic level.

Emotional—insecurity, passivity, non-interest.

Mental—inadequate mental age.

What diagnostic instruments can be used?

Informal tests
Standardized tests
Observation
Conferences

What is the primary reading trouble?

Lack of experience background on which to build concepts.
Inadequate ability to understand and speak the English language.
Lack of comprehension of easy material.
Lack of comprehension of more complex material—English structure.
Inadequate sight vocabulary.
Meager meaning vocabulary.
Lack of techniques for independent work attack.
Low rate, poor rhythm.
Low recall.
Inability to read for different purposes.
No voluntary practice (recreational reading)—No books at home.

No habit of reading.
Faulty habits(vocalization, head movements, pointing.)
Poor work habits in general.

Questions

1. Do you know the **basic level** in reading of each child in your group? Yes/ / No/ /

2. Is material provided on that level for recreational and research reading? Yes/ / No/ /

3. Is the instructional level well considered so that only a **reasonable amount** of developmental work is necessary? Yes/ / No/ /

4. Is any child asked to read material on his **frustration level**, even though it correlates with social science work in progress? Yes/ / No/ /

5. Is each group receiving the proper amount of developmental reading? Yes/ / No/ /

6. Do you know the **capacity level** of your pupils? Yes/ / No/ /

7. Is provision made for growth and enrichment of your superior readers? Yes/ / No/ /

EXERCISES WITH THE METAL INSETS

Ten geometrical shapes cut out in metal are needed. The frame is one color and the inset another. Have also two sloping stands to hold the insets and frames, squares of colored paper exactly the size of the frames, and colored pencils.

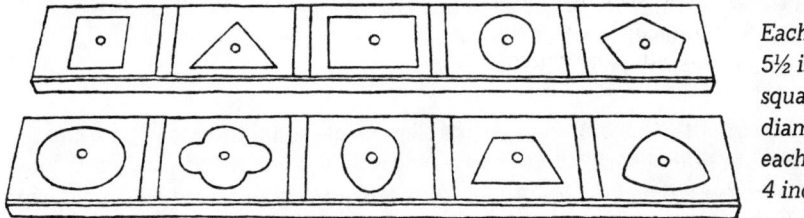

Each base is 5½ inches square. The diameter of each inset is 4 inches.

The teacher takes one shape, a piece of colored paper and two colored pencils to a child's table. She shows the child how to place the frame exactly over the paper, then how to hold the pencil and to draw round the inside of the frame. The teacher then removes the frame and shows the child how to fill in the figures entirely by drawing light parallel strokes from one side of the figure to the other.

The child does the exercise as shown. He chooses his own paper, pencil and shape. When the child has done many drawings using one figure only, the teacher can show him how to make patterns, e.g. she can show him how to draw the rectangle as before, and then turn the frame round sideways and draw it again. The resulting pattern can be filled in with any color that the child likes.

In the third step of the exercise, the child draws the shape of a frame and is then shown how to place an inset exactly over the drawing and to draw round it with a second color. A second figure appears outside the first. The child is interested to see that the hollow frame and the solid inset give a similar result when drawn round.

Later the child can be shown how to make patterns with two or more figures. He can make patterns which fill in the whole sheet of paper. He can make designs on large sheets of paper and repetitive border patterns. From time to time the teacher can show the child how to improve his work and give him fresh ideas.

This exercise prepares the hand for writing. The child gains control of the pencil through an enjoyable exercise. It is an excellent exercise for older children who write badly or dis like writing. They acquire good control of a pencil while enjoying the exercise.

Working with these insets is an indirect preparation for reading and writing.

It also leads to the discovery of the similarity of block letters with geometric forms.

Instructions for "Do-it-yourself"

These insets are commercially made of metal, but 1/8" tempered Masonite is an excellent substitute. Masonite is available in 4' X 8' sheets and should be cut in the actual sizes and shapes of the patterns which are shown.

The edges of the cut-outs should be beveled at a slight angle so that they can be sanded smooth. The smooth side of each cut-out and all edges should be primed. The insets should be painted—the frames red and the insets blue. Simple knobs should be added to the insets. These are available at hardware stores and at dime stores. According to Montessori, these knobs aid in the development of the fingers which are so important for use in handling things and in writing.

Several little boards of Masonite should be cut in the same size as the frame. These are for the children to use for design work with paper and the insets. The paper should also be cut the same size. This structures the exercise and eliminates the anxiety and guilt which the child often encounters in his efforts to make a good design and to decide where on the paper it should be placed. The child is helped in his indirect preparation for writing, geometry, and artistic design. If Masonite is not available, the insets could be cut out of stiff cardboard. Brass fasteners could serve as knobs.

One pattern of actual size and shape is given. The remaining nine can be made accordingly.

Personal Experience: Geometric Insets

In one of my special classes, we used the geometric insets in many ways. At first, of course, the children traced the shapes and colored them in to prepare for writing and for learning the basic alphabet shapes. This work continued throughout the year and by late spring, many of the children had learned to write the alphabet.

But we did not put the geometric insets away. Instead, we reversed the historical development from pictorial to alphabet writing by using our new-found knowledge to make pictures, combining geometric shapes and alphabet shapes. The children who were very inhibited and never thought that they could create a picture by themselves tended to like this type of drawing the most. Eventually, they became less inhibited and more creative in their work—a nice paradox for those who claim that the geometric insets are too rigid to allow for creativity! Actually, the definite outlines and shapes are quite comforting for children with learning problems.

I used a recording of Edward Lear's NONSENSE ALPHABET to stimulate the children, and each letter resulted in a lot of art activity. They drew all types of cartoon characters, beginning with the geometric shapes as a firm base, then adding alphabet shapes. This was very appealing because the children shared a happy experience and were able to relieve their emotions without any fears of mockery. They could laugh freely at each other's pictures without causing any anger on the part of their fellow classmates. At the same time, of course, they were getting excellent practice in writing and also in recognizing the shapes of the geometric insets.

SANDPAPER LETTERS

Each letter of the alphabet is cut out in fine sandpaper and mounted on strong cardboard. The vowels are mounted on blue cards and the consonants on pink. The large letters are mounted on larger cards and the small on smaller. The letters are on the right hand side of the cards so that there is a space on the left hand side for the child to hold the card steady.

The teacher takes any two letters to the child's table. She chooses two which contrast in shape and sound. She sits beside the child and shows him how to feel the shape of the letters with the index and middle finger of the hand which will hold the pencil in writing. At the same time she tells him the sound of the letter. She gives each letter in turn, using the Three Period Lesson. At each stage she asks the child to feel the letters. At the end of the first lesson she gives the child the idea that words are composed of these letters and starts him analyzing words in their component sounds.

Suppose the teacher has taken *c* and *s.* She will say "Can you hear *c* when I say *cat*?" "Can you hear *c* when I say *car*?" "Can you think of any words with a *c* sound in them?" She should do the same with the *s*.

The child takes any letters he knows, traces the form of the letters with two fingers and says the sound of the letters. The teacher gives him more letters as he is ready for them, or he can take any letter and go to her to be shown how to feel and sound it.

He learns to recognize the forms by touch and sight and to know the sounds of all the letters of the alphabet and gains muscular memory of the form of the letters through touch, as a preparation for writing. He begins to understand the composition of words and to analyze them into their component sounds.

If the child's fingers move off the sandpaper, he knows at once by the different texture of the surface. He learns through the three senses: hearing, touch and sight. Great care must be taken when teaching the child to feel the letter to see that he starts where one would normally start in writing and to see that he traces the letter through in the direction of writing. He must keep his fingers on the letter from start to finish except for the dots on the *i* and *j* and the cross on the *t* and *f* (where the script alphabet is used). The simple cursive form of the letters is recommended by Dr. Montessori, but the script ones are also made for those teachers who prefer them.

Script Sandpaper Letters

Sandpaper and velour alphabets are simply letters carefully cut out and pasted on cardboard, pink for vowels and blue for consonants. The child traces the letter outlined with his fingers until he knows it thoroughly. If he slips, he can feel the difference between the sandpaper and the smooth cardboard. Using these alphabets we gained understanding of another Montessori principle—the control of error and the importance of devising means for such control; in other words, those principles which are built into programmed learning.

When this happens, the teacher takes the child's hand and shows him how to follow with his two forefingers the contour of the letter, just as he would do if he were writing it. At the same time she has him pronounce distinctly the sound of the letter.

By the time the alphabet has been taught with sandpaper letters via the three-period lesson, the child has learned to associate the sound of each letter, with the muscular movements necessary to reproduce it.

Variations can be introduced as the child is ready for them—large letters and small letters. Or the child can be blindfolded, so that he learns to recognize the shape of the letters solely by touch. Such modifications and additions, however, will come only after the child has thoroughly mastered the basic exercises and has gained the confidence of achievement.

Indirect Preparation for Writing with the Sandpaper Letters

In working with the sand paper letters, the child is learning to reproduce letter forms through sensory imagery: visual, auditory, tactile, kinesthetic.

> The child sees the letter
> The child hears its letter name as the teacher says it
> The child repeats the word (this auditory feedback is important)
> Tracing the letter with two fingers, the child gets a tactile image
> Tracing the letter while blindfolded adds a kinesthetic image

The sandpaper letters and the movable alphabet help the child develop the skills necessary for handwriting:

    Eye-hand coordination

    Associating letter names with their form

    Associating capital and small letter forms   C c

    Associating type and manuscript form   a a

    Learning similarities and differences in letter forms

                          m n — d b

Developing memory of letter forms through the sensory imagery discussed above.

Actual size of letter, form is 6¾" wide.
For left-handed child reverse letter location.

Introduction to Montessori Language Skills

In the period before reading, the child is being prepared for language skills through the sensorial exercises. The child has been associating **words** with all the sensorial material. Montessori defines reading as, "the interpretation of an idea by means of graphic signs." She suggested that reading must be silent before vocal and that reading aloud requires two mechanisms: articular and graphic.

The movable alphabet exercises follow the sandpaper letter exercises in the period before reading. The movable alphabet thus becomes the appropriate tool for bridging the gap between readiness for writing and the actual command of the use of the pencil.

With the movable alphabet, the child can reproduce words he has read, can form the words he speaks, can compose his own stories and see them before him, can read these stories back as part of his work in reading. He experiences a sense of great achievement as he understands that with these letters he can compose words and sentences that others— his teacher, his parents, his friends—can read, so that he is able to communicate with them via the printed word, which is a badge of acceptance in our society.

FIRST MONTESSORI READING EXERCISES

The first lesson will make use of these materials: 1) phonetic pictures or objects of which the child has been building words with the movable alphabet, 2) the red and blue movable alphabet, and 3) labels and pencil or magic marker.

When presenting the lesson invite a child who can use the movable alphabet to work on this first reading exercise. Bring all the materials to the mat or table and let the child build a phonetic word such as "cat". Continue as follows:

>   1. Let the child read the word "cat" by matching it to its corresponding picture card or model.
>
>   2. Take a blank piece of paper or label, and write the word "cat" on it. (This gives a distinct relationship between the word built and the word written.)
>
>   3. The child reads the label and matches it to his built word, already matched to a picture or model.
>
>   4. The built word is returned to the box (making sure that each letter is put in its proper partition.)
>
>   5. Place the newly written word on the mat and have the child match it without the built word. (Other words may be written on the labels, making sure that they are all phonetic words with which the child is familiar.)
>
>   6. Place three words on the mat and have the child match them to their corresponding picture cards.

Control of error will be automatic when the child:

>1. Sees that the label, when read by the teacher, does not match the model to which he placed it.
>
>2. Sees two different labels under one object.
>
>3. Realizes that the built word does not have the same letters as the written word.
>
>4. Becomes aware of using the movable alphabet for the rest of the labels.
>
>5. At the end of the exercise realizes that the last word does not match the last label.

Direct aims of this exercise are 1) learning to read written words, 2) further practice in sounding words, and 3) further practice in mechanical reading. (Reading and Matching.) Indirect aims are 1) seeing the relationship between the written and built work, 2) vocabulary building, 3) preparation for spelling and writing, 4) giving a motive for activity, and 5) development of abstract concentration.

SECOND READING LESSON

Unphonetic Words: Phonogram Booklets

Materials needed for this exercise are drawers divided into three sections: one for the color coded movable alphabet to be used with the black movable alphabet, another for objects and pictures, and a third for phonogram booklets. The drawers should correspond with the types of phonograms and digraphs to be introduced. All things in the drawer should correspond to one type of sound.

During some activity described in the first reading lesson, and after the child has become familiar with the phonetic words, slip in an object with corresponding label for an *unphonetic* word with the phonetic words, for example, S N A K E. Confronted with the difficulty of matching what he may phonetically read S N A C K, the child will try to place it next to a picture of a snake. Through an inductive discovery the child is lead to see that some words are not pronounced just as the letters sound.

Then pick up the pictures and/or models of plate, cane, vase, rake, skate, and ask the child to name them. Look at them and say the names often, slowly, clearly, to get the sound of the long *a*.

Using the movable black consonants and light blue vowels, begin with the child to build the word working out the rule of long *a* with silent *e*. (The rule need not be articulated.)

At another time or in the same lesson ask the child to think of more words like those he is saying, reading, and matching on the mat. Spell them with the same alphabet. If the child suggests a word such as "train", begin *ai* group or put that off to later period and continue with "save, stake, lace", etc. according to the individual child.

Next pick up the labels and match them to the words made with the movable alphabet to see a printed configuration. (Writing them out on labels would be a good idea, too.)

For testing and further practice put away the movable alphabet, mix the pictures and labels and have the child match them. If the child is fairly successful give him the phonogram booklet with these and more words to read. He could also be given appropriate books if they are available. This form of lesson may be used for all the sounds.

Control of error will come when he hears the unphonetic word does not sound like the name of the picture, or when he sees light blue vowels and hears short sounds.

With this exercise it is hoped he will begin to read unphonetic words.

MOVABLE ALPHABET

The letters for the movable alphabet may be cut from stiff cardboard, or heavy construction paper. Cut out enough vowels to help the child build words. Provide a box or carton with sections so letters can be kept alphabetically. Paint or draw a pattern of the letter on each section of the box to help the child keep the letters in order. The vowels should be in a contrasting color — for example, blue for the vowels and red for the consonants.

With the movable alphabet and pictures or models of objects that have phonetic names invite the child to work with the movable alphabet. He should be already experienced with sandpaper letters and words used frequently before working with the movable alphabet. If necessary, teach the sounds of the movable alphabet in a three-period lesson. Associate sandpaper letters with movable alphabet letters. Bring a few pictures and/or models with the box of letters to the table. Let the child see the letters and give you their sounds. If he wishes, let him pick out letters to look at them.

Present a picture (giving a one word nominal description) or a word to the child. By sound analysis, break it up into its component parts. The teacher then says, "Let's pick out the letters." Take them out, one at a time, and while saying their corresponding sounds, place them on the mat, or directly under the picture, in sequential order. If while working the child does not keep the letters in sequence, do not correct him directly. Continue building more monosyllabic, three-letter words until 10 or more examples of each vowel sound have been built or the child tires. Poly-syllabic words follow.

While performing the exercise the child will be selecting letters one by one from the box and placing the symbol of the sound being heard and repeated on the mat. He will see that the sequence of symbols is from left to right, noticing that the vowels are blue and will realize the word symbolizes, explains, or is a definition of the picture.

The exercise will teach him to analyze a sound and to build words and component sounds. Indirectly he will learn vocabulary and an association of sounds with words as a key to further exploration of words. He will be involved in a preparation for reading, spelling and writing.

A MONTESSORI EXERCISE: The Movable Alphabet

(Photo courtesy of Sunday Sun Magazine, The Baltimore Sun, Maryland, and Montessori Children's House, Baltimore, Maryland.)

A child working with the Movable Alphabet

hat

Actual size of letters of movable alphabet.

ONE OBJECT, ONE NAME

Words are complex units—the elements of thought. Montessori told a story of a retarded child to whom the teacher had just taught the word "book", showing him at the same time a book. She then sent the child into the library to get a book: but the child came back saying, "It isn't there." Evidently he meant the particular book you have just shown me is not there.

He had no idea of a name belonging to more than one object. Indeed the first rule of language is: "One object, one name." We need a special concession to enable us to use the same name for many objects. It is a particularly subtle application of our power to *see similarities in unlike things.*

The retarded child is puzzled since, however alike the objects may be, there are always some differences, for example, the position they occupy in space. Yet often it is more convenient to say "girl" than Mary, and for this a corresponding word lies ready. The normal child makes use of it with unconscious ease, but it remains a difficulty to the retarded child.

LABELLING

"Labelling is the first developmental step of language. ...One study, investigating the ability of normal and retarded youngsters to handle problems with perceptual or linguistic solutions, showed that the retarded did as well as the normal children on problems with perceptual solutions; however, the retarded were clearly inferior to the latter on the language relevant problems."[1]

In teaching the mentally retarded, one should go from the object to the pictorial representation, and then to the symbolic representation. Below is an example.

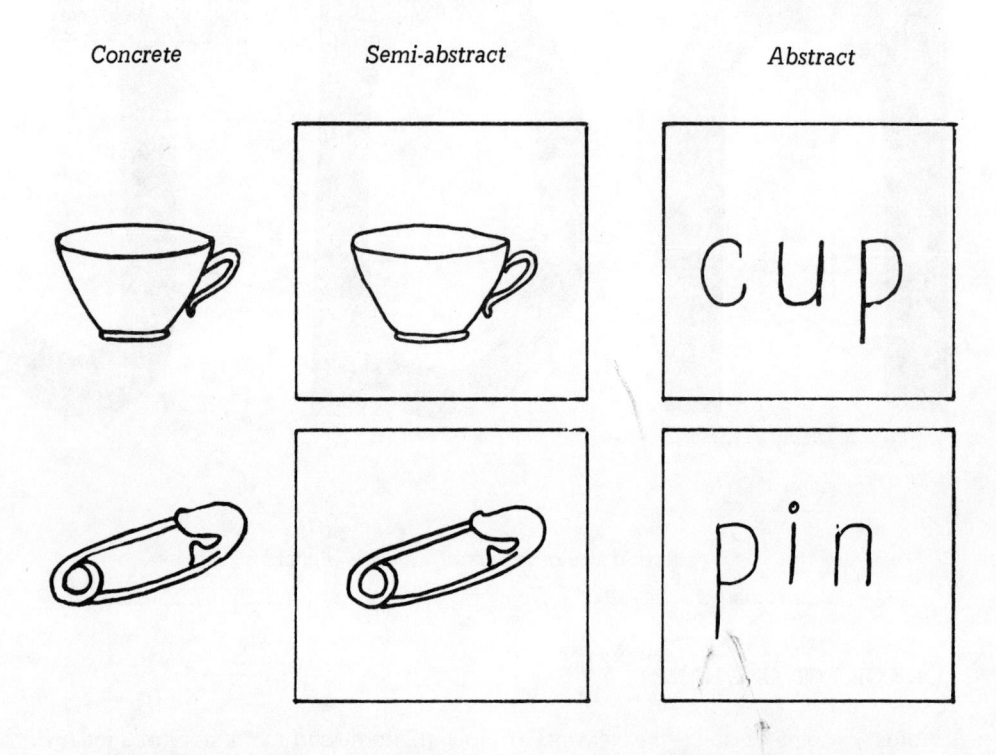

Concrete	Semi-abstract	Abstract

"Children like and remember the classifications, which confirm the idea that it is natural to collect words, and also the need for having mental order based on the sense of the words."[2]

The nomenclature cards are a set of cards with pictures to name. The set may concern transportation. There will be two each of cars, airplanes, trains, bicycles, etc. The picture of the car being represented will be alone on the card so there will not be a driver or a gas station with attendants to confuse the child. This follows the principle of isolation of difficulties.

---

[1]McCarthy, J.L., "The Importance of Linguistic Ability in the Mentally Retarded." MENTAL RETARDATION, 1964, Vol. 2, pp. 90-96.

[2]Montessori, Maria, DISCOVERY OF THE CHILD, Adyar, India: Kalakshetra Publications, 1948.

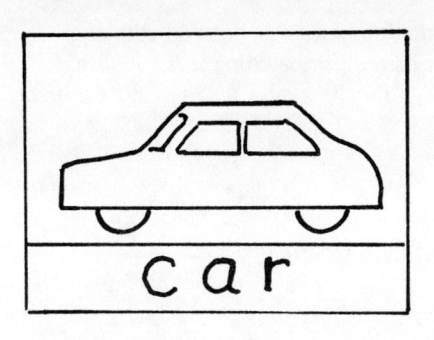

First these pictures without names are matched. When the child can do that, the teacher will give him a set of the same pictures, only this time one of the pictures will have a name and the other will not. The child will match the picture with a name to the one that has no name.

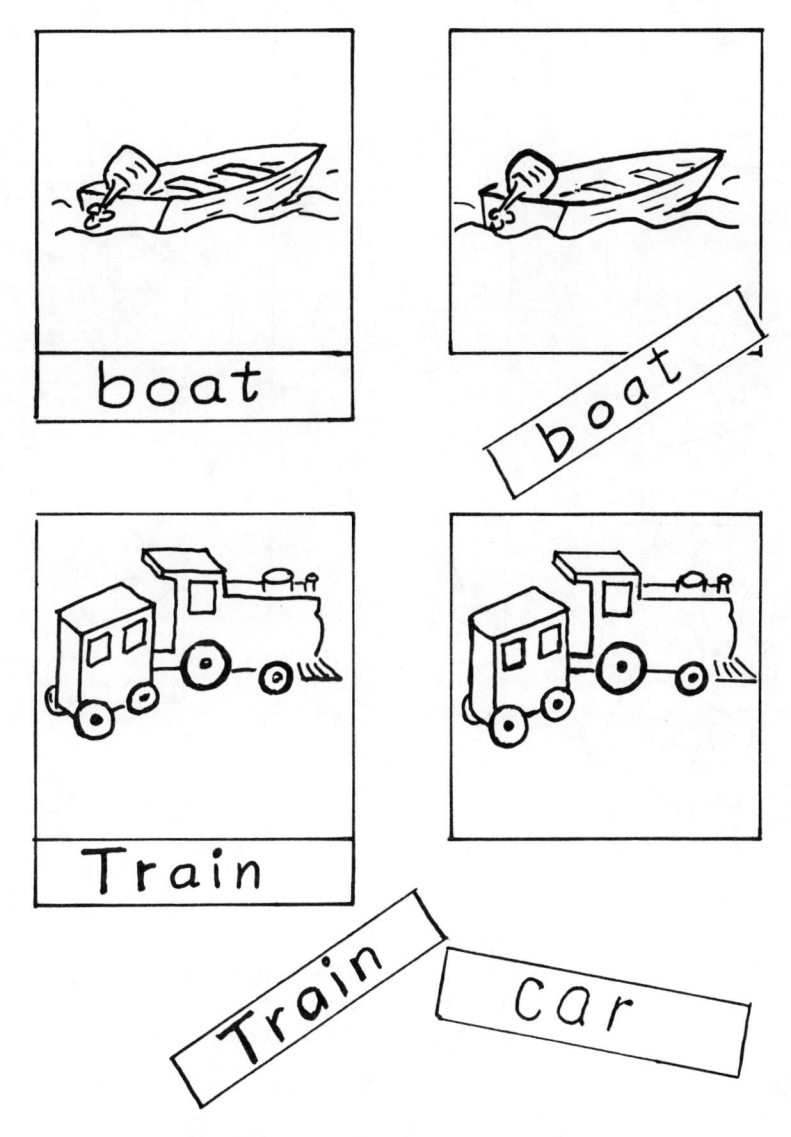

The third set will use the pictures with names and without names, but will add labels which must be placed under the pictures without names for matching with what may be called a control picture with the name.

A MONTESSORI LABELLING EXERCISE

This is another Montessori Labelling Exercise designed to help the child understand that the size of print of a word does not change its meaning and that the size of a drawing does not change the form of the object.

A MONTESSORI MATCHING EXERCISE: Teaching Safety

A LABELLING EXERCISE FOR PERSONAL CARE

This is an exercise to help young or retarded children towards independence in personal care, a task which usually presents some difficulty.

Then the child will have only pictures without names and labels and will try to match them. One can see how the child has learned the names and their configuration through labelling the cards. This may be compared to the method of learning to read by "look and say". This is the theory behind having the child label things in the environment.

As the child progresses and is familiar with more common objects, the teacher may prepare cards of animals, plants, buildings, art cards, musical instruments, the biology of his own body, and any others which seem appropriate. The child could be encouraged to cut pictures from magazines and to label them. The teacher can observe the interests of the child and prepare sets that way.

Through labels, the child's vocabulary and knowledge of his environment will be enriched and this will help him bring a wealth of information to his reading. Reading will be more meaningful and the children enjoy "playing cards." Other games can be played—several sets can be mixed together (for example, transportation and animals), and the pictures can be arranged according to their classification.

(Photo courtesy of Larendon Hall School for Exceptional Children, Denver, Colorado.)

Labelling of concrete objects by a retarded girl.

DEFINITION CARDS

| A   has a long handle and is used to sweep floors |

| A [ ] has a long handle and is used to sweep floors |

| A   has | a long handle | and is used to sweep floors |

| A   has eight legs and spins a web |

| A [ ] has eight legs and spins a web |

| A   has | eight legs | and spins a web |

COMMAND CARDS

The first reading a child is given in the Montessori classroom is the reading of command cards. These cards are also the first full sentences the child is given to read. The teacher knows that the child has fully comprehended the reading by his being able to carry out the command. The teacher should be careful to choose words and commands that the child knows and also that he can obey in the classroom environment. Children test each other and make up all sorts of games with a boxful of command cards. It is their first awareness of how reading can change their situations and relationships. Command cards can also be used to help children with low incentive to do assignments.

> Place your pencil here.

> Put the crayons on the desk.

Single command cards

> Write six words beginning with c.

> Fill in the 100-square paper with numbers.

Single assignment command cards

> Put the chair next to the window.
> Sit down on the chair.

> Paint a picture on the easel.
> Put it on the red table to dry.

Two-commands card *Two-commands Assignment card*

SOUND TABLE

A Lesson Plan for Teaching Phonics

Teach with concrete objects and contrasts first. This exercise should be taught by the three-period lesson.

The following is a week's lesson plan devised for the workshop of one of the mothers participating in the Montessori Workshop in Mississippi. This plan was helpful with the disadvantaged children, but can be used for all children with learning difficulties.

We collected several objects whose names began with the same sound for the sound table. We tried to have one of the objects be something to eat. This helped secure the beginning knowledge of sounds, because it made the language lesson a satisfying experience. The idea to use food is derived from the idea used in speaking, as when we say, "He devoured that book."

The sound we are studying with the children is *t-t-t*. This is the lesson plan for one whole week. We don't care about the *name* of the letter, *tee*, we care about the sound it makes, *t-t-t*, like the beginning sound of *table*.

First, you need a special table, your sound table, painted or covered with a very bright color to attract the children's attention. Nothing should ever be put on the sound table except items starting with the sound you are studying.

Make a letter *T*; four inches high, straight and neat with black on white. Copy, draw or trace a large table next to it. Make sure it looks like a table. Copy one from a library book, if you need to. Fasten this to the wall eight inches above your table. Collect five or six objects that start with the sound *t-t-t*. (For example, tractor, telephone, television, tricycle, tomato, tent, trumpet, turkey, turtle.) Be sure to choose things where there is no chance of making a mistake, there is only one name it could be called. Be sure one of your objects is something to eat.

First Day, Monday

Smile and be friendly, no matter what else you do. Invite a group of about seven or eight children to your sound table. Trace the letter *t* with your finger as if you were writing it. Tell the children that every time they see this mark it will say *t-t-t* like table. Let them do it again and again until all are joining in. Each time the teacher says it with them. Then tell the children that every single thing on this table starts with the same sound, *t-t-t*, like the way *table* starts, *t-t-t*.

Pick up each item. Lift it up as you call its name. After each item say *t-t-t*. Then let the children call each item's name *with* you as you lift it up. If any child wants to name one or more objects alone, *lifting each as he names it,* let him. Then do the whole game again.

Give each child something to eat off the sound table, saying *t-t-t* and the name of the food as you give it to each child. (Tomato is a good food. Give each child a slice.) Tell the children that you will be playing this game again tomorrow. Tell them you still need their help to find more things that start like **table t-t-t** (not **tee**; do not say **tee.**)

Place some objects around the room and find those already there which start **t-t-t.** Be sure you know where at least seven or eight are.

Second Day, Tuesday

Do the whole lesson again, from beginning to end, exactly as you did it yesterday. When you are finished with everything, tell the children you are going hunting for things to go on your sound table, things that start like **table, t-t-t.**

Take the group slowly walking around the room with you. Ask them if glass begins **t-t-t,** then say "No, glass, **g-g-g,** that's **not** the same as **t-t-t.** Let's look till we find something, walk around till you have found all the things starting **t-t-t.**" Let each child carry an item back to the table. Name the items you have found. Name them again as you ask each child to place his object on the table. Give each child something to eat **off the table** that starts with the sound **t-t-t.** Maybe you will give them turnip. Tell them you will play again tomorrow.

Get empty tin cans, two per child and a long piece of string for each. In the bottom of each tin can, punch a hole.

Third Day, Wednesday

Do everything you did Monday, starting with tracing the letter and naming each item and letting the children answer. Tell the children that they are going to make "toy telephones out of tin cans." Have each child take two tin cans and say this as he takes them. Have them also take a piece of string. Tell the children to put a tin can on each end of the string by putting the string through the holes in the cans. Then tie a large knot on each end of the string. Have each child find a partner to talk with on the phone. The children will pretend to call each other and say, "Hello, we are talking on our toy telephones made from tin cans." Give each child his food off the sound table that starts **t-t-t.** (It could be tuna, turkey or even tea. Tea would be especially fun if served like a fancy tea party in dolly cups and saucers.) Make sure he understands you are giving it to him because it starts **t-t-t.**

Make an engineer hat and a conductor's hat out of construction paper.

Fourth Day, Thursday

Do everything all over again like Monday. Then tell the children we are going to make a train, **t-t-train.** The first one who can think of a word beginning with **t-t-t,** as in train will get to be the engineer of the train, the second will get to be the conductor. After these two are chosen give each his cap. The conductor then holds on to the engineer's waist and both chug around the room shouting **t-t-toot, t-t-toot** as they go. Take the children back to the table and give them their **t-t-t** good, toast, or taffy, or tootsie rolls. Ask the children if they can bring something tomorrow from home that starts **t-t-t,** like table, for your sound table.

Trace the large letter *T* on separate squares of paper, one for each child in the group. Use black on white. Trace the table next to the *T* on the same square of paper, so each child will have one. Get sandpaper and make exactly the same letter, the same size, out of sandpaper. Cut it out, one for each child. Get Elmer's glue. Cut out old magazine pictures of things starting with *t*. Make a **book** with empty pages for each child.

Fifth Day, Friday

Ask if any child brought something starting *t-t-t* like table. If anyone did, say the name of the object, and put it on the sound table. If a child brings something, but it doesn't start with the right sound, say the name of it, explain why it is different from *t-t-t* and say, "we will talk about that sound another time, bring this back then, but today we only want things that start like **table,** *t-t-t.* Trace your *T* again. Name each object on the table again. Give each child his book and let him glue in his *T* sign, his sandpaper *T,* and his picture cut from a magazine starting *t-t-t.*

Let each child trace over his *T* with his finger while you watch. Then let him draw a page of the letters, as big as he wants. Collect the books. Tell the children to **t**ip-**t**oe out of the room, **t**ip-**t**oe starts like **t**able. Tell the children to tip-toe back in and the books are returned.

To help children with phonics, using isolation of difficulties, the teacher prepares these cards which the children can copy or the teacher can have mimeographed so that the children can make booklets. They love to use colorful construction paper and the stapler to make their booklets.

The sound to be taught is written in red. The rest of the word is in black. Lists for these phonograms can be found in: MONTESSORI LANGUAGE EXERCISES IN WORD-BUILDING by Sylvia O. Richardson, Montessori Materials Center, Greenwich, Conn., 1962.

ch

chin

children

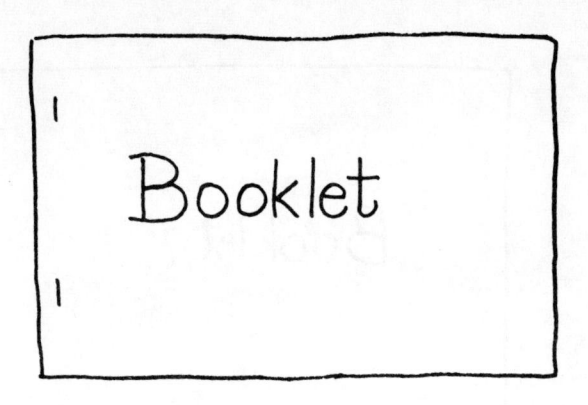

The pages of the first reading booklet are one word, one picture. The first book should be very short, not more than ten pages, so that the child will be sure to finish making it.

Booklet

a small chair

a sand pail

The second booklet is three word phrases with a picture.

My Book

I read my book.

I am going to the store.

A simple sentence with picture comprises the third booklet.

ADJECTIVE GAME[3]

This exercise interests the children who laugh delightedly at the absurd combinations that can be made, and come to realize the necessity of logical agreement between the adjective and noun. The adjectives may be placed logically or illogically with the nouns, e.g., industrious bee, rectangular mother.

Logical use	Metaphorical use	Illogical use
A strong man	A strong heart	A strong house
A thin child		A thin car
A level street	A level head	A level flower
A high building	A high hat	A high girl
A tight spot	A tight wad	A tight school
A small boy	A small person	A small sidewalk
A narrow street	A narrow viewpoint	A narrow lady
A tall book		A tall day
A slow meal		A slow suit
A happy day		A happy sandwich
A long time		A long nickel
sweet butter	sweet heart	A sweet chair
A furry mouse		A furry nose
A cheap hat	A cheap skate	A cheap dream
A short story	A short cake	A short steak
A young child		A young book
A fast driver		A fast package
A hard job	A hard person	A hard pool
pale color	pale face	pale music
A good man	good news	A good page
A low table	the low down	A low dog
A fat girl	fat foods	A fat dress
A tall tree	A tall tale	A tall coat
A wise man		A wise train

This game can also be played as a verbal game for children who cannot read yet.

A Concrete Way of Teaching Adjectives

While teaching of adjectives is difficult, the retarded child needs to know correct usage of a basic list, at least, so that he does not make obvious, embarrassing errors. The following adjectives can be taught in concrete situations by the use of the appropriate Montessori apparatus.

[3]Claremont, Claude A., THE CHEMISTRY OF THOUGHT. George Allen and Unwin Ltd.: London, 1935.

Positive	Comparative	Superlative
broad	broader	broadest
dark	darker	darkest
deep	deeper	deepest
heavy	heavier	heaviest
large	larger	largest
light	lighter	lightest
long	longer	longest
narrow	narrower	narrowest
shallow	shallower	shallowest
short	shorter	shortest
small	smaller	smallest
tall	taller	tallest
thick	thicker	thickest
thin	thinner	thinnest

ALPHABETIZING EXERCISES

Aimed at developing dictionary and encyclopedia skills this exercise will teach the concept of position of a given letter in the alphabet and the concept of alphabetical order. It will also teach the principle of filing, filing by initial letter, and filing words beginning with the same first letter by the second letter. The child will also learn how to use a telephone directory and similar information books.

The materials needed will include small filing boxes, file card, cards with pictures of an isolated object, cards with single words, and cards with one letter.

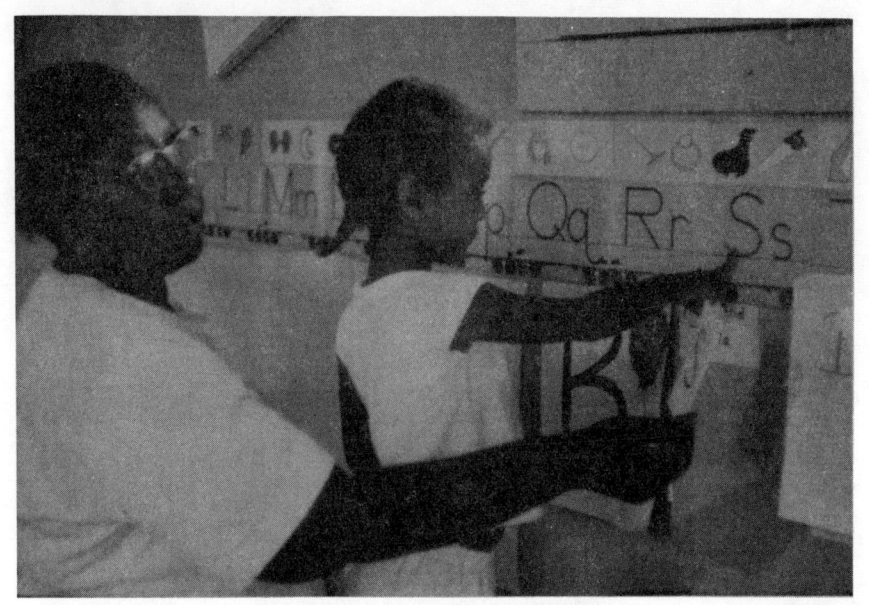

(Photo courtesy of Headstart Program, Pascagula, Mississippi.)

akmg du

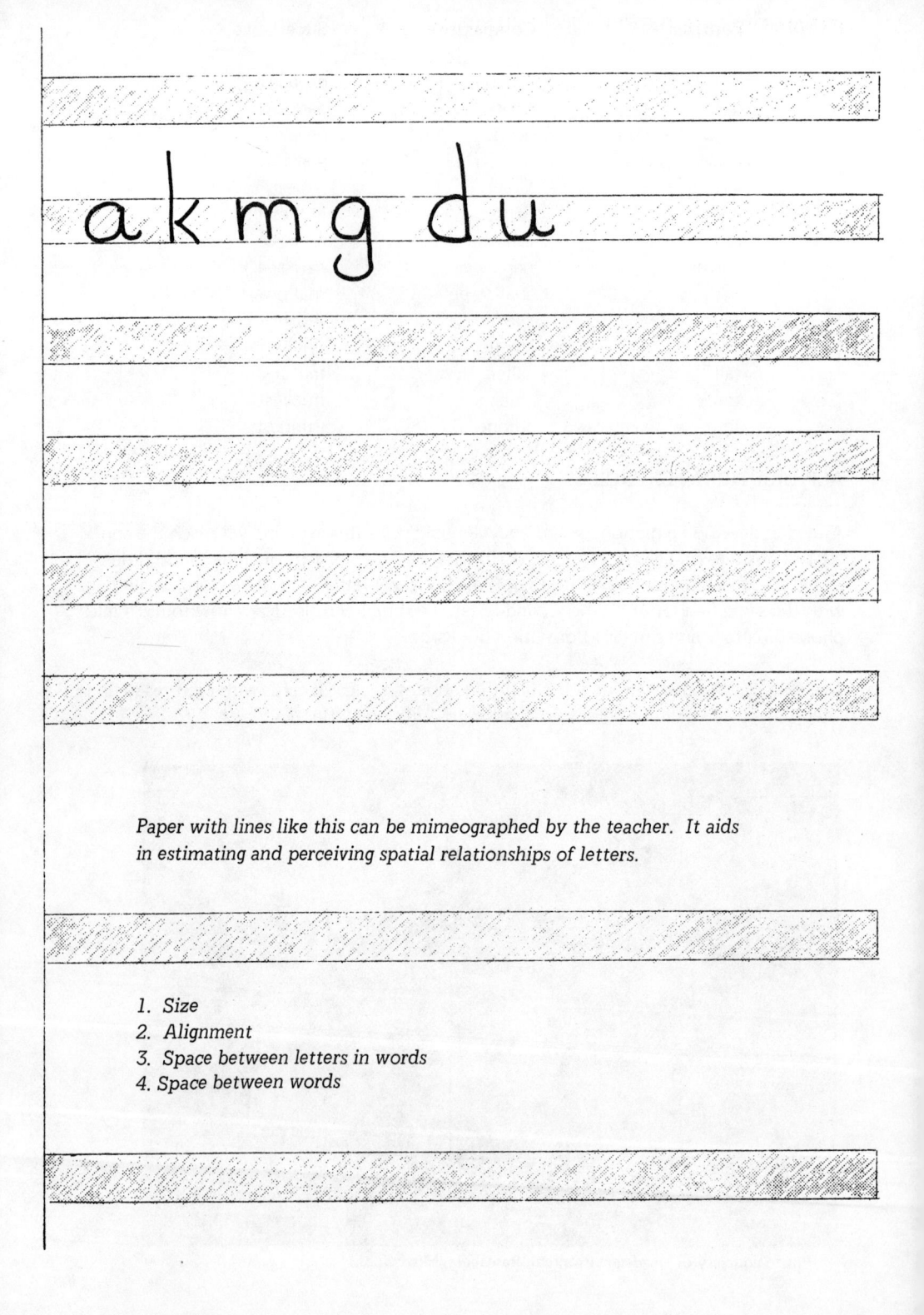

Paper with lines like this can be mimeographed by the teacher. It aids in estimating and perceiving spatial relationships of letters.

1. Size
2. Alignment
3. Space between letters in words
4. Space between words

PRELIMINARY EXERCISE IN ALPHABETICAL FILING

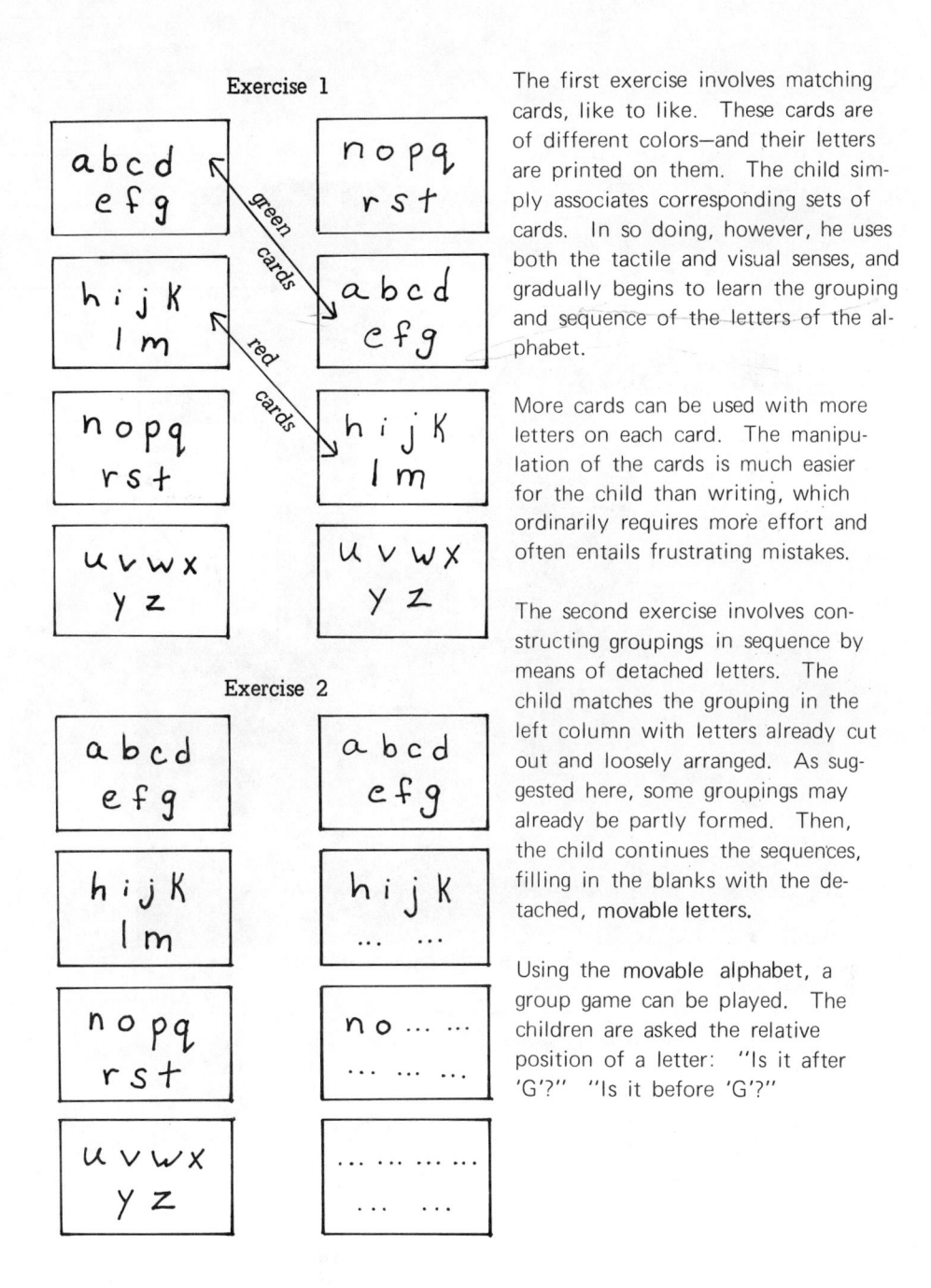

Exercise 1

| a b c d | n o p q |
| e f g | r s t |

green cards

| h i j k | a b c d |
| l m | e f g |

red cards

| n o p q | h i j k |
| r s t | l m |

| u v w x | u v w x |
| y z | y z |

Exercise 2

| a b c d | a b c d |
| e f g | e f g |

| h i j k | h i j k |
| l m | ... ... |

| n o p q | n o ... ... |
| r s t | ... ... |

| u v w x | ... ... |
| y z | ... ... |

The first exercise involves matching cards, like to like. These cards are of different colors—and their letters are printed on them. The child simply associates corresponding sets of cards. In so doing, however, he uses both the tactile and visual senses, and gradually begins to learn the grouping and sequence of the letters of the alphabet.

More cards can be used with more letters on each card. The manipulation of the cards is much easier for the child than writing, which ordinarily requires more effort and often entails frustrating mistakes.

The second exercise involves constructing groupings in sequence by means of detached letters. The child matches the grouping in the left column with letters already cut out and loosely arranged. As suggested here, some groupings may already be partly formed. Then, the child continues the sequences, filling in the blanks with the detached, movable letters.

Using the movable alphabet, a group game can be played. The children are asked the relative position of a letter: "Is it after 'G'?" "Is it before 'G'?"

(Photo courtesy of Larendon Hall School for Exceptional Children, Denver, Colorado.)

Boys practicing card matching exercise.

DEVELOPING LIBRARY SKILLS

Dewey Decimal System

To isolate the difficulties for the slow learner, color coding is suggested in all areas for a quicker orientation to the Montessori classroom or library. Assigning a symbol and color to each classification and carrying it through on the books speeds up finding the book and orderly return of books. It is also a preparation for using public library facilities.

green	000-099	General Works
yellow	100-199	Philosophy
blue	200-299	Religion
red	300-399	Social Science
turquoise	400-499	Language
amber	500-599	Science
orange	600-699	Useful Arts
purple	700-799	Fine Arts
pink	800-899	Literature
brown	900-999	History

A HEADSTART IN READING

In the Montessori system, the environment is prepared for reading just as it is for all other activities. The teacher is faced with remarkable assistance in preparing the environment for reading—but in order to make maximum use of these aids, she must structure them carefully so that the child with learning problems is not overwhelmed by too much information, too many sensory stimuli.

Montessori discovered that her children began to write before they began to read, and Sylvia Ashton-Warner[4] found the same true of her Maori children. Once children are introduced to words with emotional significance for them, they will remember them and want to use them in constructing their own materials for reading.

The basic Montessori apparatus for this stage of development is the movable alphabet, with which children can construct their own stories. Those children who have worked with the sandpaper letters may be able to write brief essays. But even for those children who cannot write because of motor handicaps or slow development, there is a way of introducing them to the joy of reading their own words, for the tape recorder can be used in the structured Montessori classroom in the same way as the movable alphabet is used. The child can read his material into the tape recorder. Someone else can type it and there it is—his own words in front of him, ready to be read.

If an electric typewriter is available and the child can use it, the teacher will be able to offer another valuable way of producing writing. This is especially helpful for older children and those with motor handicaps who can nevertheless strike one key at a time.

There are many records of folk tales and children's classics. If a headphone arrangement can be worked out, children can listen to records of their choice individually; this is helpful to the slow reader who can obtain oral assistance for his aural difficulties. Or the teacher can use the records if she cannot read well. In my own case my accent in English prevents me from being a role model in language so I have not hesitated to use available records as story tellers. Parents with good speech should be persuaded to record favorite stories on tape for storage in a tape library.

Today's teacher has another excellent means of introducing the joys of reading—films and film strips. These are particularly useful when the child associates books with a hated chore or when the culture simply does not include books or book-reading and the child must be introduced indirectly. But they offer pleasure in all classrooms; where the children are familiar with the book, the film gives one of childhood's most pleasant experiences—repetition and familiarity.

For the child without learning problems, this introduction to books should lead further and he will be able to travel on his own road with less and less help once the basic attitudes which govern love of literature have been learned.

The special child may take a long time to attain even minimal reading ability and may remain at that level. However, in our technological age, this is not necessarily a tragedy, for book

---

[4]Ashton-Warner, Sylvia, TEACHER, N. Y.: Simon & Schuster, 1959.

reading can be supplemented with the films and film strips, the records and tapes which extend his senses.

I would like to call attention to the unusual work of Weston Woods Film Studios in Weston, Connecticut. Morton Schindel of Weston Woods has developed a technique for making films and film strips with sound from the actual illustrations of the books themselves. These materials have been received with great joy wherever I have shown them. Not only do these films offer an experience in learning to those who will never be at ease with books but they give delight to parents and children of all ages and prepare the ground for taking the child to a regular film theatre.

Books for young children and for the special child should be chosen with great care. It is commonly thought that Montessori was *against* fantasy and fairy tales for young children and shunned the imagination. This is not the case. Montessori advocated that young children be introduced to books through stories of everyday life because they have great difficulty in distinguishing between reality and fantasy; therefore, fantasy should be postponed until the child is firmly grounded in reality. Then there is ample time for the introduction of the great fairy and fantasy tales.

This wise restriction of Montessori's should be kept in mind when dealing with the special child whose emotional problems or whose strategies for dealing with academic failure may have imprisoned him in a fantasy world he cannot escape, even though he would like to. Montessori did not believe in denying the child his heritage of marvelous tales but only in presenting them at the appropriate stage of his development. With the special child fantasy material should be used sparingly; fearful adventures which the normal child might well take in stride cannot always be digested by the child with learning problems. We do not want to produce nightmares and terrors rather than delight!

Certain other considerations enter into the choice of books for children with specific handicaps. Books where all the pages are stiff board are helpful to the child with a motor handicap. These pages can be cleaned with a damp cloth so the child is able to handle them freely.

Teachers and parents can also make excellent picture books which can be used for teaching object recognition and vocabulary development as well as for enjoyment. Many of our magazines contain excellent photographs both in the editorial and the advertising pages. The best photographs are of one or two clear objects with no distractions. These photographs can be arranged in scrapbooks or photograph albums. If books with heavy pages are needed, they can be made from shirt cardboard with holes punched in it and bright string used to tie the pages together.

Books can be made on general topics—a book of faces, a book of children, a book of seasons, a book of birds, a book of love, a book of holidays, and so on. One or two words lettered clearly to identify each photograph is sufficient. Some pages can be left without words. These books can be covered in scraps of wrapping paper, wallpaper or adhesive paper, following Montessori's ideas about the value of neatness and beauty in the prepared environment. They can become part of the class library and can be taken home by the children. Such books are unusually valuable for the special child as they can be used as the basis for vocabulary development as the teacher and child look at a picture together and the teacher asks: What is that child doing? Do you think he is happy? Is he older than the child on this page? Why is he wearing boots? The picture becomes the concrete object kept for reference in front of the child, just as the Montessori apparatus are the concrete learning materials by means of which the child learns abstractions.

The teaching of love of poetry is part of preparing the environment for reading. There are many simple ways in which this can be done. The Japanese hang small scrolls on their walls with *haiku* poems written on them suitable for the season. On a spring day a teacher might prepare a scroll of paper to unroll between two small sticks with a short poem about spring on it, a poem composed by a child in the class or one copied from a book to give the children inspiration. Scrolls can be prepared not only for the seasons but also to suit changes in the weather.

Poems can be written to music and even danced to music. The writing of poetry is not a chore but a pleasure. If a child does not want to participate, he should not be made to feel ashamed. The poems can be bound in small booklets covered with bright paper, illustrated by the children and kept on the library table. Other small booklets can be prepared of short poems from all languages and traditions, a few poems to a booklet. These the child can handle, carry home in his pocket, learn by heart.

Our society places great emphasis upon literacy. Some reading ability is necessary to obtain and hold a job. Therefore, since we are preparing our children for lives in this society, we should try to teach them to read if this is at all possible. At the same time, teachers and parents must shield the child with learning problems from too much pressure, since the pressure will surely hinder his learning.

These suggestions for preparing the environment are offered with just this in mind. If both indirect and direct preparation for reading are seen as a long-range matter, each step an achievement in itself, with an increase in pleasure as the ultimate aim, we are more likely to discover that all children will read just as well as they are able to not because society demands it of them but because they want to read and cannot imagine their lives without the richness of the book.

Learning to Read in Today's World

After these preliminary Montessori exercises, the next step is the introduction of reading and writing. These are areas of great difficulty for the retarded or late learner and our society places maximum stress upon them.

We can keep in mind the overall purpose of developing a self-concept consistent with accomplishment, by stressing that we all can read, even the small baby can read expressions of warmth, affection, or coldness and dislike. We read expressions on other people's faces, we read weather signs of rain or wind, we read mealtimes in the smell of cooking food.

Then we go on to the reading of other non-verbal signs as the colors of traffic lights or the white stripes that mark crossing places on a street, the flame on a stove or the feel of a radiator that means hot. Properly taught, the exploration of non-verbal reading can prepare the way for expectation of success in reading that begins with alphabet recognition.

Naturally, even with this encouragement, we eventually understand that only a limited success can be expected with socially or mentally retarded people in the area of book reading and that a large part of their information will come from other media.

Reading and Story Telling

Very young children enjoy stories about themselves and their environment. One need not be concerned over repetition since the thrice-told tale is enjoyed even more by the preschooler. They also enjoy stories containing familiar characters. One might also develop stories about places visited, people seen, and things noted. The recall of a trip thus stimulated can contribute to vocabulary development and an awareness of sequences of events.

There are a number of lovely and simple stories which have been published in book form. THE TALL MOTHER GOOSE, for example, has a good selection of the rhymes. It also has the advantage of being easily opened by little hands. It is from classics such as these that the child develops a sense of rhythm and learns the fun of sounds and words which rhyme.

Today's book market and our libraries are full of ingenious and entertaining stories of the world around us. A child can learn about our world and about himself from such stories. Not only will factual information be gathered, but a love of books and a desire to read will be gained by the child.

Since the teacher can frequently best reach a child in the role of the storyteller, it is worth looking more closely into this role and how it functions in a class of children with learning problems.

The Teacher's Role as Storyteller

The teacher, in the role of storyteller, is given the opportunity to project, not a figure of authority who finds so much resistance in many slow learners, but as the vehicle by means of which the story is presented and an experience is shared.

In the experience of hearing a story being told, the child identifies with the characters in the story rather than with the teacher-image and is afforded a group feeling as opposed to a directed learning experience. The proximity of teacher and child in sharing frequent storytelling experiences can help the child accept his role in other classroom activity and activities shared by the other children.

Storytelling, as opposed to reading to children directly from a text, in its informality and the warm quality of a voice that shares an experience rather than merely repeats others' words, creates an atmosphere of cooperative exchange and affords the teacher a flexible tool in gauging reactions and emotional effects in her undivided attention to her audience.

The told story can be creatively recited to fit particular situations or meet restless behavior. It may be cut down to meet the limitations of the child's listening span, and still give the satisfactory experience of a completed story.

Despite the various studies that deal with the great difficulty experienced in developing a sensitivity to acquiring knowledge through listening and hearing, the child exposed to the storytelling experience does react to this device, does form concepts, does form mental pictures, and does partake of this learning experience. He develops good listening habits through practice in listening.

> *We recommend for the training of teachers not only a considerable artistic education in general but special attention to the art of reading ... Our teachers ... should be cultivators of the fine arts. For in our method, art is considered a means to life. It is beauty in all its forms which helps the inner man to grow ....* [5]

Definite behavior changes may be noted in the adoption of certain phraseology by the listeners, common courtesies foreign to their *normal* misbehavior, speech growth, change in cultural standards, acceptance of group responsibilities. None of these are effected by personal experience, but rather, through identification with the characterizations presented in the storytelling sessions. The listener is sensitive to the voice of the storyteller, and copies her tone, range, modulation, calm delivery, and emulates emulates either the character or the storyteller, an impressive recognition that the child is learning by example, is experiencing a change in faulty behavior patterns.

May Hill Arbuthnot[6] provides, in her introduction in CHILDREN AND BOOKS, a fine outline gauge which can be followed in evaluating the experience of children and storytelling.

The Child and His Books

The need for security; material, emotional, and spiritual

The need to belong—to be a part of a group

The need to love and to be loved

The need to achieve—to do or be something worthy

The need to know: intellectual security

Play: the need for change

The need for aesthetic satisfaction

---

[5] Montessori, Maria, THE ADVANCED MONTESSORI METHOD,—THE MONTESSORI ELEMENTARY MATERIAL, Cambridge: Robert Bentley, Inc., 1964. Copyright, 1917 by Frederick A. Stokes Company.

[6] Arbuthnot, May Hill, CHILDREN AND BOOKS, Table of Contents, Part I, Chicago: Scott, Foresman and Company, 1947.

The child's need for security is often met in the happy endings of stories, in the secure feeling that though our hero is beset by seemingly unsurmountable dangers, he will emerge successful and live happily ever after. The feeling of belonging is fostered by the group activity afforded by storytelling, mutually experiencing the hearing of the story, mutually sharing the teacher's time and attention.

Love, the need to love and be loved, is met by the proximity of the group to the teacher and each other, sitting close together with the teacher personalizing the storytelling when this is apropos with special stories for special events in the child's experiences, personal identification with the prowess and experiences of a particular character—"just like Danny did"—self-esteem in recognition by teacher of youngster's *just like* experience, achieving status through this individual identification.

The storyteller in repeating the experience with the same group of children, in getting to know the needs of the group, can bring much information into the story without giving the feeling of a teacher-student relation. She can use storytelling as a link so the children's personal experience in the storytelling situation can lead into knowledge in areas far removed from the limited sphere of interest previously shown by these children.

In seeking to define the role storytelling plays in satisfying the child's need for aesthetic satisfaction, we turn again to CHILDREN AND BOOKS, and the concluding words to Chapter One, where May Hill Arbuthnot treats this need so well:

> ... some poems must be heard and heard again. Some stories must be talked over and listened to while someone who knows and loves them reads(tells) them aloud. Then we catch the theme, savor the beauty that eluded us, and are curiously satisfied. Sometimes with children, we can watch the discovery taking place. Suddenly their faces come alive; there is a stillness about them, a rapt attention, and their eyes shine. They do not say, "This is beauty," but you see that they are moved. For a moment, they are lifted out of themselves. The moment will pass, but they will seek such experiences again.

The storyteller should seek to select the story that will be aimed toward the student with the lowest common denominator for two reasons, to hold the attention of this member of the group and to fill the needs of the other members of the group who in many cases were deprived of this experience in their early years. In this nursery level approach there is created a base on which to build towards the satisfaction of their peculiar needs.

Physical conditions that contribute to the success of the storytelling interlude are the arrangement of the children's chairs in a close circle, preferably in a **special** section of the classroom where **special** things are known to take place; the session timed to take place after a robust physical activity or freeplay recess when a change of pace is called for; and with the child most in need of the physical nearness of the teacher placed next to her in the circle thus giving the opportunity to fill this need. In time the children will be urging the retelling of favorite stories and will contribute their interest to the success of the session.

Certain criteria must be recognized before the storyteller steps into this role. She must have read the story carefully, and retold it to herself. Never try to learn the story by rote or you will stumble, though certain phrases that are essential to the story line should be memorized to give fluency to the presentation. Use a natural voice, a careful choice of words that are understandable to the particular youngsters to whom the story is directed; simple explanations of archaic expressions, that are part of the story-line, for easy acceptance; dramatization where called for; much conversation among the characters. Be very sure that you have enjoyed the story you select and will enjoy retelling it to your audience. Another rule for all performers is, be confident in your presentation, and, further, never, never, wear distracting adornments on your person which will direct the listeners' attention to a realm other than the storytelling situation.

Pellon Plays the Part

Books with colorful pictures, slides that vividly unfold a story are all excellent teaching assistants to the child who can match these aids with abstract thinking, and even better, with personal experience. But it is for the child with deep problems; limited, if any, imagination; and definite lack of personal experience in any but the most confining environment, that we ever seek new means for class presentation of the required curriculum in order to enrich his learning experience.

It has been my experience that flannel board figures cut out of pellon offer great range in utilizing the vast literature available for children, in a most meaningful manner. There is no limit to the type of story that can be so vividly portrayed, and it is strikingly effective in explaining social studies or other subjects to the class.

The commercial material of this type that is available is both costly and too well done. They have too many disturbing colors and extraneous material which are both distracting and confusing to the student with problems.

Let me share with you the ways and means that I have been experimenting with and with which I have had exciting results.

Pellon is available from yard-goods departments in many stores. Buy white, medium weight. A pencil or ball point pen will be needed to copy patterns onto the pellon; a Deco-write pen, a tube type ball point pen available from drug store, hobby or craft shops, and crayons or colored pencils.

Lay the pellon directly over the pattern (coloring books are a fine source of patterns) and copy with pencil or ball point pen. Do **not** use the Deco-write pen yet or your pattern will be ruined. Now put the picture on a paper towel or newspaper and trace all lines with the Deco-write pen. Color it and cut it out. You may wish to cover the picture with wax paper and press with a hot iron. This is optional.

Pellon is very easy to work with. The pattern can be seen through the material, making it easy to copy even complicated pictures. It is light-weight, durable, adheres to flannel or felt, easy to cut out and inexpensive.

One of the most effective uses of these pellon figures was in the study of transportation; the vast variety of trucks that contribute to our daily lives drove across the country to our home on a busy flannel board.

And trees are more than just to climb. Our pellon trees fed us, clothed us, housed us, and provided our reading material.

The student who cringes at the sight of a book, who has experienced so many frustrations through this common learning device that the mere presence of a book fills him with fear and evokes strong reactions exemplified by stubborn and complete resistance to any learning from a book, may very well react positively to the pellon figure approach to learning. I have found this to be so in a number of situations. In addition, when successive experiences with the story figures make them very much a part of the child's repertory and the child is confronted with their duplicates in their original form in a book, the book has provoked no untoward emotion; but, happily, the recognition was of the story characters. The physical form of presentation, the book, was but a secondary and unimportant background for the familiar figure.

In working with children with brain damage or with slow learners, the great need is to remove all distracting extraneous material—to be able to focus on one item, one detail at a time. Here too, pellon figures can be used with much success.

Books and Television

Books can also be made attractive to the slow learner by being linked to experiences he likes, such as watching TV.

Are programs that children watch at home woven into classroom discussions? Just the opposite. Programs that children *should* watch at home are woven into classroom discussions, and may I add, with exciting results. Peter Pan was scheduled for the holiday season during the time period when other stations featured wrestling and westerns and crime, three of the established priority viewing programs. Plans had to be fully developed to break through expected resistance. The story was told, a story with ageless appeal. The record was played with the lilting melodies quickly adopted into the children's repertory; pictures were drawn and gaily painted and amateur theatricals brought out unsung talents—Peter Pan became an integral part of the children's reality and dreams—a potent force that no parent could resist. Wrestling, westerns and crime took a holiday. The results were that this opportunity presented by TV for school and home hand-in-hand participation stimulated the way for other such occasions with the hoped-for results. The happiness that family living, in this instance family participation, has for the children is the most valuable result. The deprived child with parental problems is most directly shown to have favorable reactions—this opportunity to please both his parents and his teachers is a most valuable emotional release. TV at its creative best becomes the media of closer understanding in parent-teacher relationships.

Parents and Teacher Foster Creativity in the Language Arts[7]

The fact that there is no technique, no method for developing creativity in the language

---

[7]Murray, Michele, From the lecture notes. Unpublished paper, Summer 1968, Montessori workshop, sponsored by the Montessori Society of Greater Baltimore, Maryland.

arts argues persuasively for the theory that it is not a subject like chemistry or history—it is more. A genuine love for books implies a certain attitude toward life.

How do we develop this attitude? In no other area of learning is personal relationship more important. Who are we? What is our own attitude toward books? As Montessori knew, children read non-verbal signs with an audacity and genius that is terrifying.

Therefore, we learn and teach, balanced between regard for the child as an individual and our own submission to the beauties of language. Love of literature and language is a continuum, beginning when the baby cannot talk, exploding when language appears and continuing throughout life.

Literature is *not* a guarantee of cultural superiority, gentility, moral uplifting or anything else. It does not promise happiness or goodness. It is not religion. It is not a sign of a special social class. It is not a subject to be grimly mastered.

In our society particularly, we must realize that we begin from scratch. Only a tiny minority of children come from homes where books and reading are taken for granted, where the English language is loved and spoken with pleasure. The fact that so many of our children are second- or third-generation Americans is important, as is the fact that many parents are the first ones in their families to have leisure, to have some money, to be *aware* of books, even if not of their value. But as Montessori said of poverty, this ignorance is also a fruitful condition, for we do not have to erase false ideas but can begin with a white sheet of paper.

Absolute honesty is needed for values are subjective. We use great literary art to find ourselves. This is true of the best children's books, too. There is an important role for the minor books which should not be overlooked. Each person develops according to his needs and a variety of books, like a variety of food, must be provided for his nourishment.

We live in a time of unprecedented development in children's literature, which is a challenge, requiring us to take time to see what is available because the child cannot choose from the enormous mass.

Language is our prison, true, but it is also our liberation, our means of escape from the narrower prison of self. Language makes us human. Our own English language is in a process of frightening deterioration which can be arrested by devoted teaching when children are small. The mass media can be allies or enemies but they cannot be neglected. Marshall McLuhan defines the challenges and the strength and the joy of books which nothing can replace.

Love of Reading

Begin by caring about language—the fun of language. Read to the children every night. If father will do it, this is even better than mother; children frequently do not associate reading with masculine activities. Also, an opportunity for father-child closeness.

Take them to the library as soon as they can go. Let them choose their books. Take out as many as allowed. Go frequently. Read their books. Learn about children's literature.

Take down children's books in dictation. Print in large letters. Let children illustrate them. Bind them as books. Let them feel that they are part of the world of literature, that it is acceptable to verbalize their feelings.

Buy books. This is a consumer-oriented society. If you do not buy books, children will sense that you do not value them. Give books at birthdays and for Christmas. Give books as prizes in school.

Can Language Develop Every Facet of the Curriculum?[8]

Language is taught in all areas, in practical life, in sensorial, in science, in geography, in history and in all the curriculum subjects.

The development of language goes from a labelling stage to a more fully spoken language, to a stage of definition. Then it progresses to a written stage of labelling, and of reading the three stages of definition cards.

Language work usually takes place within a group, and is reinforced through group and individual activities. It is important to do a great deal of group work when teaching language. It is important, also, to remember that motor activity must be a part of the lesson. For instance, with the geometric solids, the teacher can ask the child to "Put the pyramid on the table," or "Put the sphere on the chair," or "Go find the sphere."

The teacher should also examine the depth of experience in each area. What more is there to the science program beyond an experience or two with magnets? The teacher must learn how to enrich the curriculum with simple experiments and experiences, such as watering plants and observing their growth.

The teacher must realize the variety of language that is present in the classroom. The teacher can go beyond labelling and classifying and teach problem solving, discussions, dramatizations, and role-playing. The teacher must not forget the importance of non-verbal communication in the classroom—through painting, and music, through clay and woodworking, and through dance.

An important aspect of the teacher's role is to present information to the child. Her presentation must be lively and at the interest level of the children, so that the children will want to express what they have learned. To do this, she should present new poems, new stories, new songs, each week. If the child is to develop a lively imagination, he must get his ideas from somewhere.

---

[8]Drawn from an unpublished paper given by Elizabeth Stephenson, Director, Montessori Training Institute, Washington, D. C., and Atlanta, Georgia.

THE NUMBER ENVIRONMENT

Developing Mathematical Ability in the Special Child

Montessori was especially ingenious in the mathematical materials she devised. Basing her work on Seguin, she developed a vast array of concrete materials for the teaching of abstractions. This method of working is particularly important for the retarded child and helps to eliminate the child's fear of mathematics.

The special child needs to learn how to operate with numbers in his daily life and in normal social situations. Even simple daily activities, like dialing a telephone or accompanying a parent to the gas station to "fill 'er up" involve knowing place values and the use of large-digit numbers.

Montessori felt that all this could not be accomplished if the study of mathematics was considered beyond the power of the special child. It is natural for man to count and to measure. Numbers are symbols that help us to think; the special child is entitled to learn the use of these tools of thinking just as far as he is able.

The following paper lays the groundwork for an understanding of the value of number.

> *... several basic curriculum characteristics ... should be taken into account in the selection of materials for the mentally retarded: scope, sequence, balance, and general organization.*
>
> *Scope: The mathematical scope of the curriculum should not be limited to the basic number operations. In a recently completed five-year project conducted at the University of Connecticut by Professor John F. Cawley, mentally retarded pupils were successfully taught mathematical concepts in the areas of geometry, arithmetic, set theory, number theory and measurement. Yet a recent survey of teachers from one Wisconsin CESA District revealed that the materials presently being utilized in the mathematical instruction of*

educable mentally retardates were limited in scope to the basic number operations. Many times programs are designed to facilitate the pupil's learning to add, subtract, multiply and divide with speed and accuracy without provision for the development of his understanding of the numerals which he manipulates. Therefore, the scope of mathematics curricula for the educable mentally retarded must not be limited only to the number operations (arithmetic) but must also incorporate areas of learning such as set theory, geometry, number theory and measurement which will provide experience for the child to find meaning in the symbols which represent a number.

Sequence: The order in which the basic mathematical concepts are introduced can also either impede or greatly facilitate the mathematical learning of the educable mentally retardate. Both Gagne et al. (1962) working with normals, and Klausmeier et al. (1958) working with EMRs have shown the importance of the hierarchical structuring of mathematical content which begins at the pupils' level of achievement. Burns (1961) has further pointed up the importance of moving from the most concrete form of a mathematical idea to the more abstract form. Therefore, in the selection of materials for the EMR, the achievement level of the pupil must be determined and materials selected which begin at that level and proceed in a concrete to abstract hierarchical development from that point on.

Balance: Mathematics curricula selected for the mentally retarded should have proportional coverage among the various topics and areas of mathematics. Although a large amount of time should be allotted to number operations, unlimited amounts of time spent in this area is somewhat futile without proportionate time allotments in the development of ideas such as cardinality, face value, and place value of numerals. It is meaningless to present the symbols, 175 + 268 = ? to a pupil who as yet has no concept of the numbers these numerals represent.

General Organization: The general organization of the mathematical topics and areas in the curriculum has also been found to be a critical factor in affecting mathematical learning (Armstrong, 1968). A spiral form of organization around topics or areas systematically repeats the development of the mathematical ideas and extends and expands these ideas by using multiple and varied examples. The EMR requires both repetition of presentation and review of earlier presented ideas in both old and new contexts if he is to learn and retain certain basic mathematical concepts. Therefore, the spiral form of organization is another characteristic which complements the needs of the EMR, and thus better facilitates his mathematical learning.[1]

[1] Armstrong, Jenny R., "Mathematics Curriculum for the Mentally Retarded," THE WINNOWER, Winter 1968, Vol. 4, No. 2, A Publication of the Special Education Instructional Materials Center, University of Wisconsin.

The following report was given at a Conference of Mathematics Education and was designed with the idea that children have unlimited intellectual abilities, most notably in the area of mathematics. This is modern support of Montessori's idea and in accord with her practice of teaching the concepts of numbers to young children and not merely the arithmetic operations.

Experiences with numbers using concrete objects which can be counted, measured, and arranged in various ways should have a prominent place in the first years of school.

These early experiences can be surprisingly creative, can involve the child actively, and can deal with matters of honest mathematical merit.

... The work with real numbers ... can be closely related to work in "science" and "application," such as:

1) Measurement and units in cases of length, area, volume, weight, time, money, temperature, etc.

2) Use of various measuring instruments, such as rulers, calipers, scales, etc.

3) Physical interpretations of 1/2, 1/3, 1/4, 2/3.

4) Physical interpretations of negative numbers in relation to an arbitrary reference point as $0°$ Centigrade, or altitude at sea level, or the lobby floor of an elevator, etc.

5) Physical embodiments of inequalities in length, weight, etc., again using games where the child must use the transitive property, or the fact that $a > c$ implies $a + b > c + b$.

6) Estimating orders of magnitude, with applications related to physics, economics, history, sociology, etc.

7) Visual display of data on Cartesian coordinates, such as recording growth of seedlings by daily measurement of height, or graph of temperature vs. time for hourly readings of a thermometer.

... In the nursery school, K-2, and, indeed, at all elementary school levels, the present suggestions assume a general pattern of pre-mathematics to introduce each new topic, to be followed later by as much formal study as may be appropriate. The pre-mathematics at each level will serve to provide a background of experiences, and to help develop clear concepts for the work of the following months or following years. Nearly all the preceding suggestions for K-2 fall under the general heading of "pre-mathematics." (Probably "pre-mathematics" and "formal mathematical study" are not dichotomous categories, but extremes on a continuous interval, with increasingly detailed "informal" study leading gradually into "formal" study.)

A comment might be made on the role of physical equipment in the earliest grades. Whether one thinks in terms of the pre-mathematical experiences that are embodied in the manipulation of physical materials, whether one regards these physical objects as aids to effective communication between teacher and child, or whether one regards them as attractive objects that increase motivation, the conclusion is inescapable that children can study mathematics more satisfactorily when each child has abundant opportunity to manipulate suitable physical objects. Possible candidates include blocks, compasses, French curves, circles divided into equal sections, graph paper, paper ruled into columns, to help the child line up digits in colmn addition, geometric shapes cut out of wood or heavy cardboard, pebbles for counting, numerals cut out of wood or cardboard, circular protractors, and so on.

One important general principle appears to be this: wherever possible, the child should have some intrinsic criterion for deciding the correctness of answers, without requiring recourse to authority. In the present work, this bed-rock foundation is generally provided by the fundamental operation of counting. The child's slogan might well be: When in doubt, count!

. . . Clearly, counting and guessing both have important roles to play, and should be neither excluded from the curriculum nor unduly restricted. Rather, they should be put in their proper place.

. . . In the general area of problem solving, the primary emphasis should be on understanding the problem, with secondary emphasis on carrying out the calculations to get the "answer". For example, after the concept of multiplication has been studied, it is appropriate to consider problems involving multiplication of large numbers, even though the actual computations appearing are beyond the logarithmic skill of the pupil. (They would, presumably, be carried out by the teacher or with the aid of a desk calculator.) When computing machines of all sizes are widely available, surely it is more important to know when to multiply than how to multiply.

Geometry is to be studied together with arithmetic and algebra from kindergarten on. Some of the aims of this study are to develop the planar and spatial intuition of the pupil, to afford a source of visualization for arithmetic and algebra, and to serve as a model for that branch of natural science which investigates physical space by mathematical methods.

The earliest grades should include topics and experiences like these:

1) Identifying and naming various geometric configurations.

2) Visualization, such as cutting out cardboard to construct 3-dimensional figures, where the child is shown the 3-dimensional figure and asked to find his own way to cut the 2-dimensional paper or cardboard.

3) The additive property of area, closely integrated with the operation of multiplication.

> 4) Symmetry and other transformations leaving geometrical figures invariant. The fact that a line or circle can be slid into itself. The symmetries of squares and rectangles, circles, ellipses, etc., and solid figures like spheres, cubes, tetrahedra, etc. This study could be facilitated with mirrors, paper folding, etc.
>
> 5) Possibly the explicit recognition of the group property in the preceding.
>
> 6) Use of straightedge and compass to do the standard geometric constructions such as comparing segments or angles, bisecting a segment or angle, etc.
>
> 7) Similar figures, both plane and solid, starting from small and enlarged photographs, etc."[2]

Following are from "Maria Montessori's Contribution to the Cultivation of the Mathematical Mind."[3]

> ... the absorption of mathematical knowledge can be natural, easy and a source of joy: the joy of one who discovers in himself powers that he had not even suspected.
>
> It must be kept in mind that Dr. Montessori's experiences were not limited to one school or to one nation. They showed that children of all races in the most varied cultural environments, even very primitive ones, arrived at the same knowledge more or less at the same age.
>
> This seems to imply, as Dr. Montessori stated, that the child of man is endowed with a mathematical mind and that in developing it nature follows a definite pattern.
>
> Also that the outer expressions of this mind can be conquered by the child as easily as it conquers language. That this may occur, however, it is necessary that the same attitude as humanity has assumed for language, be assumed for mathematics: that is to provide the children with means, possibility of experiences and the facility to absorb them in their own way.
>
> This, according to Dr. Montessori, is not by means of direct lessons. At first the knowledge is absorbed subconsciously and it remains subconscious until the engrams have done their work of building and organizing. It is they that then bring it to the full light of consciousness.
>
> 1) Dr. Montessori was not interested in teaching children any particular subject. So she did not specially try to teach mathematics. Her interest was in the child itself and the task she imposed on herself was to try to discover the process of the natural development of the child in its various aspects.

[2] GOALS FOR SCHOOL MATHEMATICS, Cambridge Conference on School Mathematics, Educational Services, Inc., Watertown, Mass., 1963.

[3] Montessori, Maria M., "Maria Montessori's Contribution to the Cultivation of the Mathematical Mind," International Review of Education, International Montessori Congress, 1960.

2) She prepared an environment which contained objects the use of which caused children to arrive at an abstraction.

3) The children were of mixed ages, 3 years at least, and the different groups (three to six, six to nine, etc.) were in communicating rooms so that the children could circulate from one to the other.

4) There was no time-table as far as subject-teaching was concerned so that children could remain practising the same subject an indefinite length of time. This gave them the possibility of storing a subconscious knowledge which culminated into a conscious realization at a certain moment.

5) Abstraction was the result of individual experience and the time involved in reaching it varied with the individuals.

6) The interest in the exercise was determined not by the efforts of the teacher, but by the sensitive period of the child.

7) The apparatus she gave the children contained either an indirect preparation for something to come in the future, or the possibility of bringing into the light of consciousness certain items which the child already possessed in the subconscious.

8) The apparatus analysed complex items into their elements so that each stood out isolated from the others and therefore very clear.

The first sonscious step into arithmetical knowledge was — and still is — learning numbers up to ten with 10 square prisms whose lengths vary from 10 cm. to 1 m. and are subdivided by two alternating colours into equal sections of 10 cm. Later the child is given written symbols from 1 to 9 cut out in sandpaper to enable thim to feel and acquire the muscular memory of their shape and in a final step the child associates symbols and corresponding rods.

Nathan Altshiller Court has written:

> There is little in mathematics that ever becomes invalid, and nothing ever gets old . . . the first written symbols for numbers were, naturally, sticks: One stick, two sticks, three sticks and so on, to represent "one," "two," "three," etc.[4]

The following description using sticks is one of the many Montessori mathematical materials which is easy to construct and the most helpful piece of apparatus in the development of the mathmetical mind in the preschool child and in the slow learner.

THE NUMBER RODS

The number rods are a series of thin wooden sticks of the same thickness (square cross

[4]Court, Nathan A., MATHEMATICS IN FUN AND IN EARNEST, N. Y.: Mentor Books, 1958.

section) but differing in length, the second one being twice as long as the first, the third three times as long, and so on, the tenth ten times as long. Montessori designed them in the metric system — the first rod is 1 dm x 2 cm x 2 cm, the tenth 1 m x 2 cm x 2 cm. The rods are marked off into units, alternately colored red and blue. Rod one is red, two is red and blue, three is red-blue-red, and so on. They are the fundamental units of material purposefully designed for developing number concepts.

The children use the rods for various manipulations: counting them, comparing them, putting two of them together and finding them equal in length to a third rod or to another pair; forming them into "steps" by putting them side by side, or into a long line by putting them end to end for serial counting. When the rods have become familiar to the children, they can easily be linked with the number symbols by putting cards with the numbers printed on them to go with the proper rods.

The following concepts may be grasped through use of the rods:

    1. Quantitative relationship (with each rod in relation to the other)

    2. Concept of position in space (by organizing the rods into steps or long rows)

    3. Concepts involved in measuring (the two-rod is twice as long as the one-rod, and so on — the rods can be used as measuring sticks)

    4. Concept of a number as an aggregate of ones (the child can verify this by counting with the aid of the colors)

    5. Concept of number as a whole (the rod of four, for example, is a whole but can easily be broken down into ones by serial counting)

    6. Concept of the number symbol (by placing the number symbol next to the equivalent rod)

    7. Concept of number in sequence (serial counting of the rods, either up to ten, or if arranged in one long line, up to fifty-five)

    8. Concept of fraction (the five-rod, for example, is half of the ten-rod)

    9. Concept of addition (putting together two rods, comparing with a third, for example, three-rod and two-rod as long as five-rod. This has the additional value that the numbers of wholes are added rather than the aggregates of ones — for instance, $3 + 2 = 5$ is not derived from $(1 + 1 + 1) + (1 + 1) = 5$.

    10. Concept of subtraction (analogous to addition)

The rods have one distinct advantage over other material: At a time when big muscle movement is still very important and sitting at a table quite unnatural, work with the rods on a mat or the floor fits the pre-schooler's needs. The relatively large dimensions of the rods make the step from unit to unit very marked; thereby progression is made clear.

Some Exercises with the Red and Blue Rods

To understand the following instructions the teacher actually must work out each step in each process before introducing it to the children.

The use of the Red Rod in the Sensory Apparatus has prepared the way for the number rods. The difference between the two sets is that the Red Rods are all the same color, while the number rods are divided into two distinctive colors — rod 1 is painted red; rod 2 (which is twice the length of rod 1)has its two sections painted respectively red and blue; the three sections of rod 3 are red, blue, red. At the beginning, only these 3 rods are presented to the child.

The Three-Period Lesson

The teacher must be on the same side of the mat as the child, when giving the lesson. During the first period place rod 1 on the left hand side of the mat and rod 2 close behind it with its red end on a level with that of rod 1. Place rod 3 exactly behind rod 2. Show the child how to put the index and the middle finger on rod I and say — "This is *one*." Move the same fingers from the red section to the blue section on rod 2, saying, "One, two, — this is *two*." Show the section of rod 2 in the same way, allowing the fingers to rest on each section, while repeating "One, two, three, — this is *three*."

In the second period ask the child to touch each section while counting. "Give me rod *two*." "Give me rod *one*." "Give me rod *three*."

For the third period ask, "What is this?" (pointing to rod 3) "What is *that*?"

When the child can easily distinguish one rod from another, add rod 4, and gradually the rest of the rods, according to the readiness of the child. Be sure that the child touches carefully each section of the rod. All the red ends should be together at the left-hand side.

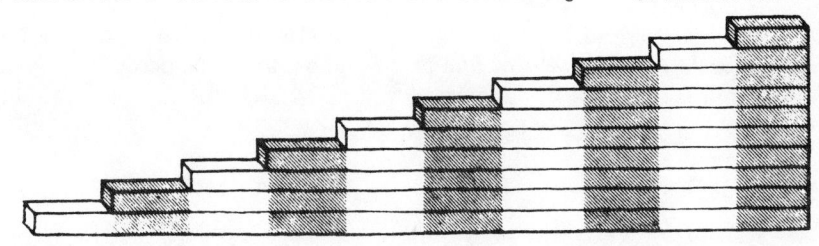

When the child can then place the 10 rods accurately in position and name, place each of the sandpaper numbers on its respective rod. Ask the child to trace over the sandpaper figures several times with his fingers before putting them into position.

If the child does not know all the symbols, begin with three numbers only, adding the others gradually, until the ten rods can be easily placed in position.

Addition to Ten

When the rods are arranged in order from 1 to 10, separate them slightly from one another, and place figure 10 in the middle of rod 10. Take rod 1 with its figure and place it quite close to rod 9 and show the child that these united rods are equal in length to rod 10. Count the divisions of rods 9 and 1 together and show that they form 10. Place rod 2 with its figure beside rod 8 making another length equal to 10. Count the 8 and 2 together and show the child that the result is 10. Treat 3 and 7 and 6 and 4 similarly, and show that 5 is exactly the half of 10. Build up the following additions and introduce the signs plus (+) and equals (=):

9 + 1 = 10	6 + 4 = 10
8 + 2 = 10	5 + 5 = 10
7 + 3 = 10	

If the child can write the numbers, ask him to write these addition facts, or prepare small slips of paper where the child will only have to write the answer:

9 + 1 =	6 + 4 =
8 + 2 =	5 + 5 =
7 + 3 =	

Subtraction

Arrange the ten rods. Take rod 4 from rod 10 and rod 6 remains. Take rod 3 from rod 10 and rod 7 remains. Take rod 2 from rod 10 and rod 8 remains. Take rod 1 from rod 10 and rod 9 remains.

Introduce minus sign (−):

10 - 1 = 9	10 - 4 = 6
10 - 2 = 8	10 - 5 = 5
10 - 3 = 7	

Addition of nine, eight, seven, six, five, four, three, two follows as described in the addition of 10; the back rod will always be that of the number to be composed:

8 + 1 = 9	7 + 2 = 9
7 + 2 = 9	6 + 3 = 9
6 + 3 = 9	5 + 4 = 9
5 + 4 = 9	4 + 5 = 9
	3 + 6 = 9

Give various examples of Addition and Subtraction with the rods. Each rod represents the quantity of unity for which it stands, thus showing that a unit can be represented by a *single* object — number five is represented by a single object, rod 5, of which the five distinct and equal parts can be easily seen by the child.

Number Rods for Learning Spatial Relationships

In the preliminary work with the number rods, building the stairs, the child is discovering the spatial relationships of the rods. The child is then introduced to the vocabulary of these relationships:

Give me the *smallest* rod.

Give me the *shorter* rod.

Give me the *shortest* rod.

Which rod is *larger?*

Which rod is *smaller?*

Prepositional relationships are also taught with these rods, using the three-period lesson:

Place 6 rod above 10 rod.

Place 4 rod below, over, beside, before, after . . . .

Each unit is a *whole.* The progression in counting in the serial order is made clear by the child's moving in counting. The rods are easier to count than loose small objects. The rods offer a concrete basis for the development of abstractions, necessary in number work, by highlighting the concreteness but detaching it at the same time from familiar objects of the environment.

While the rods are not as abstract as a spoken or written number but are real things which the child can perceive and handle, they are not of the nature of concrete objects that occur ordinarily in the child's experience, such as toys or coins. The rods, therefore, form a bridge to the higher level of abstraction represented by the number symbol. Making this next step by use of printed cards obviates reading from the blackboard or writing and brings the symbol down to a more concrete level by enabling the child to handle it by touching or placing the card, or by tracing the symbol with his fingers.

(Photo courtesy of Montessori Workshop, Natchez, Mississippi.)

The children possess all the instinctive knowledge necessary as a preparation for clear ideas on numeration. The idea of quantity was inherent in all the material for the education of the senses: longer, shorter, darker, lighter. The concept of identity and of difference formed part of the actual technique of the education of the senses, which began with the recognition of identical objects, and continued with the arrangement in gradation of similar objects. I will make a special illustration of the first exercise with the solid cylinder inserts, which can be done even by a child of two and a half. When he makes a mistake by putting a

SANDPAPER NUMBERS

(See instructions for making sandpaper letters)

cylinder in a hole too large for it, and so leaves *one* cylinder without a place, he instinctively absorbs the idea of the absence of *one* from a continuous series. The child's mind is not prepared for number "by certain preliminary ideas," given in haste by the teacher, but has been prepared for it by a process of formation, by a slow building up.

SANDPAPER NUMERALS

In the material there is a box containing smooth cards, on which are gummed the figures from one to nine, cut out in sandpaper. These are analogous to the cards on which are gummed the sandpaper letters of the alphabet. The method of teaching is always the same. The child is *made to touch* the figures in the direction in which they are written, and to name them at the same time.

The teaching of the actual figures marks an advance from the rods to the process of counting with separate units. When the figures are known, they will serve the very purpose in the abstract which the rods serve in the concrete; that is, they will stand for the *uniting into one whole* of a certain number of separate units.

The *synthetic* function of language and the wide field of work which it opens out for the intelligence is *demonstrated*, we might say, by the function of the *figure*, which now can be substituted for the concrete rods.

The use of the actual rods alone would limit arithmetic to the small operations within the ten or numbers a little higher. In the construction of the mind these operations would advance very little farther than the limits of the first simple and elementary education of the senses.

To enter directly upon the teaching of arithmetic, we must turn to the same didactic materials used for the education of the senses.

Let us look at the three sets of material which are presented after the exercises with the solid insets, i.e., the material for teaching *size* (the pink tower), *thickness* (the broad stair), and *length* (the red rods).

There is a definite relation between the ten pieces of each series. In the material for length the shortest piece is a *unit of measurement* for all the rest; the second piece is double the first, the third is three times the first, etc., and, while the scale of length increases by ten centimeters for each piece, the other dimensions remain constant (i.e., the rods all have the same section).

The pieces then stand in the same relation to one another as the natural series of numbers 1, 2, 3, 4, 5, 6, 7, 8, 9, 10.

In the second series, namely, that which shows thickness, the length remains constant while the square section of the prisms varies.

(Photo courtesy of Larendon Hall School for Exceptional Children, Denver, Colorado.)

"Is it because he can't learn, or I can't teach him?"
*Roy McGlone, Head Instructor,
Larendon Hall School for
Exceptional Children.*

ISOLATION OF DIFFICULTIES IN ARITHMETIC

To help children with poor motor coordination to practice the four basic operations of arithmetic, small sizes of addition, subtraction, multiplication and division tablets can be mimeographed so that the child need only give the answer, cutting down on the drudgery of copying. The guilt feeling of making a mistake and thus wasting paper is eliminated by using small pieces of paper and having the columns already written. This economy of time and emotional investment enhances the child's desire to learn. Color coding helps to focus attention on the arithmetical table to be learned.

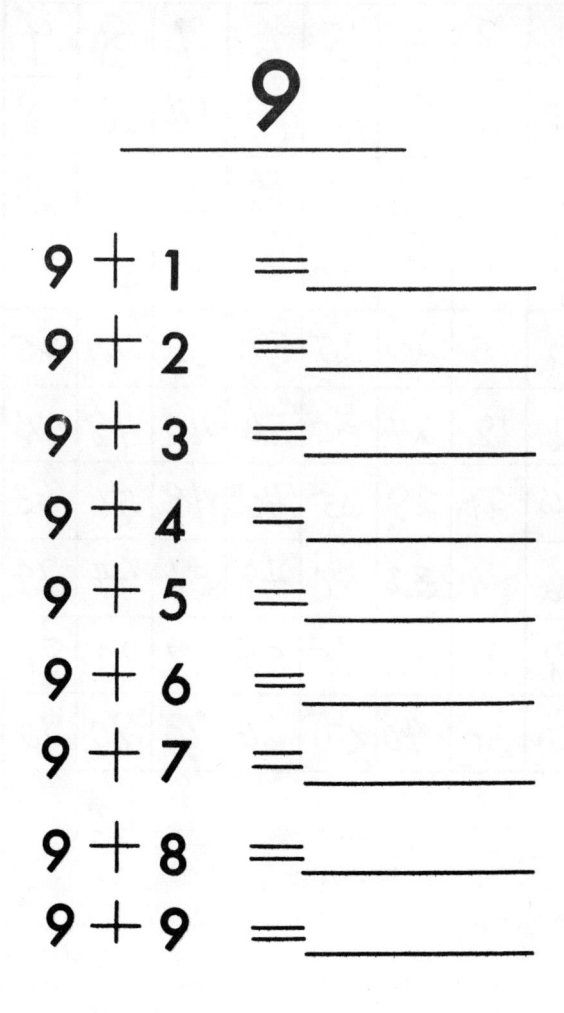

$$9$$

9 + 1 = _____
9 + 2 = _____
9 + 3 = _____
9 + 4 = _____
9 + 5 = _____
9 + 6 = _____
9 + 7 = _____
9 + 8 = _____
9 + 9 = _____

Actual size. Nines are printed in red.

THE TABLE OF PYTHAGORAS

This table is used as a control chart for children working with multiplication tables on "100 square" paper. With this check, the child can correct himself and thus gain independence and learn researching and self-checking habits. "100 square" paper may also be used for rhythmical counting.

1	2	3	4	5	6	7	8	9	10
2	4	6	8	10	12	14	16	18	20
3	6	9	12	15	18	21	24	27	30
4	8	12	16	20	24	28	32	36	40
5	10	15	20	25	30	35	40	45	50
6	12	18	24	30	36	42	48	54	60
7	14	21	28	35	42	49	56	63	70
8	16	24	32	40	48	56	64	72	80
9	18	27	36	45	54	63	72	81	90
10	20	30	40	50	60	70	80	90	100

Preparing charts with the basic operations, where the answers are given allows the child to go back and check his own answers of multiplication, addition, or subtraction facts. These charts should be easily accessible to the child to eliminate the insecurity of not knowing and not being sure of the right answer, and will not reinforce mistakes in the child's mind. Picture dictionaries and other informational books should be available. Rather than telling the child the answer, if he learns to handle reference material, he will be trained to more independent learning. This is of great importance in our expanding technological and scientific knowledge, where new words are coined every day and it is impossible for anybody to be a walking encyclopedia.

MULTIPLICATION CHARTS

1x1 = 1									
2x1 = 2	2x2 = 4								
3x1 = 3	3x2 = 6	3x3 = 9							
4x1 = 4	4x2 = 8	4x3 = 12	4x4 = 16						
5x1 = 5	5x2 = 10	5x3 = 15	5x4 = 20	5x5 = 25					
6x1 = 6	6x2 = 12	6x3 = 18	6x4 = 24	6x5 = 30	6x6 = 36				
7x1 = 7	7x2 = 14	7x3 = 21	7x4 = 28	7x5 = 35	7x6 = 42	7x7 = 49			
8x1 = 8	8x2 = 16	8x3 = 24	8x4 = 32	8x5 = 40	8x6 = 48	8x7 = 56	8x8 = 64		
9x1 = 9	9x2 = 18	9x3 = 27	9x4 = 36	9x5 = 45	9x6 = 54	9x7 = 63	9x8 = 72	9x9 = 81	
10x1 = 10	10x2 = 20	10x3 = 30	10x4 = 40	10x5 = 50	10x6 = 60	10x7 = 70	10x8 = 80	10x9 = 90	10x10 = 100

ACTUAL SIZE: 15 x 6½ inches

THE NUMBER CHART AND NUMBER GAMES

1	2	3	4	5	6	7	8	9	10
11	12	13	14	15	16	17	18	19	20
21	22	23	24	25	26	27	28	29	30
31	32	33	34	35	36	37	38	39	40
41	42	43	44	45	46	47	48	49	50
51	52	53	54	55	56	57	58	59	60
61	62	63	64	65	66	67	68	69	70
71	72	73	74	75	76	77	78	79	80
81	82	83	84	85	86	87	88	89	90
91	92	93	94	95	96	97	98	99	100

The number chart should be made on "100 square" paper. It can be mimeographed or dittoed and handed out to the children which releases the children from the strain of copying the whole number chart. These charts are particularly good for a child with poor motor co-ordination.

Many games can be played with this chart and create in the children a feeling that numbers can be fun. Children may choose a colored pencil to circle the numbers. The teacher can make up games to be played such as the following:

> Circling the times tables. For example, by circling the 2 Times Table, the child can begin to see and understand that the 2 Table is really adding two to the previous number. Patterns begin to emerge. The 2 Times Table creates columns and the 3 Times Table creates diagonals. Children are helped to fix a visual image of the multiplication tables with a minimum of effort.
>
> Finding even and odd numbers using, for instance, a red and a blue pencil and observing the emerging pattern.
>
> Add a zero to each number to multiply by ten to show that a new number chart will develop just by adding a zero.
>
> Counting by fives or tens and circling the numbers with a colored pencil.
>
> Match the numbers with real or play money.

The teacher may devise some other number games with these charts. Playing the foregoing number games familiarizes children with numbers and quantitative concepts in an atmosphere of fun. Fear of numbers can thus be eliminated.

DEVELOPING NUMBER MEMORY

A Counting Game

Numbers from 0 to 10 are written on slips of paper. The slips of paper are then folded and placed on a tray or in a box.

Each child takes a paper from the tray. He looks at it and remembers the number which is written on it. He tolds the paper again and places it on his desk. Then each child goes anywhere in the room to collect the number of beads, or counters or spindles which is written on his paper. He brings them back to his desk.

The teacher comes around to each child, and he reads aloud his numeral and counts his objects.

A Memory Game

Eleven children can play this game at one time. Needed are 11 small cards with the numbers 0 through 10, and 11 red wooden numbers of 0 through 10.

The children sit on the floor. The wooden numbers are scattered on the table. Each child picks a card from the box, looks at it, closes it, and keeps the number in his mind.

The child then goes to the table, chooses his numeral, and returns to his place with the numeral in front of him on the floor. After all the children have selected their numerals, they place their cards next to them, so that the teacher can correct them.

A Counting Game

As many children as would like to play may join in this game. The children sit in a circle. The teacher calls out one child and whispers a direction requiring that he count the number of times he hops, skips, jumps, turns etc.

By watching what that child does, the others should be able to repeat the directions. The child who can do so, has the next turn.

THE ZERO NUMBER GAMES

To teach the importance and value of the *zero* in arithmetic, several games can be played. The children, sitting in a circle, are asked by the teacher to do various things a certain number of times. For instance, "John, clap your hands 4 times," or "Mary, stamp your feet 3 times." "Karen, knock zero times." Give every child a turn and many will look very puzzled when you ask them to do something zero times.

Another game is to assemble on a table a quantity of identical objects — pebbles, or marbles, or beads, or whatever is available in the classroom. The numbers from 0 to 9 are written on small pieces of paper many times. The paper is then folded. Each child draws a folded slip of paper, sees the number written on it, and goes to the table to get the corresponding number of objects. The teacher or another child can check his objects with the number he drew. The children who draw zeros do not bring anything and this is sometimes very hard for the children to realize. Many variations of this game can be played.

Later on, when you say, "Stop that," the children will enjoy saying, "Oh, do it zero times!" The teacher will learn to create other similar games, to help the children understand the meaning of zero.

SPINDLE BOXES

The spindle boxes are two deep, wooden trays with ten compartments marked with the figures 0 through 9 in order at the back and 45 dowel sticks (known in Montessori language as spindles). They are to make associations between the figures 0 through 9 and their corresponding quantities and to introduce the concept of "0".

The child removes the spindles from the compartments and counts the correct number into each correspondingly numbered compartment. The child already has had experience with the number 10, and is not frustrated with the manipulation of the larger number of sticks (45). For the younger child and the slower learner, it is more advisable to use only the first spindle box, compartments numbered 1 through 4, and thus, only 10 spindles.

There are just enough spindles to do this exercise correctly. Thus, if the child finishes with a surplus or deficiency of sticks, he knows that he has made a mistake. He confronts himself with a self-constructed problem. He may then find the solution to this problem — by personal trial and error, with the aid of another child, or, by last resort, with the aid of the teacher.

Although not perfectly self-correcting, the use of the spindle boxes does introduce the child to the fundamentals of problem-solving: 1) Repeated personal efforts, 2) Mutual aid from peers, 3) Lastly, resort to authority.

The separate compoartments of the spindle boxes correspond to the "brackets" and "sets" in modern math. Moreover, the spindle boxes provide a concrete opportunity to spell out the concept of "0" as an "empty set". The problem presented by the exact number of spindles (45) cannot be solved without appreciating the importance of the "0" compartment, or the "empty set".

NUMBER CARDS AND COUNTERS OR CHIPS

With this exercise the child builds up the sequence of numbers for the first time. He makes the association between the figures and the corresponding quantities of the numbers one to ten and he has a visual impression of odd and even numbers.

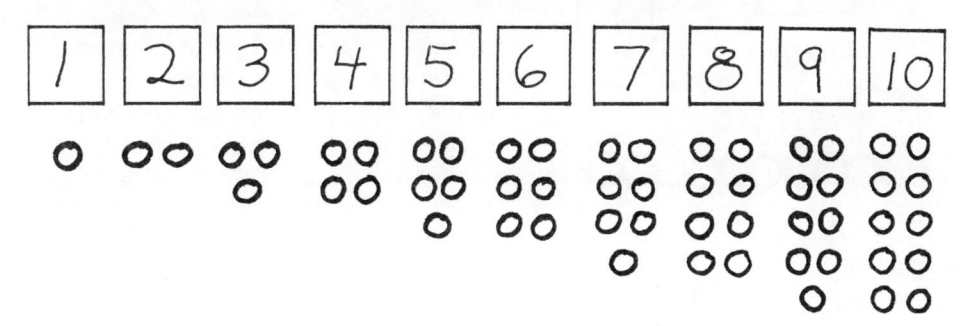

| 1 | 2 | 3 | 4 | 5 | 6 | 7 | 8 | 9 | 10 |

```
O   OO  OO  OO  OO  OO  OO  OO  OO  OO
         O  OO  OO  OO  OO  OO  OO  OO
                 O  OO  OO  OO  OO  OO
                         O  OO  OO  OO
                                 O  OO
```

Take ten number cards from one to ten and 55 counters all the same color and size. Ask the child to place the cards in their correct order starting with the 1 on the left. Show him how to place the corresponding number of counters under each card. Place the counters in pairs and where there is an odd counter place it in the middle underneath the bottom pair.

With the exact number of counters to complete the exercise given, if there are not enough, or if there are too many at the end, the child will know he has made a mistake.

GOLDEN BEAD MATERIAL: INTRODUCTION TO DECIMAL SYSTEM

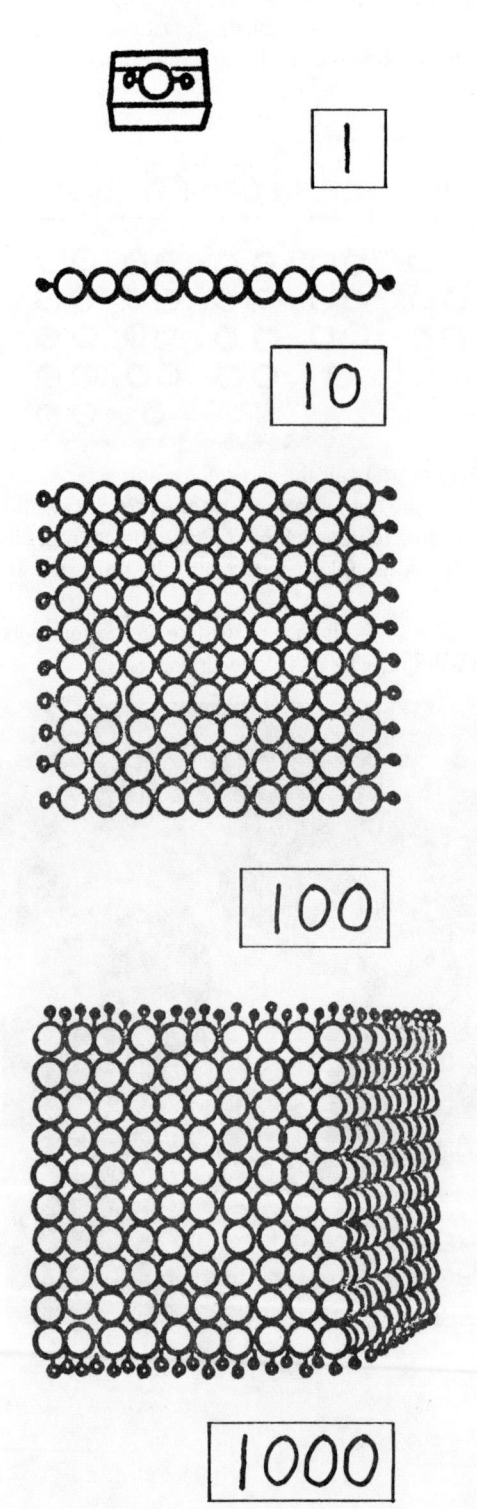

Units are represented with loose, single beads of gold. Units are also represented as symbols 1 – 9 printed in green on cards.

Tens are represented by ten unit beads strung together on a wire bar. Tens are also represented as symbols 10 – 90 printed in blue on cards twice the length of the unit cards.

Hundreds are represented by ten bars-of-ten wired together into a square shape. Wooden squares of the same size as the bead square also represent the hundreds. Printed circles on these wooden squares represent the beads. The wooden squares are of the same size as the bead squares – but much lighter, and therefore, more easily manipulated by the child.

Hundreds are also represented as symbols 100 – 900 printed in red on cards three times the length of the unit cards.

Thousands are represented by ten squares of one hundred wired together in the shape of a cube. Wooden cubes of the same size as the bead cubes also represent the thousands. Printed circles on these wooden cubes represent the beads. Again, the wooden cubes are of lightweight construction, so as to be easily manipulated by the child – stacked one upon another. Thousands are also represented as symbols 1000 – 9000 printed in green on cards four times the length of unit cards.

The Montessori teacher presents the child with three types of objects: 1) the Golden Beads, 2) Boards (representing squares of 100 beads and cubes of 1,000 beads, 3) Cards of different length and color upon which are printed the mathematical symbols. The three-period lesson is used for presenting the material: 1) Presentation of Quantity, 2) Presentation of Symbols, 3) Association of Quantity and Symbol.

In the presentations the child handles concrete objects, moves them, walks up and down (the chain of 1,000), experiences lifting the quantity of 1,000 even in his large muscles. When the beads are folded, he sees *surface* quantity (rectangles and squares), and finally, by placing folded beads on top of one another, he sees the cube, *volume.*

Appropos of this, Montessori writes:

> *The longer a material can claim and hold a child's attention, the greater promise it gives that an* abstract process *and* imaginative creation *will follow as the result of a developed potentiality . . . . Without positive replenishment in reality there never will be a spontaneous flight of the mind . . . .*
> (ADVANCED MONTESSORI, II, 225)

The purpose here is to train the child in order and precision, characteristics of what Montessori called the "Mathematical Mind". Nowadays, we would say in the same context, that the child sees relationships, and when he sees relationships ordered in a certain system (Base 10 or the Decimal System), he comes to understand mathematics. The structure of the materials permits the child to advance through the successive stages of *abstraction*: first, the basic concrete quantities (golden beads); second, the concrete-abstract image (wooden boards); thirdly, the abstract symbols (colored cards).

The child has already mastered the fundamentals of the decimal system in previous lessons — the sequence of numbers 1 through 9 and the concept of "0". These previous lessons (rods and numerals, spindle boxes, and counters game) thus provide an easy transition to the presentation of the golden beads. Thus, the child often corrects himself, simply counting or recounting. Also, in these introductory presentations he has enjoyed the benefits of mutual aid from his peers. As a last resort, he may turn to the teacher, and so be instructed to "hunt and see" if he (they) can find a mistake.

PERSONAL EXPERIENCE: NUMBER CONCEPTS

The following experiences which I had with one of my special classes demonstrate graphically the emotional importance which humbers have for children. Even those children who cannot grasp difficult number operations can be helped to an understanding of the numbers they discover around them — calendar numbers, time, place, and so on. Nor should we forget that all children enjoy the mastery which comes from understanding number operations. Mathematics is not cold, precise, unemotional, but is rather intimately tied up with the growth of a child's feelings about himself and his world.

"What Happened to August?"

"Teacher, teacher, what happened to August?" Curtis rushed away from the group that had been so busy playing Doctors and Nurses in the free play period, and tugged at my arm excitedly. "What happened to August?"

"August?" I searched my mind — there wasn't anyone by that name in the class, but perhaps a character from a recent story was August? "August who?"

"August, what happened to August?" Curtis rushed to the bulletin board where the calendar hung, pulled it down hurriedly, and then turned and turned the pages to show me his terrible discovery — the calendar did not show August! "What happened to August? We must have August!"

I tried to explain that this was a special school calendar showing only the months when there was school in session. Surely he knew that school was not held in the month of August. This did not satisfy him. I found a desk calendar with the month of August clearly visible. He elicited the following explanation: "We must have August — Marcia is going to have a baby in August — my Mommy is going to have a baby in August too. You don't think it will be a boy, do you?"

This is but one incident that shows graphically the vital role the calendar has in the classroom situation. In this particular instance I was made keenly aware of the emotional impact the days of the week and the months of the year have on these children. The calendar represents in some cases a happy time, and in others, a threat.

Curtis

Curtis is one of seven children and the only boy in the family. This role of only boy gives him a special status in his immediate family where poverty is a constant companion. What little material goods and Mother's love and attention is available, is shared by all, with Curtis having an edge on the girls as recipient. August looms large as a threat to his little arena of status — for what if the new baby is a boy? Here the calendar is a foe, not a friend, and as the months go by the dreaded outcome comes nearer and nearer. Curtis' great fear is "What happens in August?"

Carol Ann

Friday is the most wonderful day of the week. Father gets paid on Thursday. Friday, Carol Ann and Mother, hand in hand, go to the Thrift Store just a block away from the school to select some finery. This is important to this young Miss who preens in her ruffles and frills. The fact that they are someone else's cast-offs throws no shadow on her full enjoyment of them. Carol Ann watches for Friday of each week on the Calendar because it is the loveliest day of the week!

Michael

Wednesday begins with a W and so does Michael's surname. Michael, who cannot read, watches for Wednesday of each week. What is so special about Wednesday?

At news time Michael announces: "Today is Wednesday, and Wednesday is my mother's day off from work. Today when I get home from school the house will smell from something good and warm cooking, and we will have a hot supper at our house tonight. Today is Wednesday, and Wednesday is my Mother's day off!"

"Who's Boss Today?"

Dale was late on his "Boss" day. He missed conducting opening exercises and calling on his classmates for show and tell. A substitute had been assigned as Boss by the time Dale arrived in school. This was a crushing experience for Dale.

"Who's Boss today?" The calendar, at the start of each month, has each school day assigned to a boss with all important activities managed by these important assignees. Boss is a most forbidding and almost sanctified word to most of these students. He is a constant threat to Father, a worry to Mother, but also, he is the source from which all good comes. It is a wonderful thing to be a boss, and the students play the role to the hilt on their designated days. Opening exercises, show and tell, recess monitor, special errands, all of these are their very own responsibilities on their special day. This is a status that is prized beyond measure, that gives an emotional lift when one is so sorely needed. "Who's Boss today?" Count the days till your turn. The calendar offers the promise of "Boss for the day."

Happy Birthday

A day to get, and a day to give. Each birthday is marked with a miniature birthday cake and the student's name. We watch eagerly for the great day for there is much celebrating. The birthday child, who is honored, and the classmates who bring mementos share in the festivities and realize that they too will celebrate when their great day appears on this wonderful informative medium— the calendar.

Monday, Wednesday and Friday

Mr. Vespoint is due! He is young and strong and tall, the ideal of all little boys and girls. Mr. Vespoint, the Physical Education Instructor, comes on Monday, Wednesday and Friday. He is a good friend to all the members of the class. Such active games! Such hard exercises! But such fun!

Report Card Month

Here the calendar looms large as a threat. Papers to be signed have a frightening aspect and create an anxiety that the children express in many ways.

John did not bring his signed report in until well past the day it was due. The ensuing explanation was given: "Dad works in a garage and promised to bring a pencil home to sign my report card." I offered John a pencil, and he took it home. The card was signed and returned the next morning.

We fail to realize that in our affluent society there are homes without pencils, without books, without so many of the basic items of family living that we take for granted. Report Card Month triggered this graphic example of the environment in which too many of our children live. There is nothing we must take for granted — not even the pencil as being on hand to sign the report.

School Days

The security the calendar promises as it notes each school day is important. A school day promises a warm classroom, a desk of his very own, and most important, the hot lunch at noon, perhaps the only hot meal that any of these children will have that day. School days and hot meals are synonymous, an oasis of good feeling and good feeding sandwiched in between weekends and school holidays. The calendar promises security — promises school days. The calendar must promise, also, "What happens in August!"

One may think that all this material takes up a lot of space and some exercises are troublesome to teach, and perhaps it is rather an elaborate waste of time over something so simple. Or one may say that children of this age ought not to do lessons. Instead, they should amuse themselves with toys. But Montessori said that this is a mistake. Children are not really interested in toys for long without the real intellectual interest of associating them with sizes and numbers. When children playing with blocks achieve the manual dexterity to build them up securely, they want to go on to some new difficulty. So, this is the time to give them numbers. One greatly underrates the intelligence of the four or five year old if one thinks that this learning is too much. If one does this, one is also likely to make the mistake later on and expect the child of five-and-a-half or six to grasp the numbers in a few short lessons. The units may seem obvious to us after years of practice, but they are not so to the child. If his initiation is hasty and unprepared, he will learn the names by rote and it may be years before he gets a real conception of the different numbers and their relations to each other. The names of numbers tend to be associated with figures only, and the child's arithmetic is a succession of verbal formulae connected precariously by counting on the fingers. Because we have a decimal system it seems possible that there is good precedent for counting on the fingers in pre-history. Whether this is so or not, we cannot avoid the conclusion that today, counting on the fingers is not a success. Counting **with** the fingers, definitely yes, but **on** the fingers, no.

Now all this finger counting, that lets us down so often and causes so many disappointments when we find that the laboriously achieved answer is wrong, is only necessary for the combinations of the nine units — adding and subtracting the numbers from one to nine. If the child knows these combinations and knows them correctly, he need not count on his fingers. If he starts with a real concept of the numbers, gained from the use of the number rods, that is a great help. He learns from this which combinations of numbers make up ten. Then later, he can do all kinds of exercises with the small bead bars and the addition board that will teach him many more little additions and subtractions, until finally, all the combinations of the nine units are perfectly familiar, as familiar as the linear counting itself, so that it becomes easier and more natural to say at once fourteen and two are sixteen because the child has mental conceptions of four and two, than to embark on the precarious operation of adding two (or four!), fingers to a misty conception of the numerical sixteen in the imagination.

ADVANCING THE CURRICULUM

Science for the Mentally Retarded

It is impossible, in the scope of this book, to detail each subject taught in the early years of grammar school. The good Montessori teacher will always remember that there are not really separate subjects to be taught, but that all the subjects have an integral unity and interconnection. For example, if the teacher is teaching leaf shapes in the botany class, she can also teach the geometric shapes which are evident. Even the vocabularies are similar and this should be pointed out.

As K. D. Wann et al. said so well,

> ... the great expansion of knowledge in modern times makes it virtually impossible to teach all there is to learn about a body of knowledge. To use as a basis for teaching the key ideas from which all other ideas in a body of knowledge emanate and to which they all relate would give learners a fundamental understanding of a subject so they can grasp the meaning of the facts and ideas within the subject quickly and effectively. ... The learner is thus given a conceptual framework on which he can fasten new facts and information and against which he can test the pertinency and relevancy of ideas. Early beginning toward a development of this framework provides a base for later learning and understanding .... Merely acquiring facts is not so important as how they fit into a conceptual framework.[1]

From the guides and outlines in this book it is hoped that the teacher can see how to build a framework for his students and in this way teach specific subjects, as well as the skills of mind and body that have been taught through the Montessori exercises.

For further help and references, see the bibliography included at the end of this book.

[1]Wann, K. D., Dorn, M. S., Liddle, E. A., FOSTERING INTELLECTUAL DEVELOPMENT IN YOUNG CHILDREN, Bureau of Publications, Teachers College, Columbia University, 1962.

We are living in a world in which we receive daily news of another scientific achievement. This generation of children that we are now teaching will increasingly feel the impact of science technology upon their lives. Successful adjustment to this mode of life will depend to a large extent upon the quality of science education they receive today. The significance of what we as teachers, yes, even as teachers of the mentally retarded, can contribute toward this effort and toward our nation's progress in science, has been thrown more sharply into focus.

In preparing these boys and girls for further training and future adequacy in even the simplest tasks, we are contributing toward the scientific progress of our country, and toward the fulfillment of the individual child. It is very possible that these children may also find a place in the activities of expanded research in a world which puts a premium on science. Through the child's growing awareness, or even through his familiarity with scientific terms, meaning may be given to the simplest responsibilities which he as an adult can be trained to perform in the laboratory; washing test tubes or caring for research animals. He too, can be an essential part of the team. It should be remembered that *every* experience can be meaningful to a child, and that everything he learns or does will broaden his awareness and promote his personal and social fulfillment.

Following are a few cases in point that the author has experienced, and which might serve as helpful examples for the teacher of mentally retarded children.

LEARNING TO ASK WHY

Curtis asked why are there no leaves on the trees in winter. Vincent asked where do the leaves go? Michael asked how are the trees fed when the snow is on the ground. For Michael, being fed is the symbol of his mother's love.

Even the mentally retarded can learn to ask why.

Each child must have a desk, a pencil, a piece of paper and eventaully a book. These are the basic tools he uses in learning. The significance of the desk is ownership. "A desk for me." For Carolyn, who has moved many times in her young life, it is disturbing to find her desk moved from its customary place. Her desk is a little island of security. For Michael, the desk is an object to be defaced and scratched or, at other times, a barricade from which he can direct an attack — pencil and paper are weapons of defiance. From such things as these, we can begin. Hostility and frustration can be turned to wonder.

We talk about the wood from which the desk, the paper, and the pencil are made. We go outside to the adjoining woods and look at the trees. We feel the roughness of the bark; we put our arms around the trunk; we sense the strength of the tree. We notice the elasticity of the branches and twigs. We look up and measure the height with our eyes. We examine the leaves.

Someone may see a bird's nest. Someone else sees a squirrel. We learn that the tree has many uses. It is a protection for the soil. We have seen the exposed roots.

Now the pencil and paper are used to draw the tree just as much later on they will be used to write a sentence about it.

Filmstrips show us that there are many kinds of trees. To Rocky, it was a great discovery when he exclaimed, "Look at the bananas on that tree!" To John, photosynthesis could be compared to what goes on in his mother's kitchen where food is prepared. The sun serves as a stove to cook the food. The roots were reminiscent of the root cellar on his grandfather's place where potatoes were stored.

The green of the chlorophyll reminded Bonita, who loves to paint and responds readily to colors, that green (so her mother says) is the color of hope. This, in turn, reminds the teacher of the primitive notion about the evergreen as a symbol of everlasting life. To the scientist, the life-cycle is dependent on the green of the plant.

The baby rabbit lost his home when the bulldozer dug up the ground around Hanky's home. This led to a discussion about how many animals have been evicted in order to make room for homes for us. The children were readily involved in the rabbit's predicament because they too, have been forced to move for drastic reasons. Father may have lost his job or deserted his family.

Interest in the bulldozer would have offered an opportunity to study machines, but the teacher felt that the emotional indentification with animals and their homes offered more fertile ground for learning about animal life and the comparison with human needs for shelter, food, protection, and care of the young.

Here again, film strips were a tremendous help. ANIMAL BABIES showed how a wide variety of animal young are nurtured and grow to maturity. The children's reactions were strong and uncontrolled. The suckling baby pig was not something they could easily accept, and they expressed their revulsion in obscene language. It is not my purpose to analyze the reasons for this. It is enough to observe, however, that their notions of human reproduction and growth are based on superstition and distaste, on fears and half-knowledge.

The time came for the eggs which had been kept in the classroom to hatch. When we saw that the baby chick appeared after twenty-one days, someone asked about human babies. Bonita refuted the teacher's explanation with the statement that her mother had told her "babies come from heaven." As the children were exposed more and more to the scientific explanation of the "miracle of life" observed in plants and animals, their feelings of "something nasty" were replaced by an awareness of and respect for the "miracle" and the beauty and tenderness which accompany the nurturing mother and her offspring.

We are told that the mentally retarded are the most destructive — with this group there is more incidence of accidents, more vandalism. By stimulating a greater awareness of nature and science, we may lessen this destructiveness. All living things, birds for example, have a function from which we humans benefit. When this is understood, there will be less of an inclination to destroy the eggs in the nest or use the birds as a target. The child, even in his limited way, is made aware of his environment and the interdependence of all of nature.

We talked about static electricity when the children discovered that they received a shock after touching something when they came into the room on a cold day. We then did further experimentation — combing Johnnie's hair, rubbing paper on the desk and then making it adhere to the chalkboard. This was terribly exciting to the whole class. They never tired of repeating it over and over. Only Ricky wearied of using his hands and transferred to crayon on his own initiative. When he ran to the board with his colorful results, the others became so excited that *it* has now become a popular leisure-time activity. Beautiful designs have been created, and equally important, the children's other art activities have taken on new dimensions. Their awareness of color combinations has somehow increased.

Through these various experiences with Science, these children have begun to see relationships. It does not matter that they were crude or simple relationships. Now the pencil, the paper, the desk have taken on new meaning and become instruments for positive self-expression — if only through drawing. Later on the first sentence will be written.

To use a scientific precept, energy is broken down and rearranged for other uses through continued exposure and reinforcement.

The child has been given his first awareness that trees, animals, machines, people — all give him something. Knowledge of this engenders a feeling of security and satisfaction. Some of the superstition — the folklore brought from the home — is replaced by factual knowledge which he is able to accept with less disbelief from the teacher. At first, he said she was crazy.

It is very possible that these children too, may find a place in the activities of expanded research which are going on in a world which puts a premium on science. Simply through the child's growing awareness — or even a familiarity with the terms — can meaning be given to the simple tasks which as an adult he can be trained to perform in the laboratory — washing the test tubes, or caring for the animals. He too, can be an essential part of the team.

A rudimentary knowledge of science has significance for the growing child's own personal life whatever the limits of his capacity. Of all the things there are to learn at school, science touches most frequently on his every-day living.

In this profession of teaching, we wish to give knowledge and understanding to all children. Those with greater or lesser capacities will use this understanding and make their contribution to the best of their ability.

With the mentally retarded, we see that the child is giving when he is able to express what he understands about his environment. We know that he is using his limited understanding when he becomes more aware of the world around him and is able to find a place for himself in that world. His curiosity can be stimulated through science. This is happening, and it can be done.

The following examples of drawings, labels and definition cards show how the teacher can break down a subject into small parts. The child first learns through his visual sense, then learns the name of the part and then progresses to the definition. The children can also make their own definition books and thus have a handy reference as well as practice their writing skill.

Several examples of the definition cards and their accompanying drawings are given so that the teacher will see that they can be used in every subject, not just biology or

(Photo courtesy of Las Nereidas Montessori School, Puerto Rico.)

"The need of children to understand reality must be recognized by adults . . . This involves, of course, opportunities to handle, to observe the world of plants and animals, of weather phenomena, of gadgets and machines . . . . Adults support the child's questioning and testing . . . who delight with children in the process of discovery and encourage their attempts to verbalize their opinions and ideas." (From: Wann, K. D., Dorn, M. S., Liddle, E. A., FOSTERING INTELLECTUAL DEVELOPMENT IN YOUNG CHILDREN, Bureau of Publications, Teachers College, Columbia University, 1962.)

geography. The cards, labels and drawings are a method of teaching that moves from the simple, visual idea to the abstract idea of word symbols.

The definition cards, as with most of the teacher prepared material, are particularly helpful to the child with problems in motor coordination. Even very bright children often have difficulty making their hand keep up the pace of their mind. The already prepared definition cards enable these children to develop their reading and vocabulary skills without the frustration of actually writing.

Zoology, anatomy, geography — introduction to all these subjects can begin in the Montessori classroom.

INSETS OF LEAF OUTLINES

Besides introducing biology this exercise stimulates visual and muscular discrimination of form.

Use the same general procedure as with the Geometric Cabinet. Take the presentation tray and place on it 3 contrasting leaf forms and their wooden frame. Pick up the leaf form by its knob with the left hand. With the right hand trace around the leaf inset. Trace around the cut-out also. Add more shapes, gradually, until all the shapes have been presented. Return the leaf inset, carefully, into drawer, by point of leaf point or by point of stem.

These may be used for matching with cards or as patterns for drawing or coloring (green leaves, unless it is autumn).

Following is a list of leaf shapes with one example of each shape.

reniform — ground ivy	elliptical — apple
aciculate — fir	obriculate — marsh penny
linear — grasses	obovate — wood sorrel
ovate — lilac	obcordate - white clover
cordate — dead nettle	spatulate — daisy
sagittate — morning glory	hastate — cuckoo-pint
lanceolate — wall flower	triangular — beech

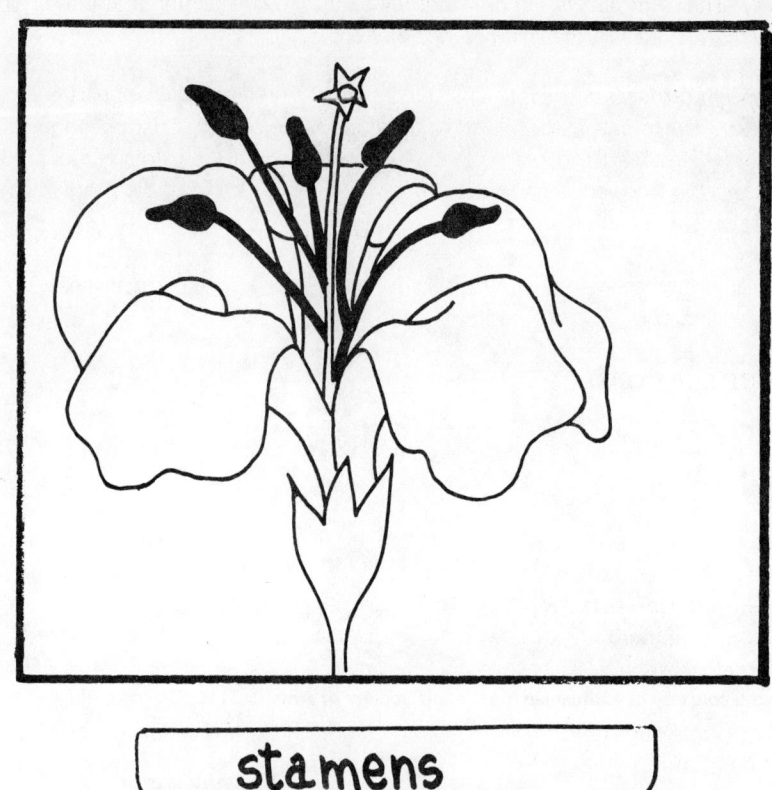

stamens

The stamens form the male part of the flower and produce the pollen.

The word defined and that part of the flower should be in the same color.

(Photo courtesy of Lithuanian Montessori Society of America, Inc., Chicago, Ill.)

A botany lesson.

A Montessori geography lesson.

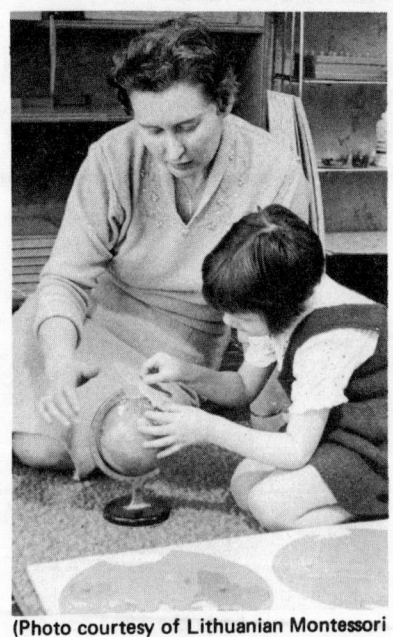

(Photo courtesy of Lithuanian Montessori Society of America, Inc., Chicago, Illinois.)

First the child works with geography puzzles, with a control map next to her. This is done in the period before reading.

(Photo courtesy of Lithuanian Montessori Society of America, Chicago, Illinois.)

"It were far better to sail forever in the night of blindness with sense and feeling and mind than to be content with the mere act of seeing."

from THE SOUL IS WHAT COUNTS, by Helen Keller.

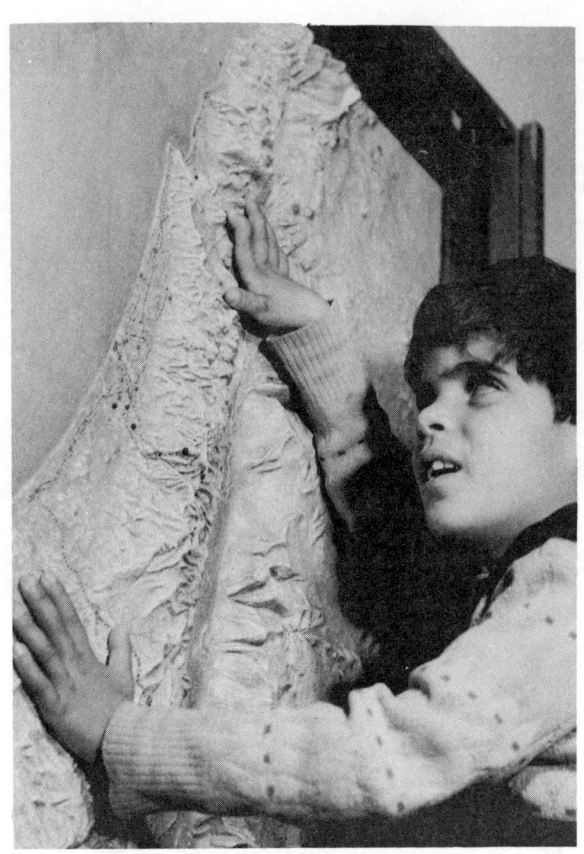

(Photo courtesy of Fred Csasznik, Jerusalem.)

isthmus

An isthmus is a narrow neck, or strip, of land by which two larger portions of land are connected.

This and the five following pages are illustrations in geography, but could be applied to any subject needing graphic definitions.

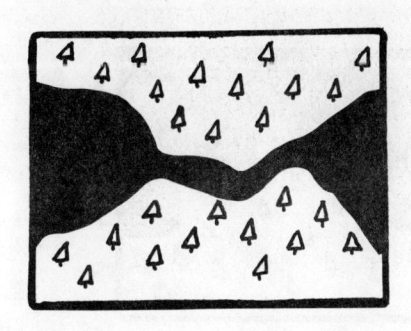

strait

A strait is a narrow strip of water connecting two large bodies of water.

peninsula

A peninsula is a long, narrow neck of land extending into the water.

gulf

A gulf is a long, narrow inlet of water extending into the land.

island

An island is a piece of land surrounded by water.

lake

A lake is a body of water surrounded by land.

PUZZLE OF THE HUMAN ANATOMY

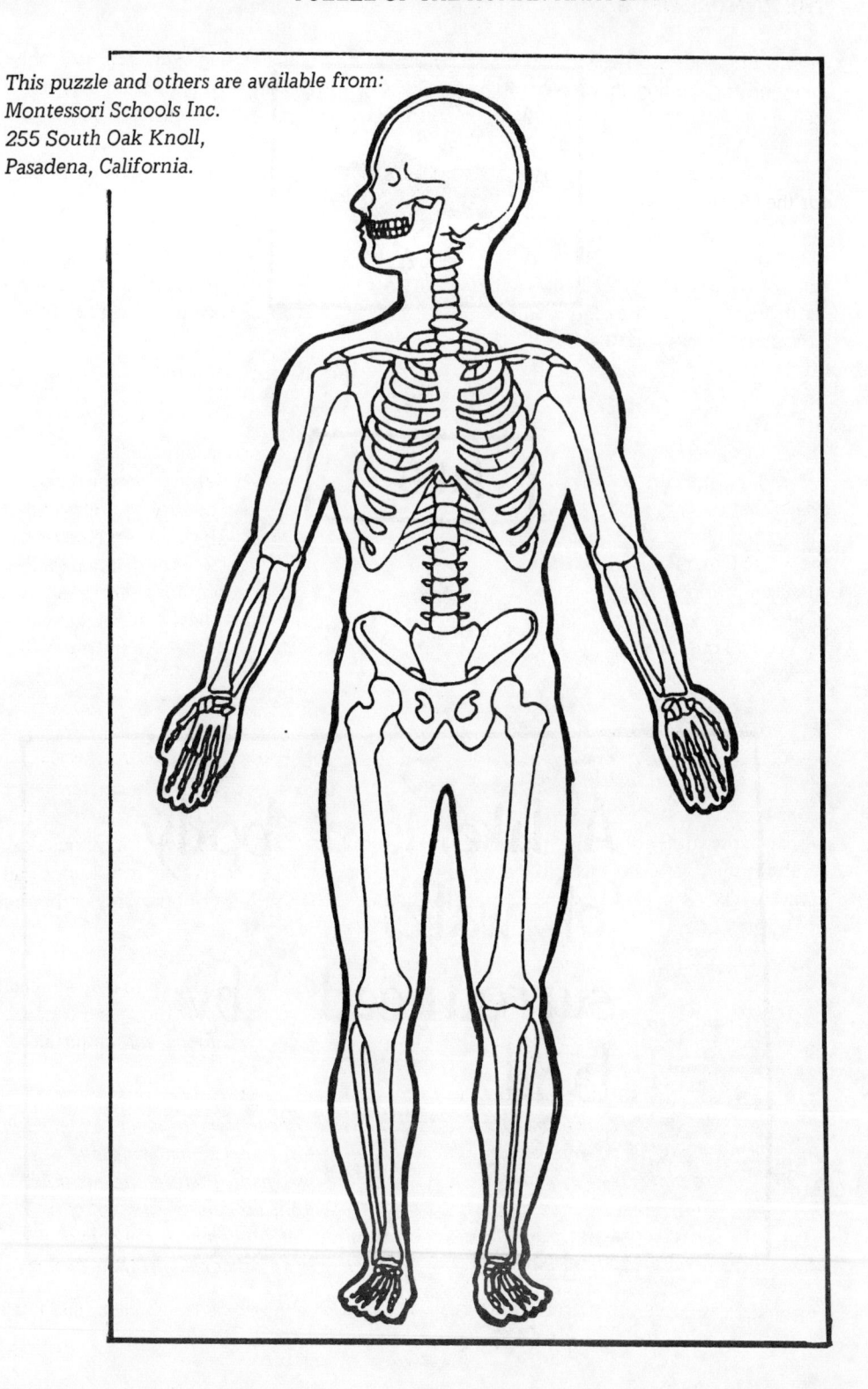

This puzzle and others are available from:
Montessori Schools Inc.
255 South Oak Knoll,
Pasadena, California.

THE MONTESSORI WAY

What is the Montessori way? Is it only a collection of techniques and exercises? Is it only a method for keeping children orderly and the classroom quiet? Is it applicable only to special education? Is it limited to young children? Is it a branch of pedagogy?

It is all of these things — and something more. And without that something more, it is *not* the Montessori way.

In this book I have touched on different areas of the curriculum; in science, for example, what I have given is only a beginning. And there is nothing on art, music, and drama, for another book would be required to do justice to those subjects. But I hope that I have indicated, however briefly, that all the subjects I have treated are part of what Montessori called "cosmic education" and it is in pursuing that cosmic education that we find the essence of the Montessori way.

The Biblical injunction warns that "the letter killeth but the spirit giveth life," and so it is with Montessori. Underneath her particular techniques lay a view of life which perceived that everything in nature, including every human being, had a task to fulfill and a role to play in the great chain of life. A century after Montessori's birth others all over the world understand as she did that to forget the human connection with nature is to invite destruction. The science of ecology deals precisely with relationships in the great chain of life and brings to our attention in a particularly urgent way right now just how far we have ruined our country and our planet by lack of awareness of natural laws and limitations.

Montessori's cosmic education is scientific, not to develop scientists or to advance technology, but to teach that reverence for all life without which we cannot grow and develop as human beings. In this way of looking at the life around us, we come to understand that the special child also has his task to fulfill in life, which is uniquely his. He is the one who eagerly and joyfully does those tasks which are boring to others. Because he develops slowly, scientists have been able to conduct careful studies which teach us a great deal about all human development by working with these children. They are part of our common humanity.

Cosmic education also leads to greater sensitivity of the needs of others, both individually and as nations. Montessori's greatest desire was that her educational method should lead to peace. In 1918 she was invited to speak before the League of Nations, and at that time she said: [2]

> But now that man has entered into the realm of the stars, he can rise to his full height; he can present himself to the universe as a new being. He it is who is the child, the new child. He it is who is the new man, entering into the third dimension, the man predestined to undertake the conquest of the infinite. Such a conquest is a work of great magnitude and it demands the help of all men. But to bind them together they will find no other cement than love.

[2] Montessori, Maria, PEACE AND EDUCATION. 2nd Ed., Madras, India: The Theosophical Pub., 1938.

Such is the vision that we see in the real facts of today. We who are the last men to live in a two-dimensional world must make a strenuous effort to rise to the understanding of the vision. We have fallen upon a period of crisis, inserted between an old world which is drawing to its end and a new world which has already begun and has revealed all three elements that go to build it up. The crisis we are witnessing is not one of those that make the passage from one era to another, it can only be compared with the opening of a new Biological or Geological period, when new beings come upon the scene, more evolved and more perfect, ... At the same time we must gather together all the elements of this new world and organize them into a science of peace.

The survival of humanity depends on our ability to achieve peace and to fit ourselves into nature rather than to destroy our environment as we have been doing. Both of these efforts require deep understanding of the truly human needs of all children so that their education can prepare them to be adults with this comprehension.

And the Montessori way is truly found in her cosmic education, the aim of which is just that, a growth and deepening of what is most human in all children. In using Montessori in our classrooms, we should try to understand her by studying what underlies the specific techniques and methods which are themselves so full of riches. Studying her own writings will make her spirit even clearer, of course, and the Montessori training programs available in this country offer the living tradition.

More and more it is possible to see that Montessori was far ahead of her time and is only now coming into her own as other thinkers discover in their own way and in their own fields what she perceived so many years ago.

BIBLIOGRAPHIES

References	252
Additional Reading	256
Magazines and Journals	259
Films, Slides and Filmstrips	260
Children's Books	261

BIBLIOGRAPHY

This is not a complete listing, but it includes Montessori's own writings on education as well as the work of our contemporaries, the research materials I have drawn on in preparing this book, and publications of basic interest both in the field of special education and in the area of poverty and minority education. Journal articles and magazines are included as well as books.

REFERENCES

Arena, John I., TEACHING THROUGH SENSORY-MOTOR EXPERIENCES. San Rafael, Calif.: Academic Therapy Publications, 1969.

Arena, John I. (Ed.), TEACHING EDUCATIONALLY HANDICAPPED CHILDREN. San Rafael, Calif.: Academic Therapy Publications, 1967.

Aries, Philippe, CENTURIES OF CHILDHOOD. trans. Robert Baldick. New York: Knopf, 1962.

Armstrong, Jenny R., "Mathematics Curriculum for the Mentally Retarded." THE WINNOWER, Vol. 4, No. 2, Winter 1968. A publication of Special Education Instruction Materials Center, Univ. of Wis.

Ashton—Warner, Sylvia, TEACHER. New York: Simon & Schuster, 1959.

Beck, Robert H., "Kilpatrick's Critique of Montessori's Method and Theory," STUDIES IN PHILOSOPHY AND EDUCATION, Vol. I, No. 4, 1961.

Brazelton, Dr. T. Berry, PEDIATRICS, Vol. 29, No. 1, Jan. 1962.

Bryan, J. Ned. "Gifts Are For Use", a speech. U.S. Office of Education. Presented before Williamsburg Student Burgesses on Feb. 10, 1962.

Bruner, Jerome S., ON KNOWING. Cambridge: Belknap Press of Harvard Univ. Press, 1962.

Burt, Sir Cyril, THE BACKWARD CHILD. London: Univ. of London Press, 1950.

Carinato, Sister Mary Matthew, et al., MONTESSORI MATTERS. Cincinnati: Ohio Province, 1967.

CHILDREN LIMITED, "Seaside's Program Geared to Individual Child's Potential." April-May, 1963.

Claremont, Claude, THE CHEMISTRY OF THOUGHT. London: George Allen & Unwin, Ltd., 1935.

Court, Nathan Altshiller, MATHEMATICS IN FUN AND IN EARNEST. New York: Mentor Books, 1958.

Dewey, John, SCHOOLS OF TOMORROW. New York: E. P. Dutton and Co., Inc., 1962.

Donahue, Gilbert E., "Montessori and American Education Literature: An Unfinished Chapter in the History of Ideas." Distributed by the American Montessori Society, 1962.

Focillon, Henri THE LIFE FORMS IN ART. New York: Wittenborn, Schiltz, 1948.

Focault, Michel, MADNESS AND CIVILIZATION. New York: Pantheon, 1965.

Frankel, Max G., Happ, F. William and Smith, Maurice P., FUNCTIONAL TEACHING OF THE MENTALLY RETARDED. Springfield, Ill.: Charles C. Thomas, 1966.

Fromm, Eric, THE ART OF LOVING. New York: Harper and Row, 1956.

Gitter, Lena L., MONTESSORI RENAISSANCE IN AMERICA, Johnstown, Pa.: Mafex Associates, Inc.

Gitter, Lena L., READYING YOUR CHILD FOR SCHOOL THE MONTESSORI WAY, St. Meinrad, Ind.: Abbey Press, 1969.

Gitter, Lena L., A STRATEGY FOR FIGHTING THE WAR ON POVERTY, Johnstown, Pa.: Mafex Associates, 1965.

GOALS FOR SCHOOL MATHEMATICS, Cambridge Conference on School Mathematics, Educational Services, Inc., Watertown, Mass., 1963.

Hendrick, Joanne, "The Pleasures of Meaningful Work for Young Children." YOUNG CHILDREN, The Journal of National Ass'n. for Ed. of Young Children. Sept., 1967.

Holbrook, David, ENGLISH FOR MATURITY. Cambridge: Cambridge Univ. Press, 1961.

Holbrook, David, ENGLISH FOR THE REJECTED. Cambridge: Cambridge Univ. Press, 1964.

Itard, Jean Marc Gaspard, THE WILD BOY OF AVEYRON. trans. George and Muriel Humphrey. New York: Appleton, Century, Crofts, 1962.

Koegler, Ronald R., "The Psychology of Mental Retardation." Paper delivered American Montessori Society Seminar, Wash., D. C., 1964.

Martin, Wm., Jr., "Language and Literature." Department of Elementary, Kindergarten, Nursery Education, Washington, D. C., 1968.

McCarthy, J. L., "The Importance of Linguistic Ability in the Mentally Retarded." MENTAL RETARDATION, 2, 1964.

Miller, Leonard M., Ed., GUIDANCE FOR THE UNDERACHIEVER WITH SUPERIOR ABILITY. U. S. Dept. of Health, Ed. and Welfare, OE - 25021, No. 25, 1961.

Minor, W. F., MONTESSORI IN NATCHEZ. Special Report to the National Catholic Reporter, March 22, 1967.

Moholy-Nagy, Laszlo, THE NEW VISION AND ABSTRACT OF AN ARTIST. New York: George Wittenborn, Inc., 1947.

Montessori, Maria, THE ABSORBENT MIND. Adyar, India: Theosophical Publishing House, 1949.

Montessori, Maria, THE ADVANCED MONTESSORI METHOD. New York: Frederick A. Stokes Co., 1917.

Montessori, Maria, Ed., THE CALL OF EDUCATION. Amsterdam: H. J. Paris and Van Holkema en Warendorf, Vol. 1, 1924, Vol. 2, 1925.

Montessori, Maria, "On Discipline — Reflections and Advice". Trans. Sheila Radice. THE CALL OF EDUCATION.

Montessori, Maria, "The New Mistress." THE CALL OF EDUCATION.

Montessori, Maria, DISCOVERY OF THE CHILD. Adyar, India: Kalakshetra Publications, 1948.

Montessori, Maria, DR. MONTESSORI'S OWN HANDBOOK. New York: Schocken Books, 1965.

Montessori, Maria, EDUCATION FOR A NEW WORLD. Adyar, India: Kalakshetra, 1965.

Montessori, Maria, THE FORMATION OF MAN. Adyar, India: Theosophical Publishing House, 1955.

Montessori, Maria, PEDAGOGICAL ANTHROPOLOGY. New York: Frederick Stokes & Co., 1913.

Montessori, Maria, PSICO-ARITMETICA. Araluce, Barcelona: Casa Editorial, 1934.

Montessori, Maria, PSICO-GEOMETRIA. Araluce, Barcelona: Casa Editorial. 1934.

Montessori, Maria, THE SECRET OF CHILDHOOD. India: Orient Longmans Ltd., 1964.

Montessori, Maria, "Maria Montessori's Contribution to the Cultivation of the Mathematical Mind." International Review of Education, International Montessori Congress, 1960.

Montessori, Maria, WHAT YOU SHOULD KNOW ABOUT YOUR CHILD. Major Montessori principles interpreted by A. Gnana Prakasam. India, 1961.

Plank, Emma N., REFLECTIONS ON THE REVIVAL OF THE MONTESSORI METHOD. Journal of Nursery Education: New York. Vol. 17, No. 3, May 1962.

Rambusch, Nancy McC., LEARNING HOW TO LEARN. Baltimore: Helicon Press, 1962.

Sandburg, Helga, SWEET MUSIC: A BOOK OF FAMILY REMINISCENCE AND SONG. New York: Dial Press, 1963.

Schachtel, Ernest, METAMORPHOSIS. New York: Basic Books, 1959.

Seguin, Edward, IDIOCY. New York: William Wood & Co., 1866.

Seguin, Edward, "New Facts and Remarks Concerning Idiocy." A lecture delivered before the N. Y. Medical Journal Ass'n., Oct. 15, 1869. New York: Wm. Wood & Co., 1870.

Stennett, R. G., "Chances Are He Won't Grow Out of It." AMERICAN ACADEMY OF GENERAL PRACTICE. London: Board of Education. Vol. 35, No., 5, May 1967.

Tomlinson, R. R., CHILDREN AS ARTISTS. London and New York: Penguin Books Ltd., 1947.

Walsh, William, THE USE OF IMAGINATION. London: Chatto & Windus, 1959.

Weill, Blanche C., "The Montessori Method and Sub-Normal Children." THE CALL OF EDUCATION. Amsterdam: H. J. Paris & Van Holkema en Warendorf, Vol. 2, 1925.

Weiss, Paul, THE MAKING OF MEN. Carbondale, Ill.: Southern Ill. Univ. Press, 1967.

Young, Marjabelle and Buchwald, Ann, WHITE GLOVES AND PARTY MANNERS. Washington, D. C.: R. B. Luce, 1965.

ADDITIONAL READING

On Montessori

Fisher, Dorothy Canfield, MONTESSORI FOR PARENTS. New York: Bentley, 1964.

Fleege, Urban H., MONTESSORI IN THE LIGHT OF CURRENT RESEARCH. Paper presented June, 1963 at AMS Seminar. Available American Montessori Society.

Gitter, Lena L., MONTESSORI AND THE COMPULSIVE CLEANLINESS OF SEVERELY RETARDED CHILDREN, N. Y.: The American Montessori Society.

Gitter, Lena L., ART IN A CLASS FOR MENTALLY RETARDED CHILDREN, N. Y.: The American Montessori Society, 1964.

Gitter, Lena L., MONTESSORI VIEW OF ART IN EDUCATION, N. Y.: The American Montessori Society, 1964.

Rambusch, Nancy, LEARNING HOW TO LEARN. Baltimore: Taplinger Co., 1962.

Smaridge, Norah, THE LIGHT WITHIN: THE STORY OF MARIA MONTESSORI. London: Hawthorn Books, 1965.

Standing, E. M., MARIA MONTESSORI, HER LIFE AND WORK. London: Hollis and Carter, 1957.

On Art

Dover, Cedric, AMERICAN NEGRO ART. Greenwich, Conn.: New York Graphic Society, 1965.

Radin, Paul and Sweeney, James Johnson, AFRICAN FOLKTALES AND SCULPTURE. New York: Pantheon Books, 1964.

Read, Herbert, ART NOW. Revised edition. London: Faber & Faber, 1960.

A GALLERY OF CHILDREN, portraits from The National Gallery of Art, Wash., D. C., with text by Marian King. Washington, D.C.: Acropolis Books, 1967.

In The Classroom

Holt, John, HOW CHILDREN FAIL. New York: Delta Books, 1967.

Holt, John, HOW CHILDREN LEARN, New York: Pitman Publishers, 1967.

Marshall, Sybil, AN EXPERIMENT IN EDUCATION. New York: Cambridge Univ. Press, 1966.

Current Surveys and Opinions

LeShan, Eda, THE CONSPIRACY AGAINST CHILDHOOD. New York: Atheneum, 1967.

Pines, Maya, REVOLUTION IN LEARNING: THE YEARS FROM BIRTH TO 6. New York: Harper and Row, 1967.

In The Ghetto

Gitter, Lena L., MONTESSORI IN MISSISSIPPI, Johnstown, Pa.: Mafex Associates, 1966.

Gitter, Lena L., MONTESSORI AT WORK IN THE SOUTH, Johnstown, Pa.: Mafex Associates, 1966.

Gitter, Lena L., ART AND THE MONTESSORI APPROACH IN A POVERTY-STRICKEN RURAL AREA, Johnstown, Pa.: Mafex Associates, 1968.

Greene, Mary Frances and Than, Orletta, THE SCHOOLCHILDREN. New York: Pantheon, 1965.

Hornstein, Bruce, ANIMALS FOR THE URBAN CHILD: PSYCHOLOGICAL IMPLICATIONS. Baltimore: Montessori Society of Greater Baltimore, 1967.

Kohl, Herbert, TEACHING THE UNTEACHABLE. New York: New York Review Book, 1967.

Kozol, Johnathan, DEATH AT AN EARLY AGE. Boston: Houghton Mifflin, 1967.

Language Development

Chukovsky, Kornei, FROM TWO TO FIVE. Berkeley: Univ. of California Press, 1963.

Gitter, Lena L., IT'S TIME TO RHYME, N. Y.: The American Montessori Society, 1964.

Gitter, Lena L., THE MELTING POT. N. Y.: The American Montessori Society, 1964.

Holbrook, David, THE SECRET PLACES. University, Ala.: Univ. of Alabama, 1965.

Holbrook, David, ENGLISH FOR MATURITY. New York: Cambridge Univ. Press, 1961.

Holbrook, David, ENGLISH FOR THE REJECTED. New York: Cambridge Univ. Press, 1964.

Holbrook, David, THE EXPLORING WORD. New York: Cambridge Univ. Press, 1967.

Holbrook, David, CHILDREN'S WRITING. New York: Cambridge Univ. Press, 1967.

Richardson, Sylvia Onesti, MONTESSORI LANGUAGE EXERCISES IN WORD-BUILDING. N. Y.: The American Montessori Society, 1962.

Cookbooks

Beim, Jerrod, FIRST BOOK OF BOY'S COOKING. New York: Watts, 1957.

Crocker, Betty (Pseud.), NEW PICTURE COOKBOOK. New York: McGraw-Hill, 1961.

Freeman, Mae Blacker, FUN WITH COOKING. New York: Random House, 1947.

Rombauer, Irma S. A COOKBOOK FOR BOYS AND GIRLS. Indianapolis: The Bobbs-Merrill Company, 1952.

Rudomin, Esther. LET'S COOK WITHOUT COOKING. New York: Thomas Crowell Co., 1955.

MAGAZINES

AMERICAN MONTESSORI SOCIETY BULLETIN
175 Fifth Avenue
New York, New York 10010

AROUND THE CHILD: MONTESSORI IN INDIA
18, Suren Tagore Rd.
Calcutta 19, India

COMMUNICATIONS
Association Montessori Internationale
Koninginneweg 161
Amsterdam, Holland

ILLINOIS MONTESSORI SOCIETY NEWSLETTER
Box 735
Oak Park, Illinois 60303

JOURNALS

ACADEMIC THERAPY QUARTERLY
1543 Fifth Avenue
San Rafael, California 94901
Published four times a year. Practical and theoretical articles on the entire range of educationally handicapped and socially deprived.

BULLETIN OF ART THERAPY
Box 4918
Washington, D. C. 20008
Quarterly publication. Articles on all aspects of art in therapy and education with attention paid to mentally handicapped and socially deprived.

CHILDREN'S HOUSE
2145 Central Parkway
Cinncinnati, Ohio 45214
Published six times a year. Articles on all aspects of child development, with special attention to a wide range of learning problems. Features book reviews and a summary of important research in the field.

FILMS, SLIDES AND FILMSTRIPS

A CHANCE FOR CHANGE. Produced by the Child Development Group of Mississippi, 1965.

LIVELY ART OF PICTURE BOOKS. Produced by Morton Schindel at Weston Woods Studios, 1964.

AID FOR TEACHING THE MENTALLY RETARDED. Produced by Thorne Films, Boulder, Colorado, 1964.

AMERICAN PAINTING IN HISTORY. Color film strips with text prepared by the National Gallery of Art, Washington, D. C.

AMERICA'S NATIONAL GALLERY. Slide lectures with 40 slides and a brief text to be read. National Gallery of Art, Washington, D. C.

MONTESSORI. 18 min., color. Washington Montessori Institute, 2119 S Street, N.W., Washington, D. C. 20008

A DEMONSTRATION OF THE USE OF FILM STRIPS IN A MONTESSORI CLASSROOM. Lena L. Gitter. With four film-strips. Weston Woods Films, Weston, Connecticut, 1969.

A PICTURE WINDOW TO THE WORLD. Lena L. Gitter. Weston Woods, Weston, Connecticut, 1970.

CHILDREN'S HOUSE — STRUCTURING: THE MONTESSORI CLASSROOM. Hanna Hornstein. Slides and tapes. The Montessori Society of Greater Baltimore, Baltimore, Maryland 21208.

INTRODUCTION TO MONTESSORI. Lena L. Gitter. Slides and tape. Montessori Publications, Washington, D. C. 20020, 1968.

RECORDS

FOLK TUNES AND MUSIC OF THE MASTERS. Adapted for the classroom by Elise Braun Barnett. Produced by American Montessori Society, New York.

GOLDEN SLUMBERS. A soundbook with record published by Book-Records, Inc., New York.

CHILDREN'S BOOKS

Many publishers now publish regular series of "easy-reading" books for brand-new readers. There is a very wide choice of such books. Therefore, it is necessary for the teacher and parent to acquaint the new reader with enough of these books so that he may choose the ones which interest him. To insist on a particular choice will not encourage him to think of reading as a pleasure.

Specific information on children's books can be found in the following from R. R. Bowker Company, 1180 Avenue of the Americas, New York, New York 10036.

BEST BOOKS FOR CHILDREN
CHILDREN'S BOOKS FOR SCHOOLS AND LIBRARIES
GROWING UP WITH BOOKS
GROWING UP WITH SCIENCE BOOKS

THE HORN BOOK MAGAZINE, 585 Boylston Street, Boston, Massachusetts.

The following comprehensive Booklists are taken from a guide published by the Children's Book Council, Inc., 175 Fifth Avenue, New York, which was compiled by Alice Dalgliesh and Annis Duff. Each year good new children's books are published. The following titles are only a beginning and should be considered as such.

For the Youngest Child

ABC BOOK OF THE ALPHABET
THINGS TO SEE

Both of these books are published by Platt and Munk and are available in this edition with hard covers and sturdy paper pages, also in smaller versions with hard covers, cardboard pages and spiral binding (very good for children with motor handicaps) and in a boxed set of four small washable linen books. They contain beautiful full-color photographs of common objects and are excellent for all children with learning problems.

GOODNIGHT, MOON - Margaret Wise Brown. Illus. Clement Hurd. Harper & Row. A charming goodnight story full of peace, calmness, humor.

WHISTLE FOR THE TRAIN by Golden McDonald. Illus. Leonard Weisgard. Doubleday. A repetitive story, also excellent for bedtime, about the animals who waited for the train to go by.

SUMMER IS . . . by Charlotte Zolotow. Illus. Janet Archer. Abelard-Schuman. "Summer is birds singing. Summer is bare feet and daisies and dandelions and roses full on their stems." The book touches on all four seasons in just such charming and exact language.

THE SNOWY DAY by Ezra Jack Keats. Viking. Bright, clear pictures tell of the silent wonder of city snow and Peter's joy as he experiences it. Ages 3 - 8.

WHISTLE FOR WILLIE by Ezra Jack Keats. Viking. How a boy learns to whistle for his dog. In both this book and the one above, the child is a Negro, although no reference is made to this in the text, only in the drawings. Ages 3 - 8.

Two Books for All Children of All Ages

MOTHER GOOSE, Designed and illustrated by Raymond Briggs.

A HARVEST OF RUSSIAN CHILDREN'S LITERATURE edited by Miriam Morton. University of California Press. Unbelievably rich book, with short folk tales from all parts of Russia, clever poems, fables and parables by such writers as Krylov and Leo Tolstoy, famous fairy tales, realistic stories for "middle-aged" and older children. Sturdy pages, large type, beautiful binding designed to take a lot of wear. Splendid for reading aloud, especially as a lot of the material is short.

American Heritage and Horizon Caravel Books. The American Heritage Books deal with American history, the Caravel with world history. Each volume is a large, lavishly- illustrated book on a fascinating subject—Marco Polo in China, Pirates of the Spanish Main, The French & Indian War, Russia Under the Czars, The American Indian and so on. Recommended for all children, particularly recommended for boys who have trouble reading and who find little to interest them in other early reader books. The texts are not easy, but the many pictures and charts give excellent assistance. These books are distributed by Harper & Row.

Other Series Books for Children

ADVENTURES IN SCIENCE AND NATURE. Childrens Press. Ages 8 and up.
CORNERSTONES OF FREEDOM. Childrens Press. Ages 6 and up.
ENCHANTMENT OF AMERICA. Childrens Press. Ages 9 and up.
HOLIDAY BOOKS. T. Y. Crowell. Ages 6 to 8.
LET'S READ AND FIND OUT SCIENCE BOOKS. Crowell. Ages 4 to 8.
I CAN READ BOOKS. Harper and Row. Ages 4 to 8.
SCIENCE I CAN READ BOOKS. Harper and Row. Ages 4 to 8.
BEGINNER BOOKS. Random House. Ages 4 to 8.
LANDMARK BOOKS. Random House. Ages 8 to 12.

Additional Information

A century and a half after its founding, the Library of Congress has paid tribute to the importance of children's books by organizing a separate Children's Book Section with facilities for research in the field. The section contains children's magazines and books from the past as well as much additional information to assist anyone wishing to do research on children's books. The Section also issues an annual list of CHILDREN'S BOOKS, recommended titles divided by age and subject with a brief description of contents.